Mohawk Valley Cemeteries

By Shelley D Brienza

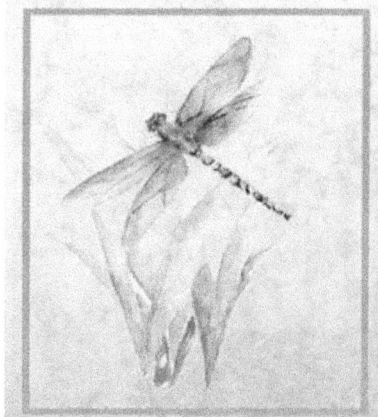

Evolve Today Publishing
Mayfield, NY
Email: sdigestpublishing@gmail.com
October 2020
Mayfield, NY
Printed in the U.S.A.

All rights reserved. This book may not be reproduced in whole or in part without prior permission from the publisher, except by a reviewer, who may quote brief passages in a review; nor may any part of this book be reproduced, stored in a retrieval system, or transmitted in any form, or by electronic, mechanical, photo-copying, recording, or other means, without prior permission from the publisher. Publisher will not be held liable for content within. All stories are the property of the author.

Mohawk Valley Cemeteries Fulton County, NY

By Shelley D Brienza

This book is dedicated to all those who have passed and left a little piece of history behind for others to learn from.

Rest in Peace.

Introduction

Mohawk Valley Cemeteries came about from my love of exploring the unknown. I enjoy looking in old cemeteries especially, because I find that each of these locations are filled with history, sculptures, and art within each gravestone seems to be present.

I think that each cemetery has a story to be told and I tried to find those through the eyes as a paranormal investigator. I am the Founder of Haunted in New York, which is a team of dedicated persons who wish to help educate others on the paranormal within each homeowners home or business. If you are interested in that you can find me on Facebook, Instagram, IGTV, YouTube, LinkedIn, Twitter and all those types of social media platforms. Or email me directly to : hauntedinny@gmail.com.

These books will focus on just the Mohawk Valley cemeteries as a picture book with some history and personal stories . This first book of the series is focusing on just Fulton County, NY cemeteries.

While taking the pictures of different gravestones I wasn't thinking about where I was particularly. I was looking at the stones architecture and those are the ones I tend to take pictures of. I will post where I was if I recall but mainly this book is just about the beauty one can find in a gravestone. These are not all the cemeteries in Fulton County, NY but rather just the ones I personally visited in the year 2020.

Other cemeteries have triggered a paranormal response in me and I have noted those as well. As an intuitive I try to "read" each cemeteries energy and that has been documented as well.

Warmly,

Shelley Brienza
Author

About the Mohawk Valley

The Mohawk Valley region of the U.S. state of New York is the area surrounding the Mohawk River, sandwiched between the Adirondack Mountains and Catskill Mountains. As of the 2010 United States Census, the region's counties have a combined population of 622,133 people. In addition to the Mohawk River valley, the region contains portions of other major watersheds such as the Susquehanna River.

The region is a suburban and rural area surrounding the industrialized cities of Schenectady, Utica and Rome, along with other smaller commercial centers. The 5,882 square miles (15,230 km2) area is an important agricultural center and encompasses the heavily forested wilderness areas just to the north that are part of New York's Adirondack Park.

The Mohawk Valley is a natural passageway connecting the Atlantic Ocean, by way of the Hudson Valley with the interior of North America. Native American Nations of the Iroquois Confederacy lived in the region, and in the 17th century immigrants of Dutch, and the 18th century German, and Scottish settled the area, joined by Italians following the rapid industrialization of the mid-19th century. During the 18th Century, the Mohawk Valley was a frontier of great political, military and economic importance. Colonists, such as Phillip Schuyler, Nicholas Herkimer, William Johnson, trading with the Iroquois set the stage for commercial and military competition between

European nations, leading to the French and Indian Wars and the American Revolution. Almost 100 battles of the American Revolution were fought in New York State, including the Battle of Oriskany and defense of Fort Stanwix. A series of raids against valley residents took place during the war; led by John Johnson they were collectively known as the "Burning of the Valleys".

The Erie Canal was completed in 1825 as the first commercial connection between the American East and West.

During the French and Indian War, the Mohawk Valley was of prime strategic importance; to the British, it provided a corridor to the Great Lakes from which to threaten New France directly, while to the French it provided a corridor to the Hudson Valley and on to the heart of British North America. In addition, many settlements of the Mohawk, Britain's crucial Indian ally at the time of the war, were located in or near the valley.

At the beginning of the war, the major British stronghold in the Mohawk corridor was Fort Oswego, located on Lake Ontario. The French captured and destroyed the fort after a short siege in 1756, and the Mohawk Valley lay open to French advance as a result. Although the French did not directly exploit this avenue of attack, its impact swayed some of the Iroquois tribes to the French side.

The original inhabitants of common day Mohawk Valley are traced back as far as 10,000 plus years and included Algonquian people that later relocated from the newly established Fort Orange Dutch trading post region as early as 1624, otherwise as the name implies, the inhabitants were and remained Mohawks. The name Mohawk Valley had its origins in the time period of 1614 and 1624-25 following the settlement of Dutch traders who established a post among the region of the Mohawk of Mohawk Valley as the Mohawk had become alliances and targets of the Indian Wars. The Mohawks of Mohawk Valley call themselves Kanien'keha'ka, and "People of the Flint" in part due to their creation story of a powerful flinted arrow. Among other things, the traditional use of Mohawk Valley flint as Toolmaking Flint is only one attribution to the Mohawk Valley People of the Flint name.

Fulton County, NY Cemeteries

Fulton County is a county that forms part of the Mohawk Valley region.

Fulton County is a county in the U.S. state of New York. It forms part of the state's Mohawk Valley region. The county is named in honor of Robert Fulton, who is widely credited with developing the first commercially successful steamboat. Fulton County comprises the Gloversville micropolitan statistical area, which is included in the Capital District.

In 1838, Fulton County was split off from Montgomery, shortly after the Montgomery county seat was moved to Fonda, New York. The creation of Fulton County was engineered by Johnstown lawyer Daniel Cady, whose wife was a cousin of Robert Fulton.

Fulton County was created on April 18, 1838 by a partition of Montgomery County, resulting in a county with an area of 550 square miles (1,400 km2).

The old Tryon County courthouse, later the Montgomery County courthouse, became the Fulton County Courthouse, where it is New York's oldest operating courthouse.

One adjustment has been made to the area of Fulton County. On April 6, 1860, 10 square miles (26 km2) on the northern border was transferred to Hamilton in the vicinity of Sacandaga Park. This resulted in the Fulton County that exists today.

In the mid-18th century, Sir William Johnson, founder of Fort Johnson in Montgomery County and of Johnstown, arrived in what would become Fulton County. Sir William Johnson, 1st Baronet, was an Irish pioneer and army officer in colonial New York, and the British Superintendent of Indian Affairs from 1755 to 1774. His homes, Fort Johnson and Johnson Hall are current New York State Historic Sites.

Fulton County was also home to Elizabeth Cady Stanton, a central pioneer in America's women's rights movement.

Shortly after the American Revolutionary War, the manufacture of gloves and leather became the area's primary industry. At one point, Johnstown and Gloversville were known as the world's Glove and Leather capital. The largest rise in population and growth came as a result of the fruits of these businesses.

Many residents of Fulton County can trace their ancestry to the glove and leather trades. Today few glovers, tanners and leather dressers remain in the area, although some companies have adapted to the changes in the market to remain competitive.

(https://en.wikipedia.org/wiki/Fulton_County,_New_York)

Ephratah Rural Cemetery

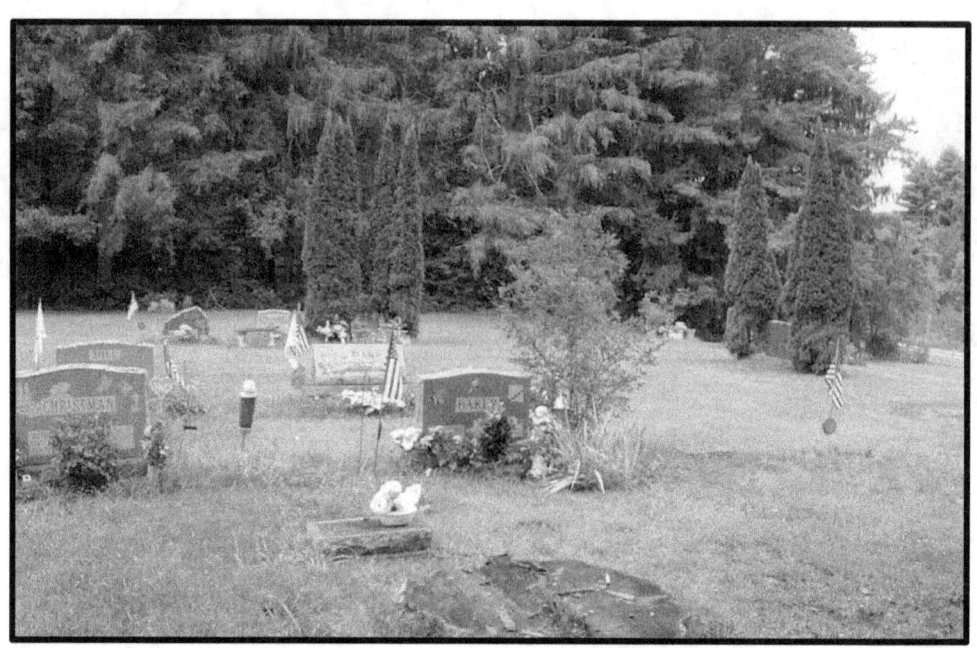

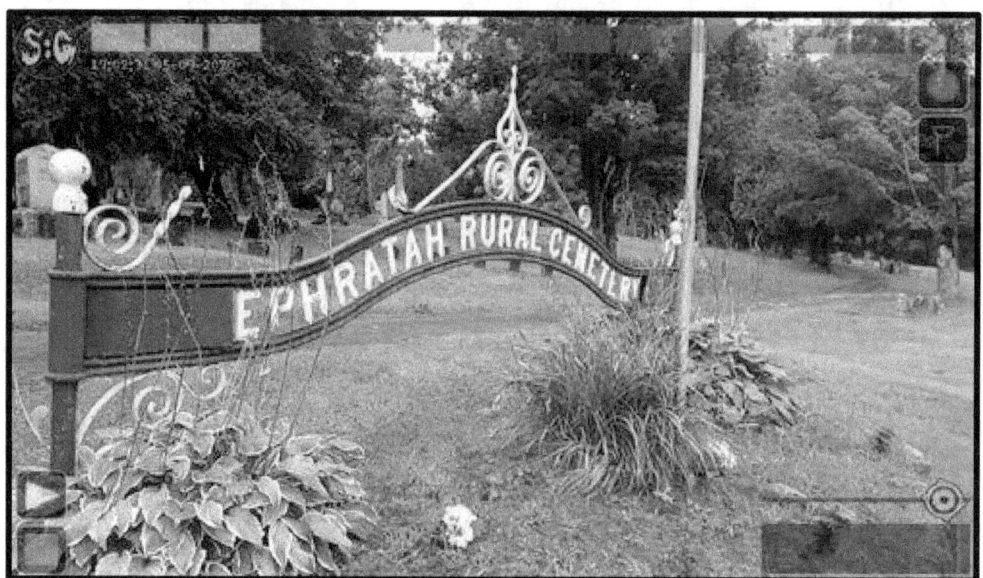

Ephratah Rural Cemetery

This was one cemetery we visited with the paranormal team. It's located in St. Johnsville, NY, in Fulton County. Above is a screenshot of one of the tools we use while on investigations that captures electronic voice phenomenon or EVPs as we call them. This shot you can see has three green bars across the top which indicated to us that spirit was indeed present in this cemetery.

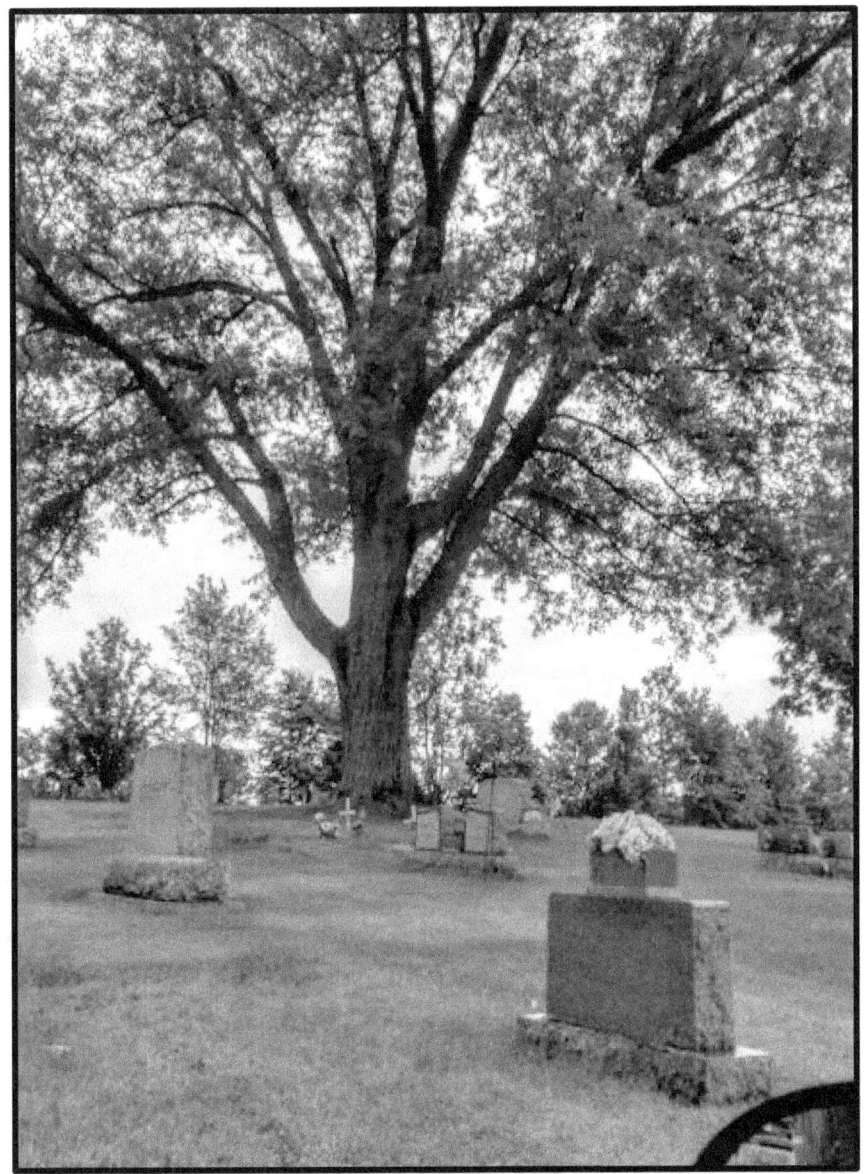

Ephratah Rural Cemetery

I like looking for what would make a picture say what each location feels like to me. This had some very old stones in it but it felt calm here even though we had picked up some spirit activity.

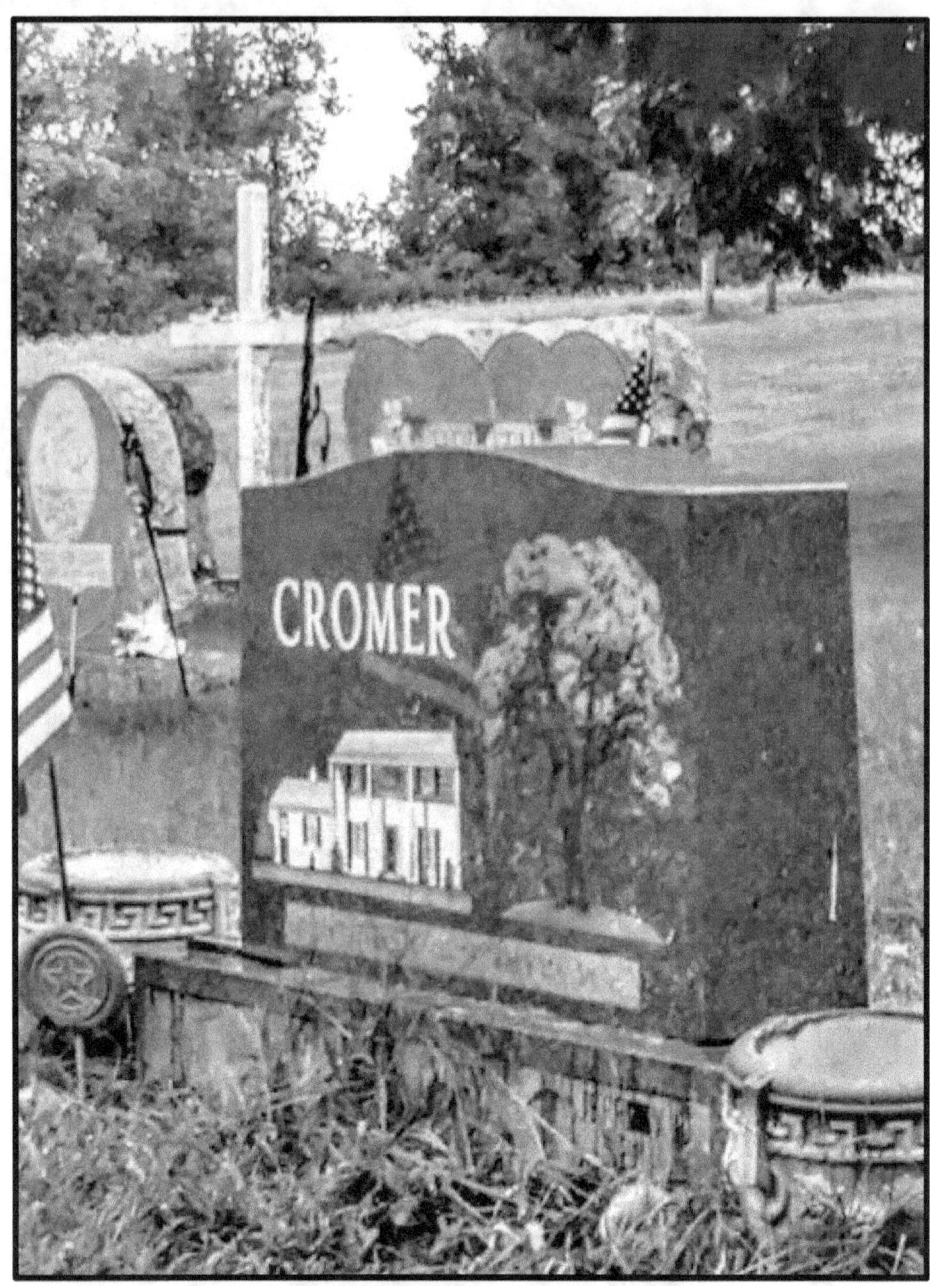

Ephratah Rural Cemetery
I like looking at gravestones that tell a story like this one.

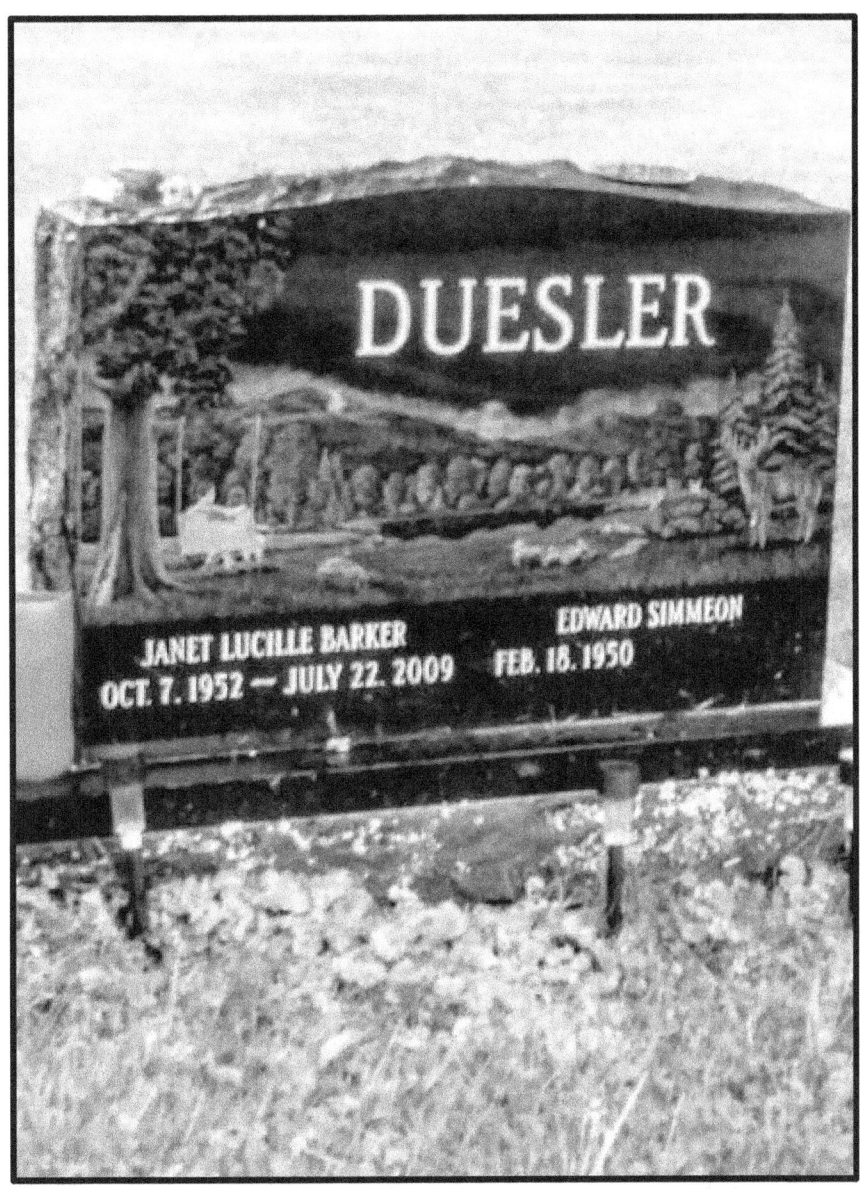

Ephratah Rural Cemetery

This was a lovely gravestone too. It definitely tells a story.

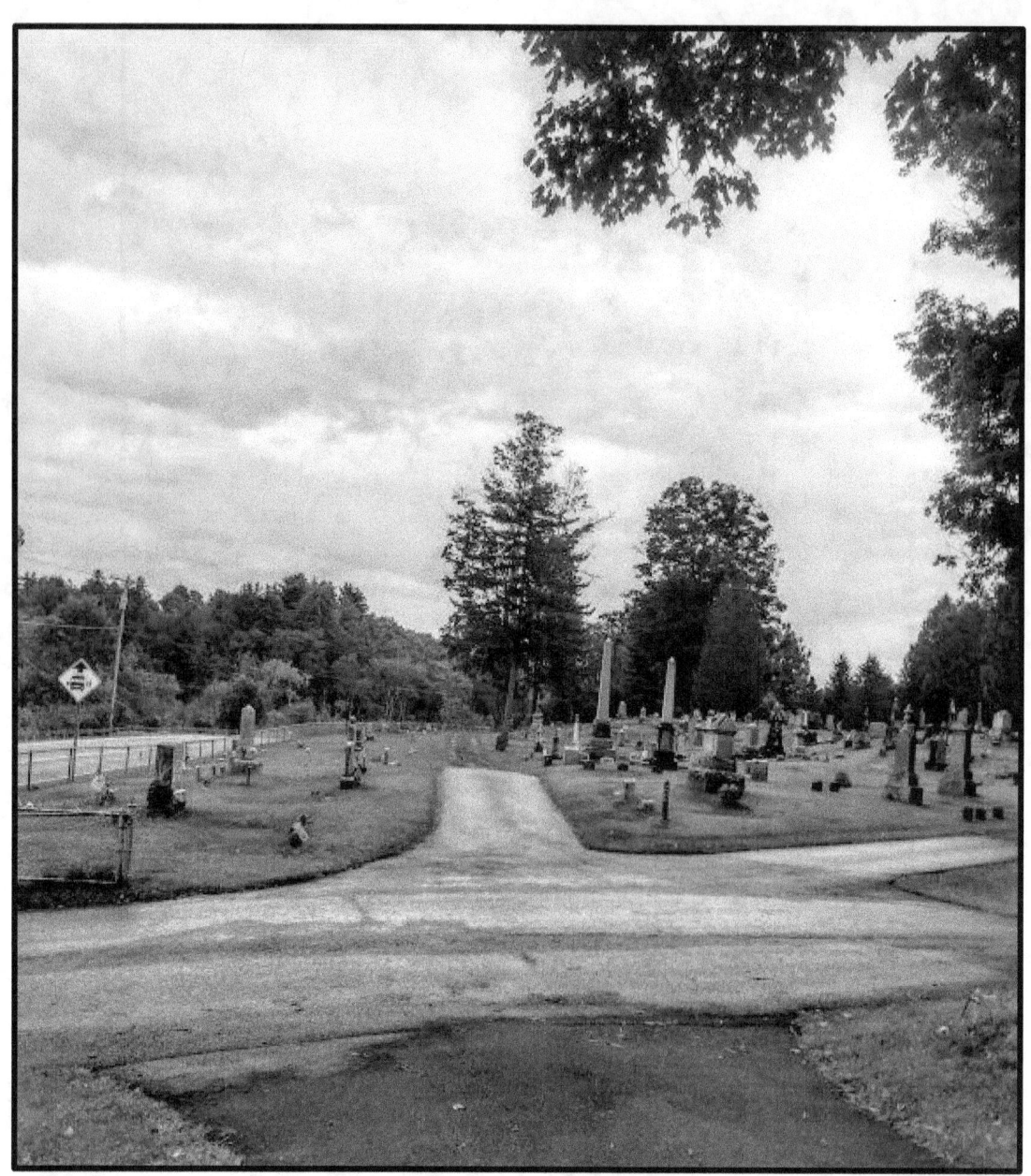

Ephratah Rural Cemetery
This shot was on the way out.

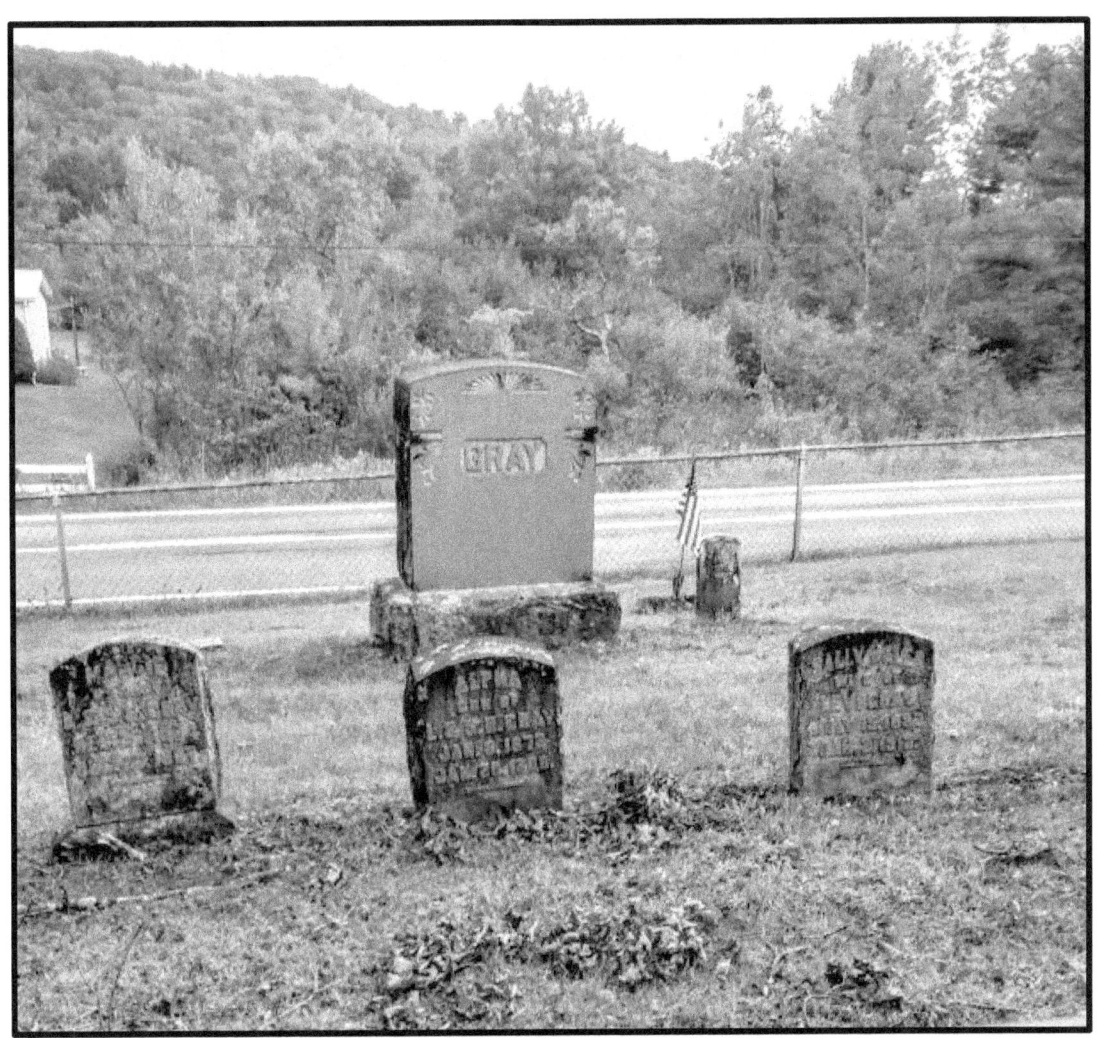
Ephratah Rural Cemetery

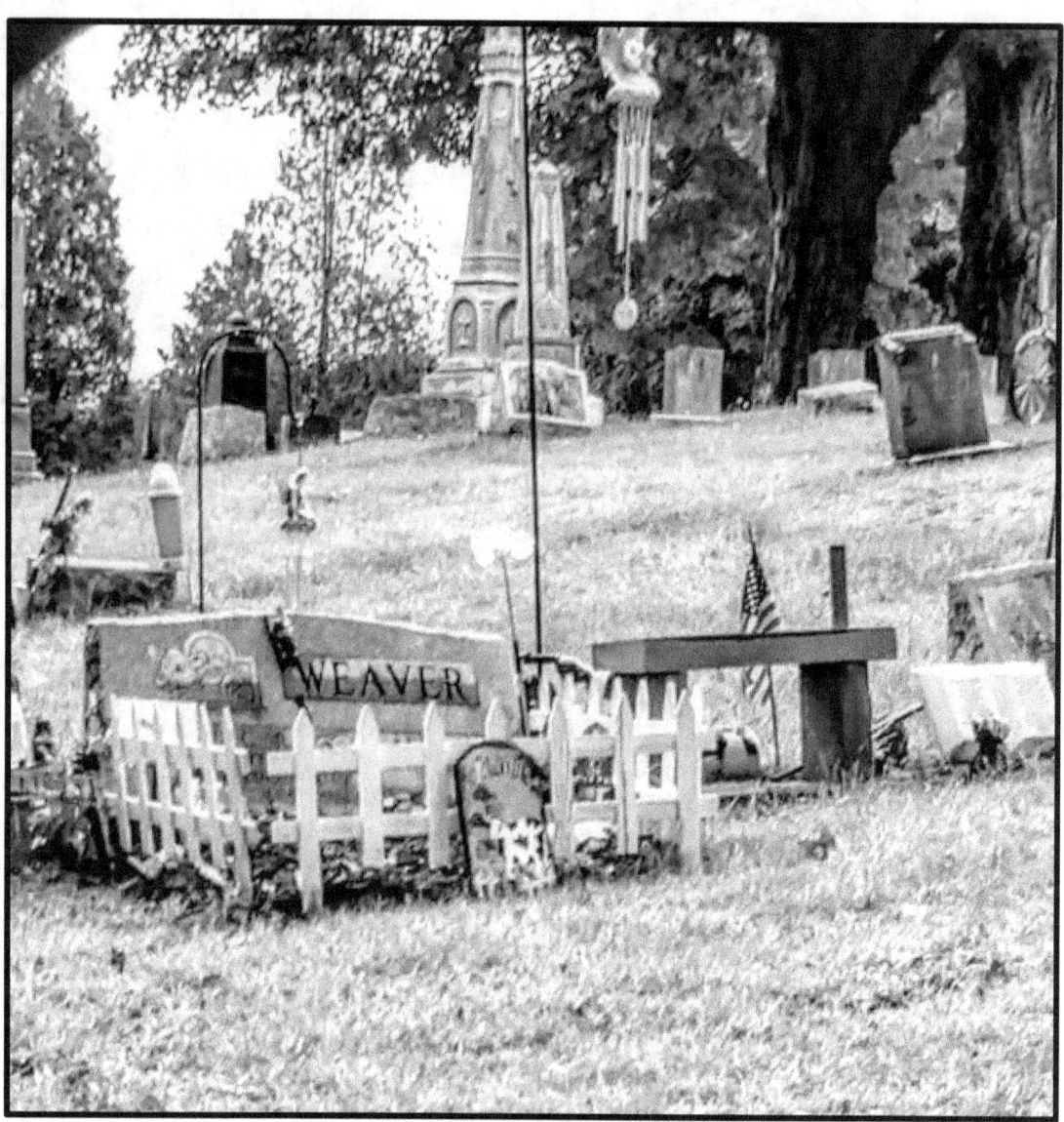

Ephratah Rural Cemetery

Even though the headstone wasn't overly elaborate, I feel the family was sharing a story by what they left for this person at their resting place.

North Bush United Methodist Church and Cemetery

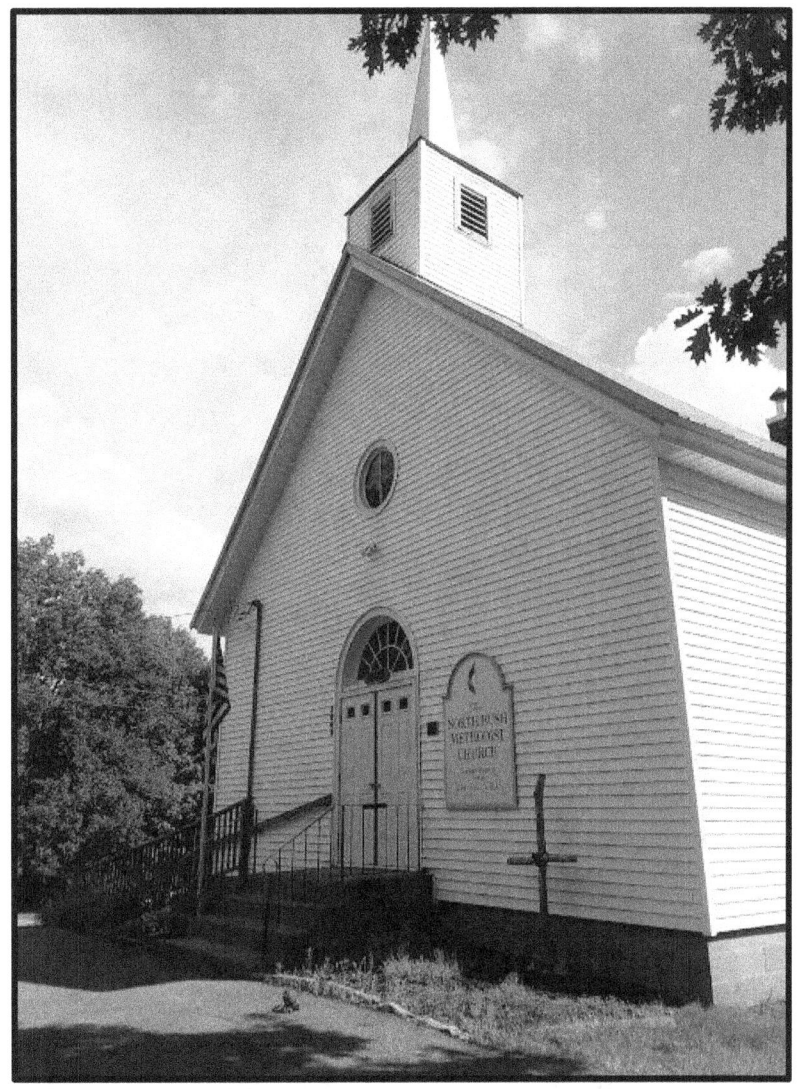

Sometimes I can "feel" that I shouldn't be entering a particular cemetery. Being intuitive or sensitive I can literally "feel" a cemetery. One not so good experience was at the old North Bush Church Cemetery, located outside of the city of Gloversville, Caroga, in Fulton County. The cemetery is really old on one side of the road and then there is another cemetery behind the North Bush United Methodist Church itself, which was built in 1898.

The old cemetery gave me the "heebie jeebies." You see I am also a paranormal investigator and that's where the love of old cemeteries was born. It is said that this cemetery holds the remains of many of the area's early pioneers and settlers. Some of the graves were unmarked. On a slight hill in the older section lies the remains of early black residents that are unmarked.

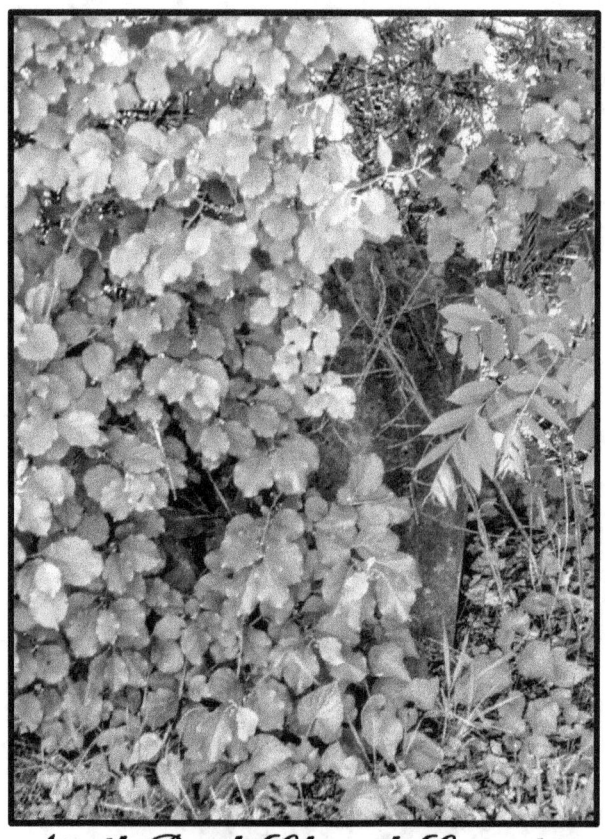

North Bush Church Cemetery

This stone was hidden in the bushes, but not forgotten. We got a lot of EVPs from this cemetery. My lead investigator, got a strange voice that came across and said, "Leave you pig!" Another one was "Why are you doing this to us?" I do believe they can see us just as we can at times see them.

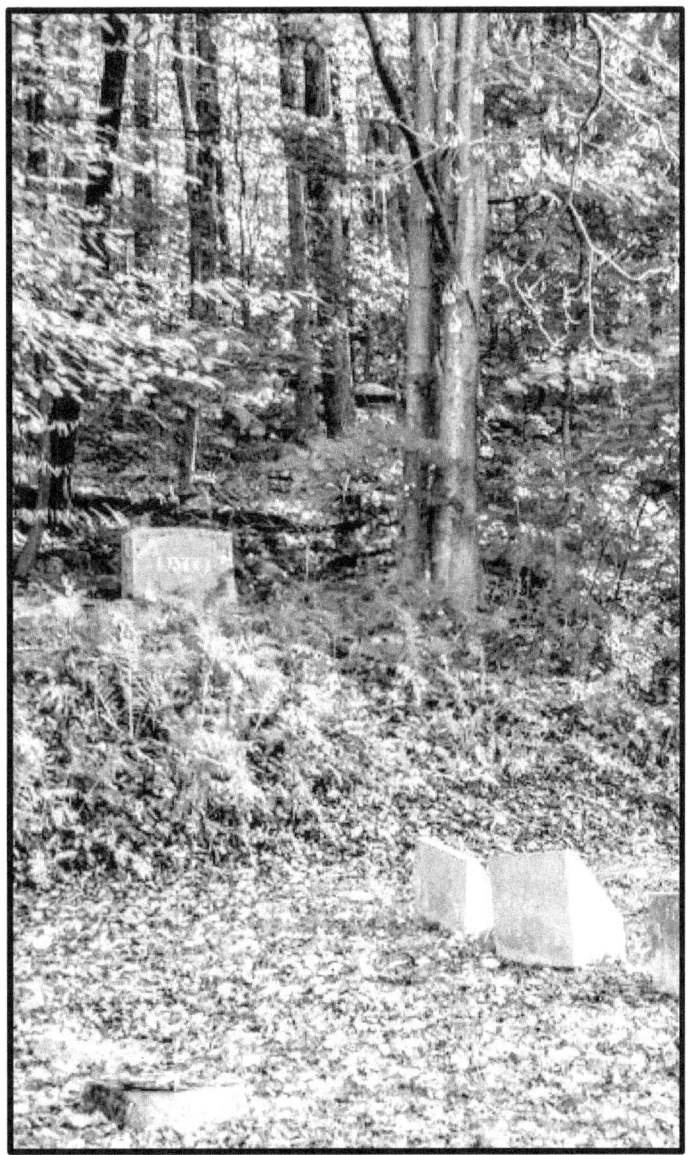
North Bush Church Cemetery

I wonder why stones are often so close to the edge of a cemetery border? Sometimes they get buried in bushes and ground coverings. I'm always looking in those places to say hello. I felt really uneasy about entering the old side of this church cemetery. Behind the church itself my team and myself felt it was calmer feeling than the more active side.

Wandering through the North Bush Cemetery was like walking through some dark, heavy air. I went back after the first time I was there and had brought my team and mediums who were also picking up on the activity there on both sides of the road. My Medium told me to just stop before entering a place and let my body "feel" the energy. I did that second time. I didn't like what I was feeling. It made me feel very nervous like. Generally for me that means I am receiving an affirmation to whatever my thoughts were at that moment, and that day, was, "I am not going in there today."

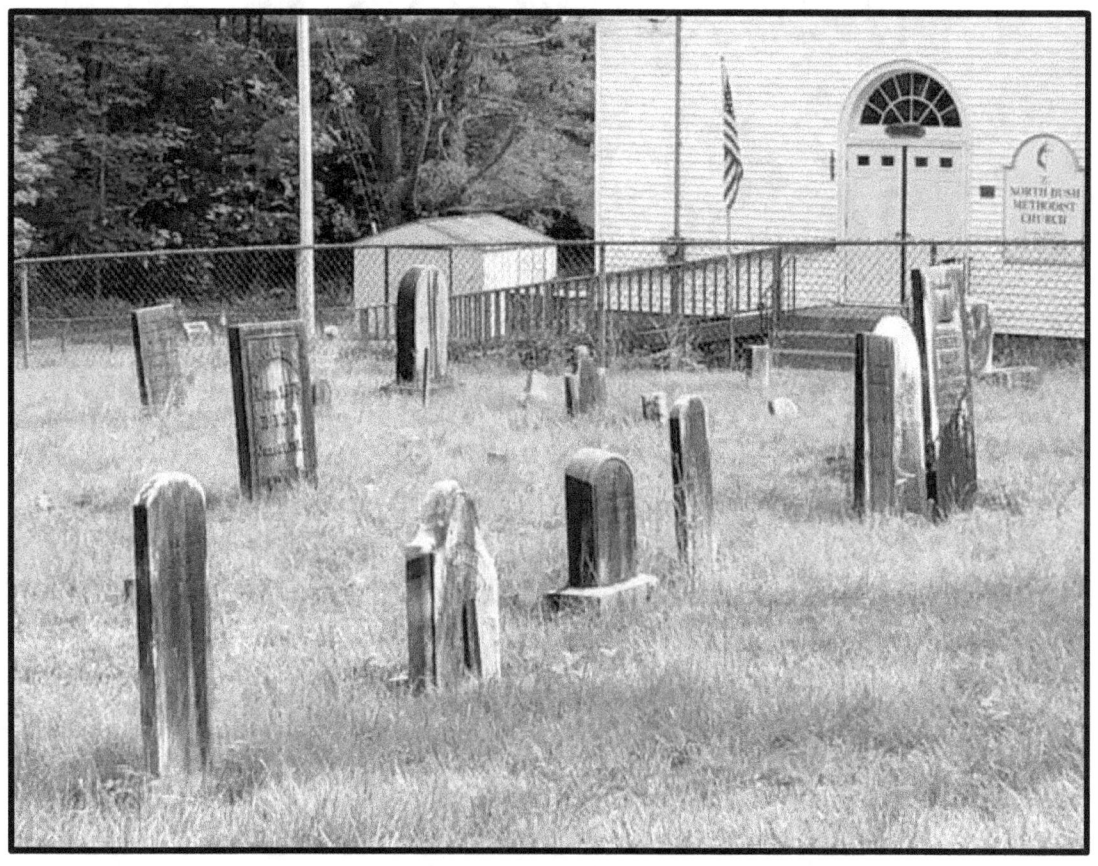

North Bush Church Cemetery

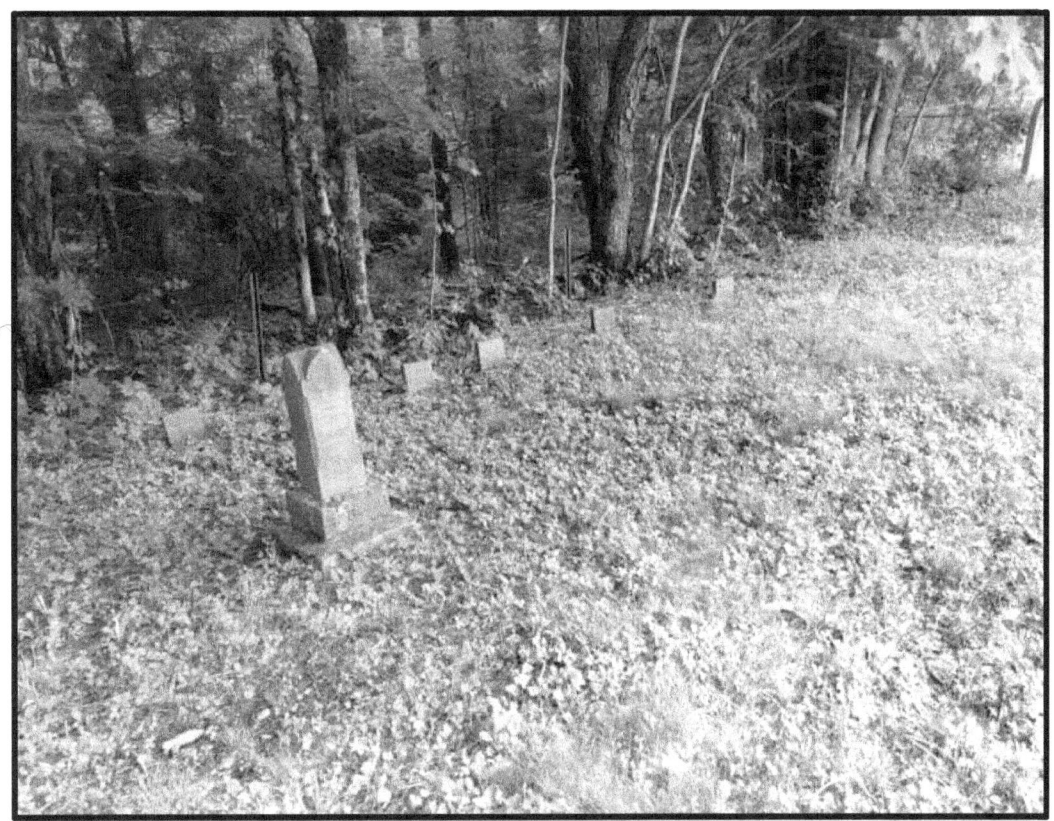

So many stones lining up against the woods line.

North Bush Church Cemetery

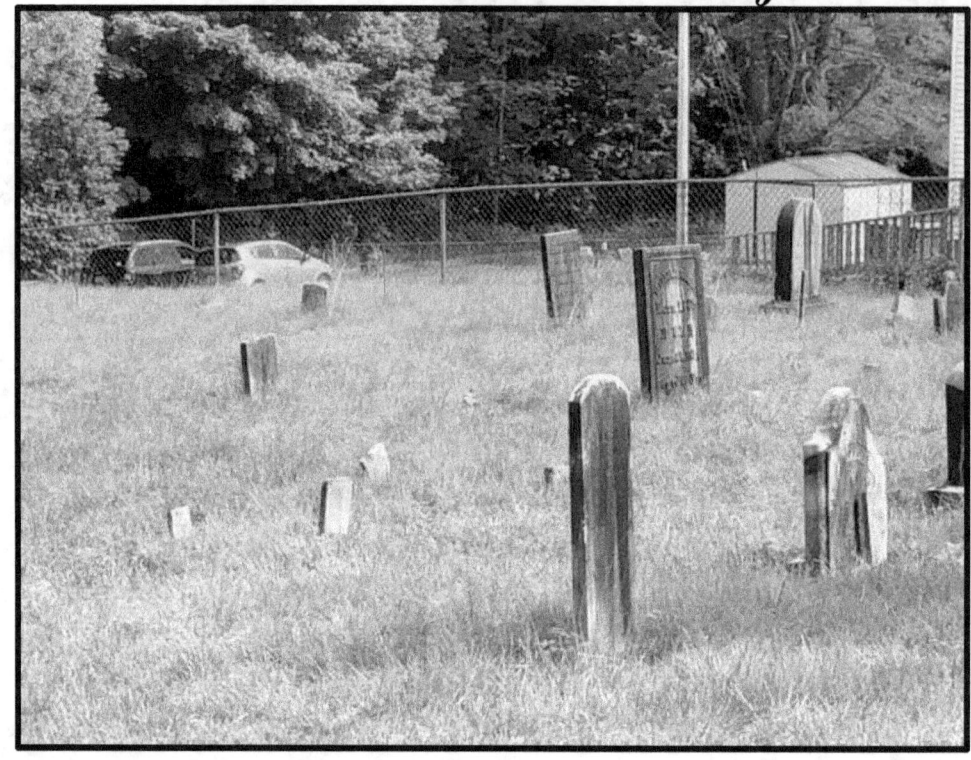

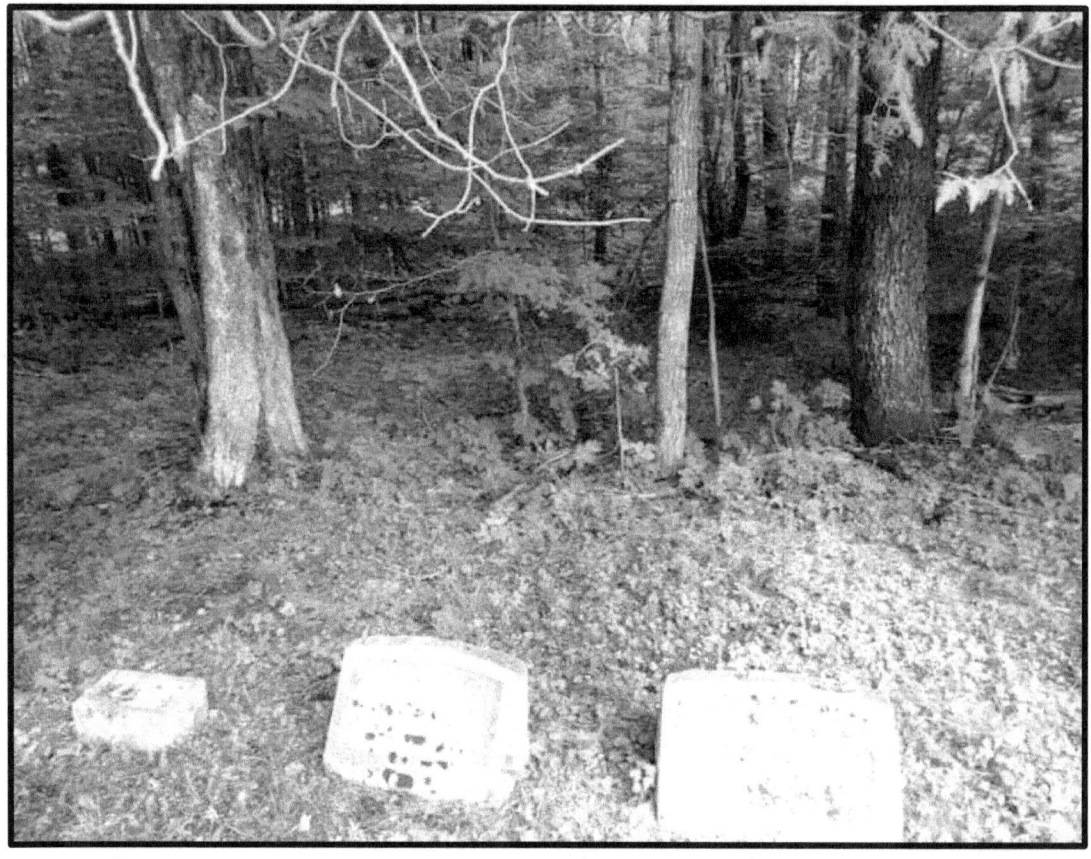

North Bush Church Cemetery

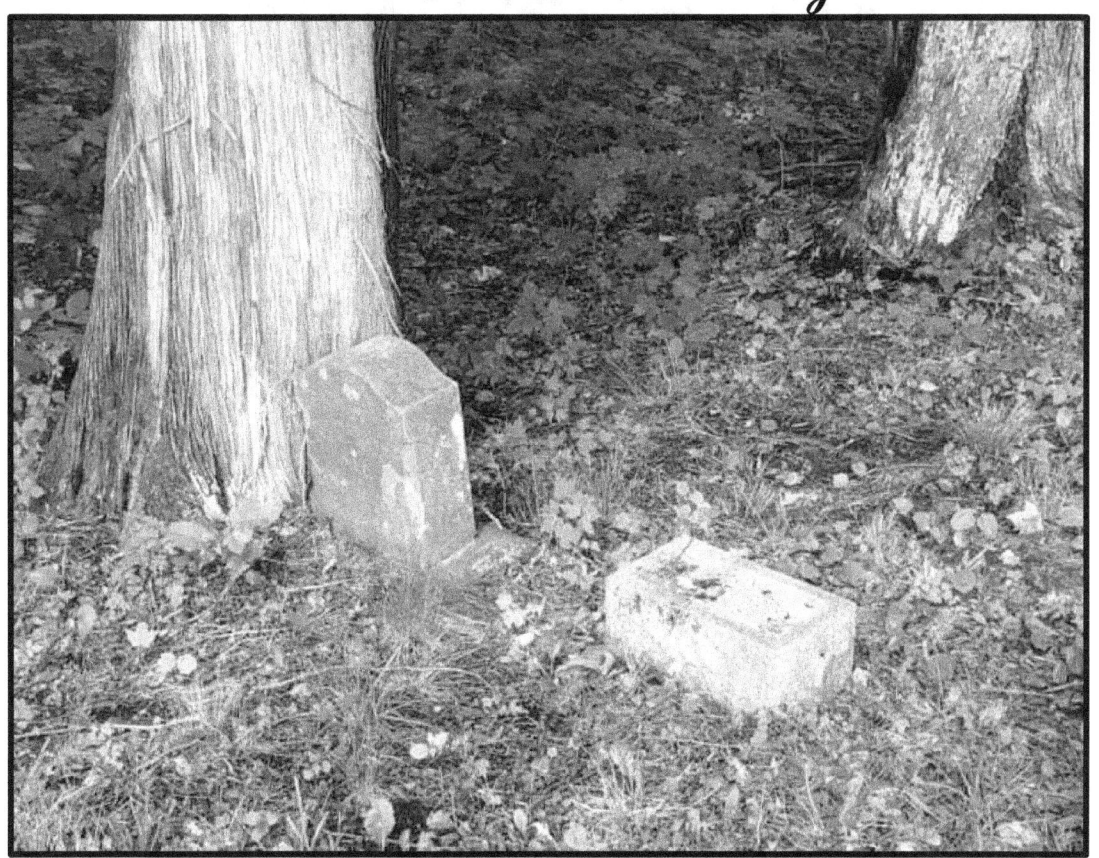

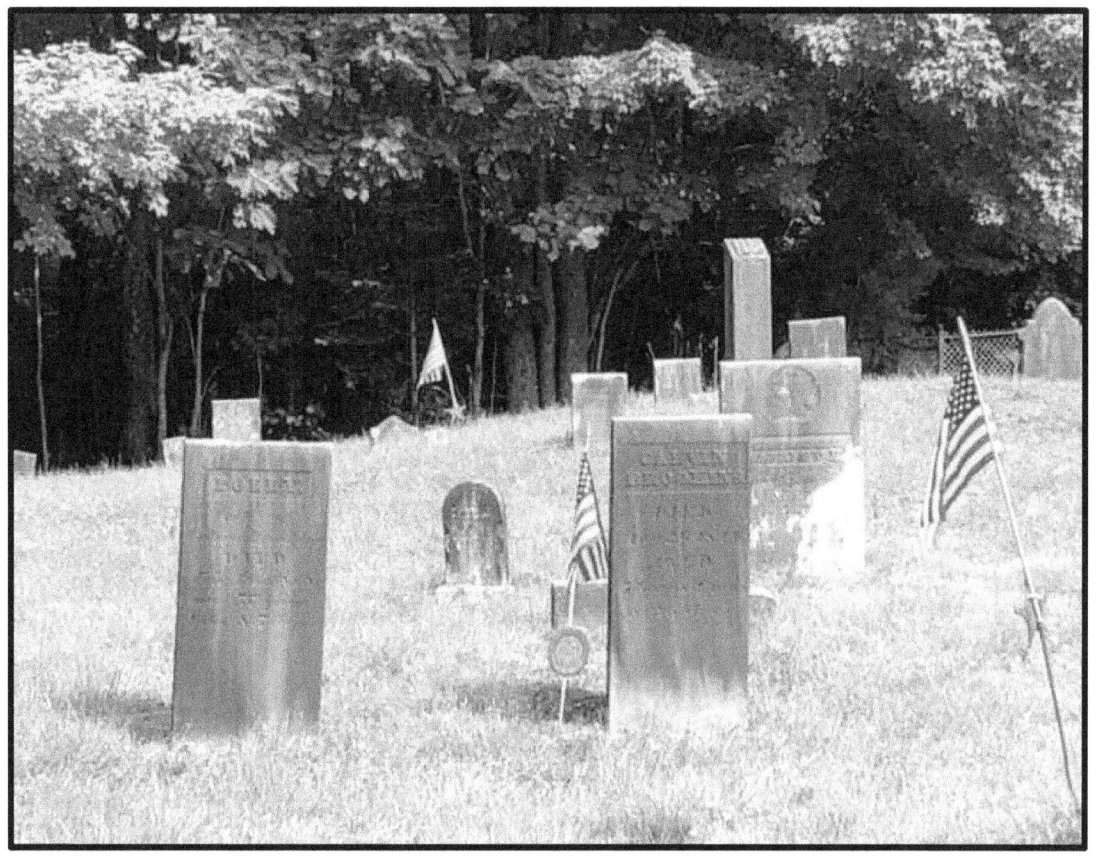

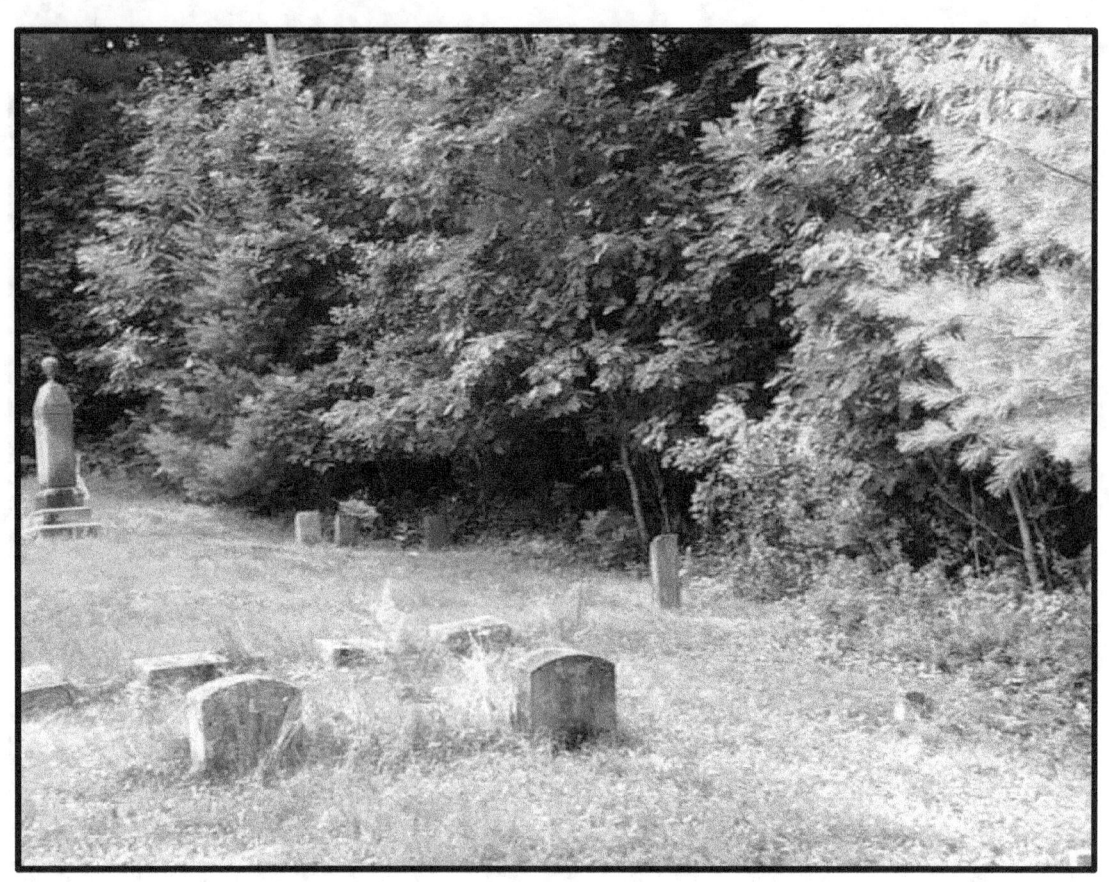

North Bush Church Cemetery

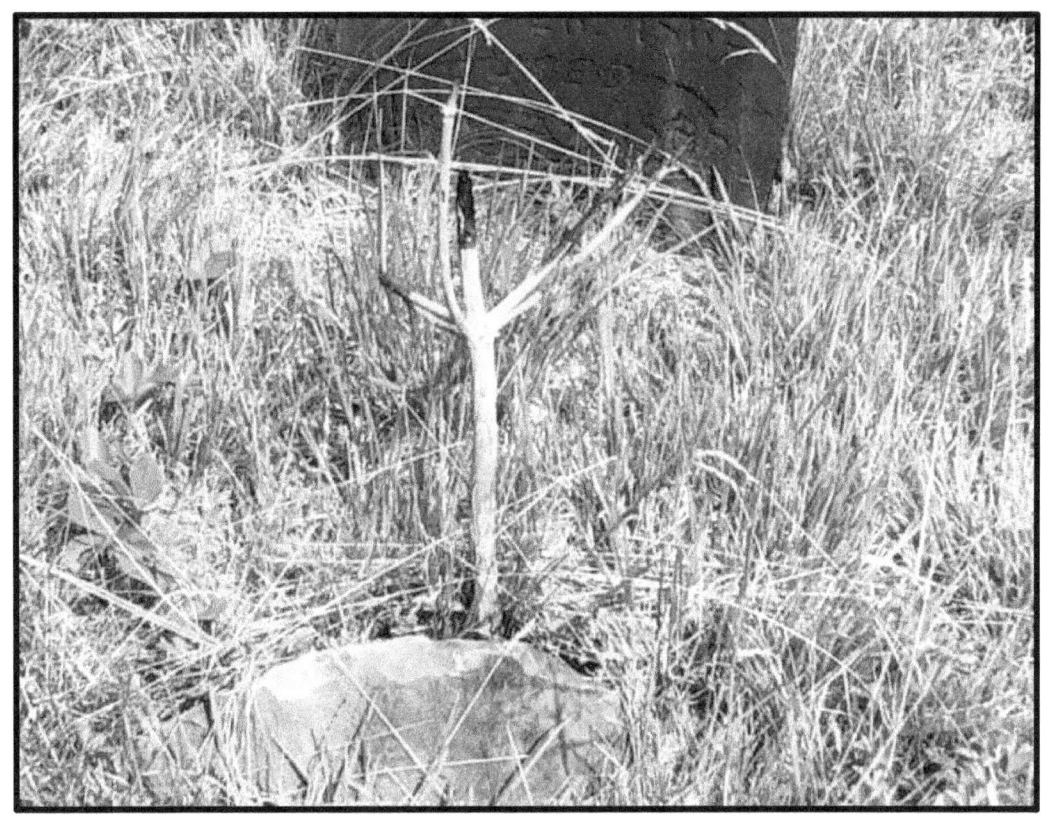

North Bush Church Cemetery

This I found very strange. Why was there a 5 pronged stick in the ground next to a gravestone? And why were 3 tips burned? What did that signify? I don't know to this day.

Hope Valley (Willard) Cemetery, Hope, NY
(Fulton County/Hamilton County Line)
287 New York 30
Northville, NY 12134

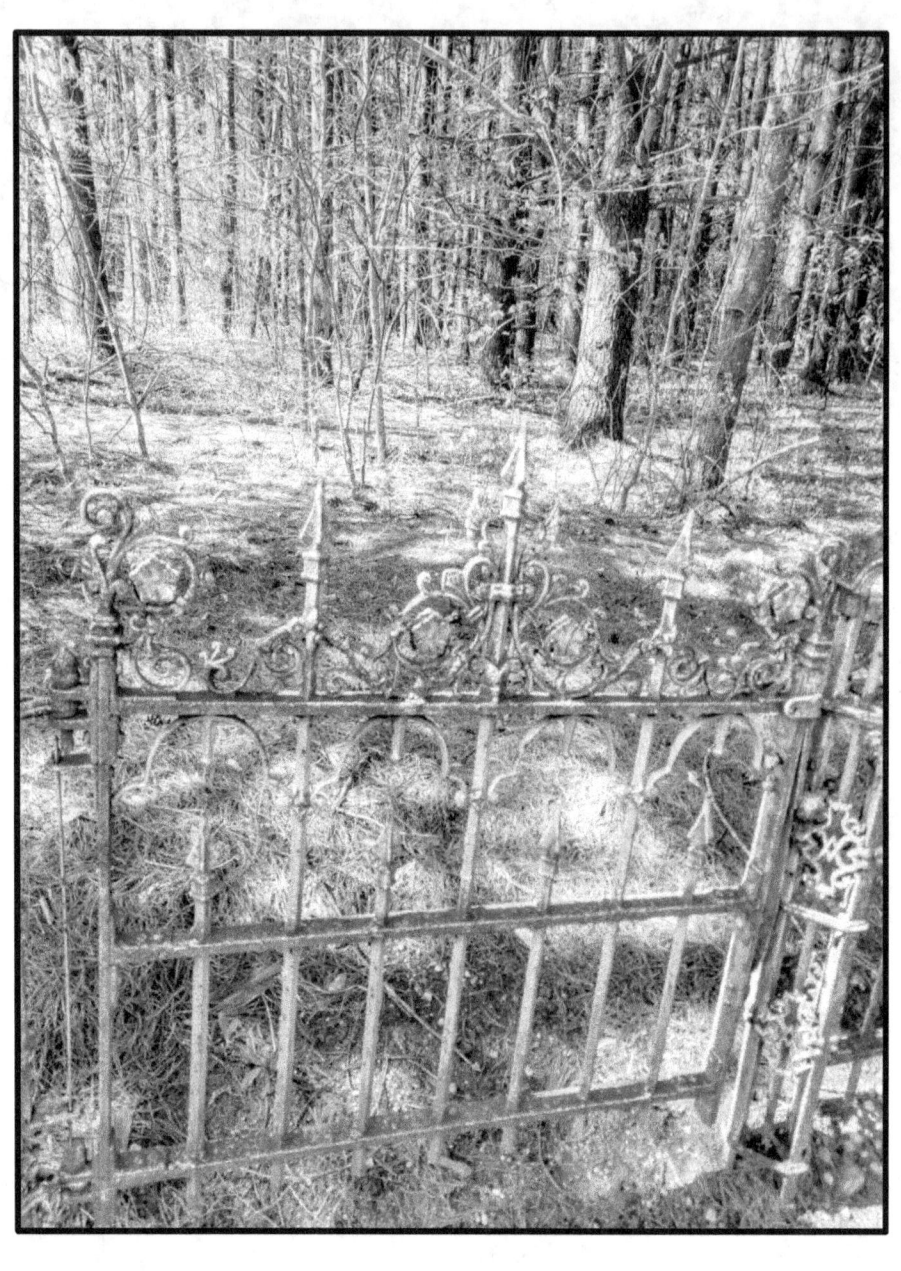

Although this cemetery is located just outside of Fulton/Hamilton County line, near Northville, NY, I found it to be very interesting. I actually found it by accident. Upon learning more about this cemetery, I learned that one of my paranormal team member's, family is buried there.

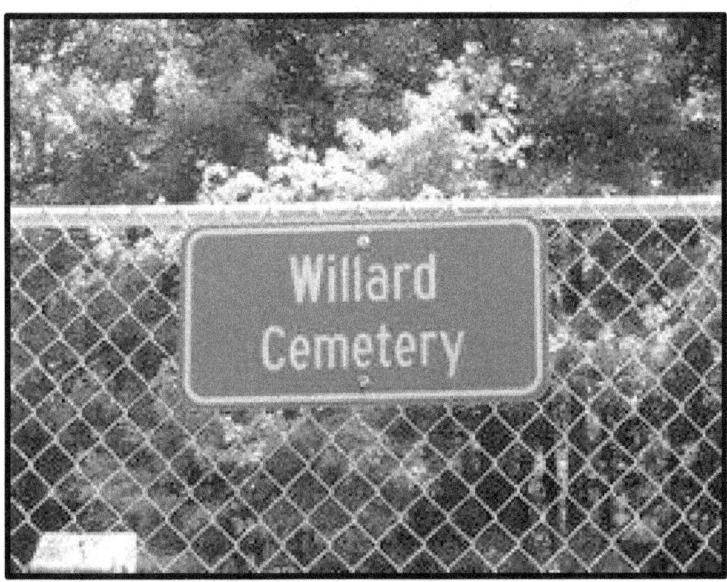

Hope Valley (Willard) Cemetery, Hope, NY

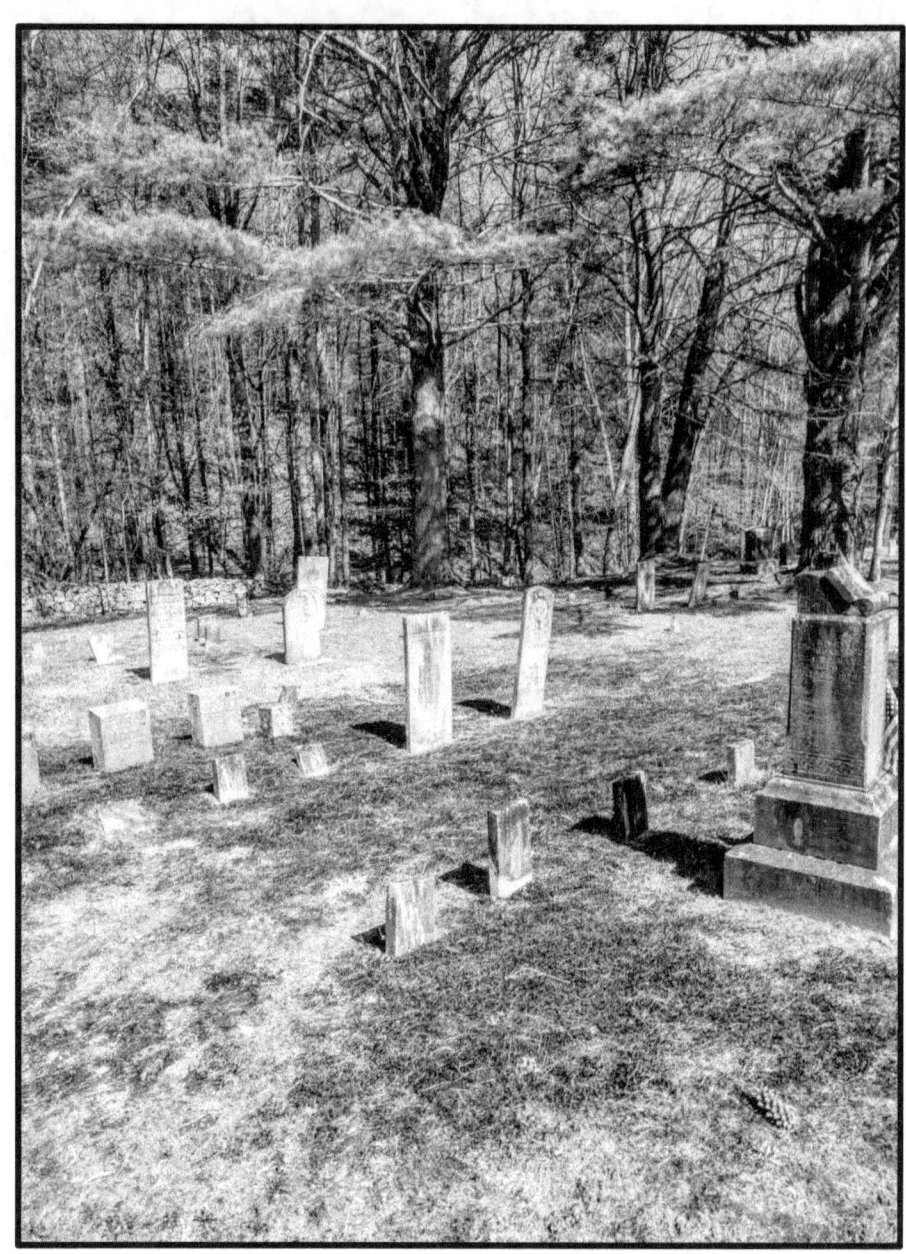

Hope Valley (Willard) Cemetery, Hope, NY

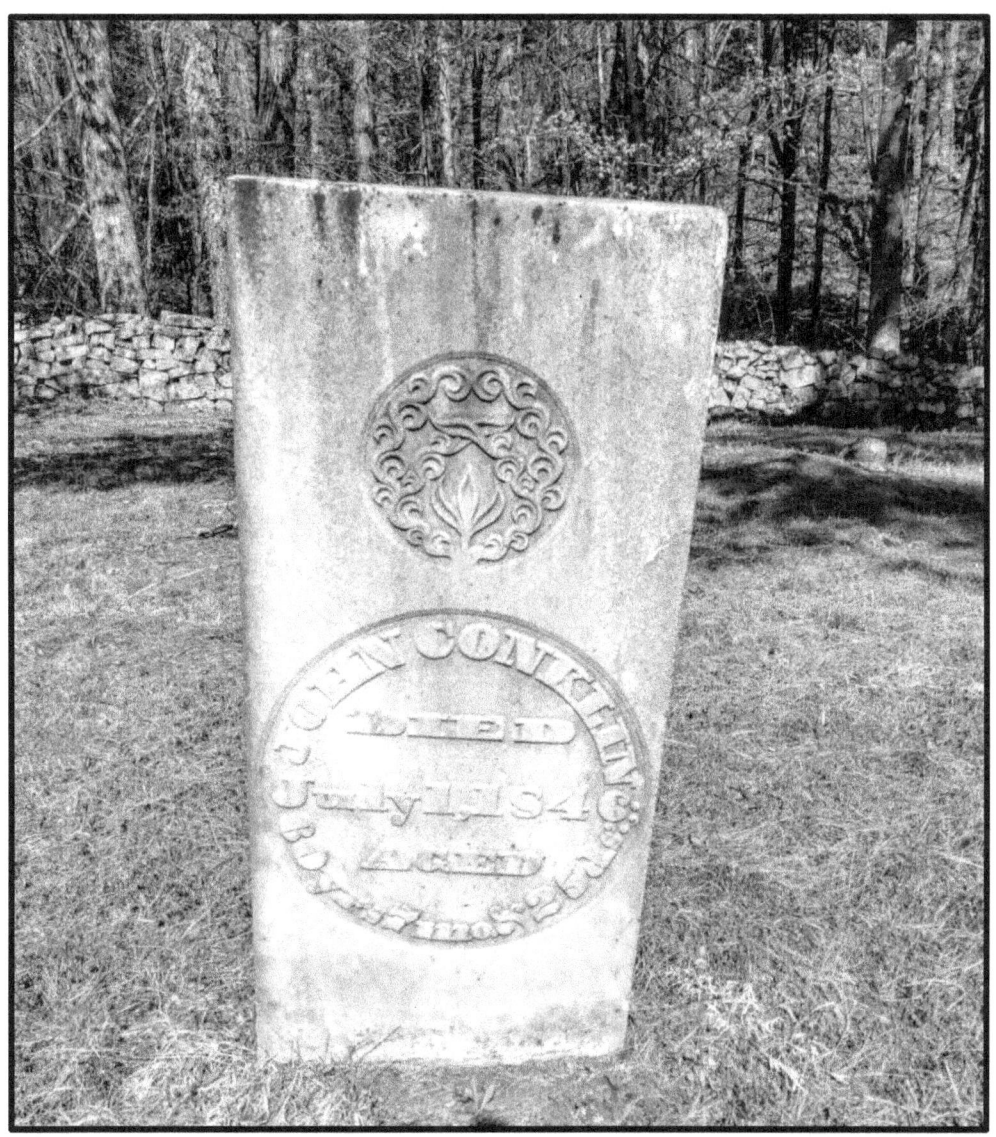

Hope Valley (Willard) Cemetery, Hope, NY

This type of stone isn't something that I had seen before. It's clear to read and obviously has some significance. Most the stones here are from the early 1800's. Sadly, what I have found out about this cemetery after the fact, is that there a LOT of children buried here. I've included the burial names and ages in the chart below but it's really sad to read. I'm going to research out why so many children died in those early years.

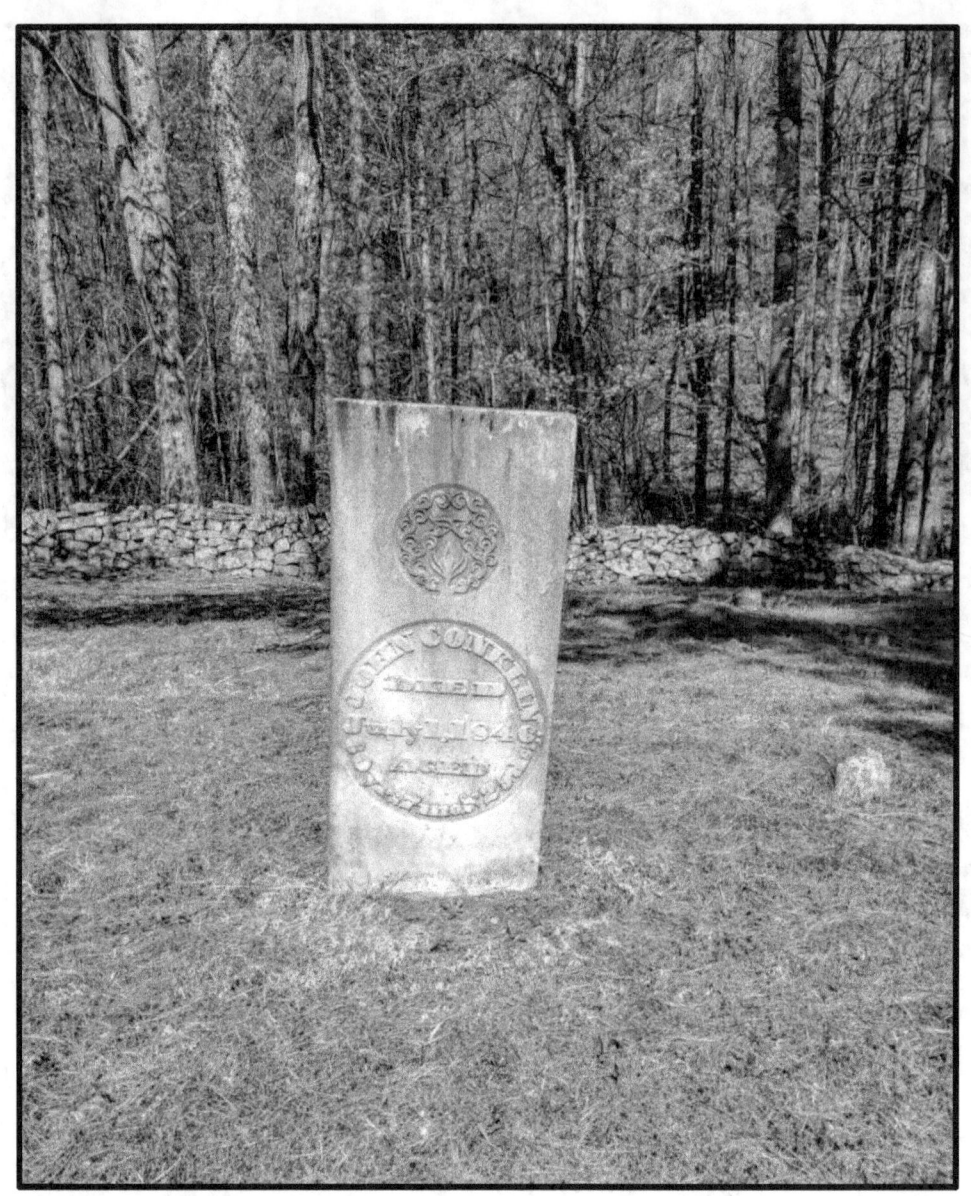

Hope Valley (Willard) Cemetery, Hope, NY

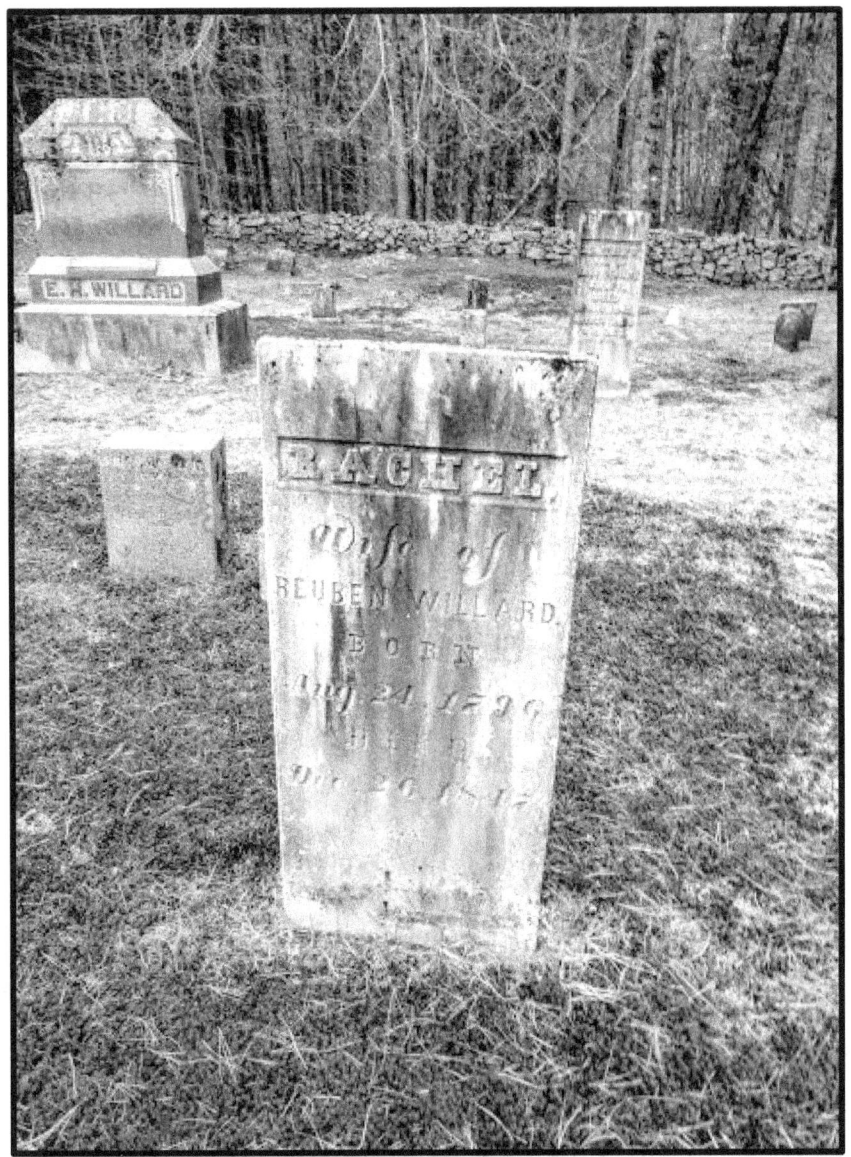

Hope Valley (Willard) Cemetery, Hope, NY

I saved some of these pictures in black and white to be able to read the stones easier.

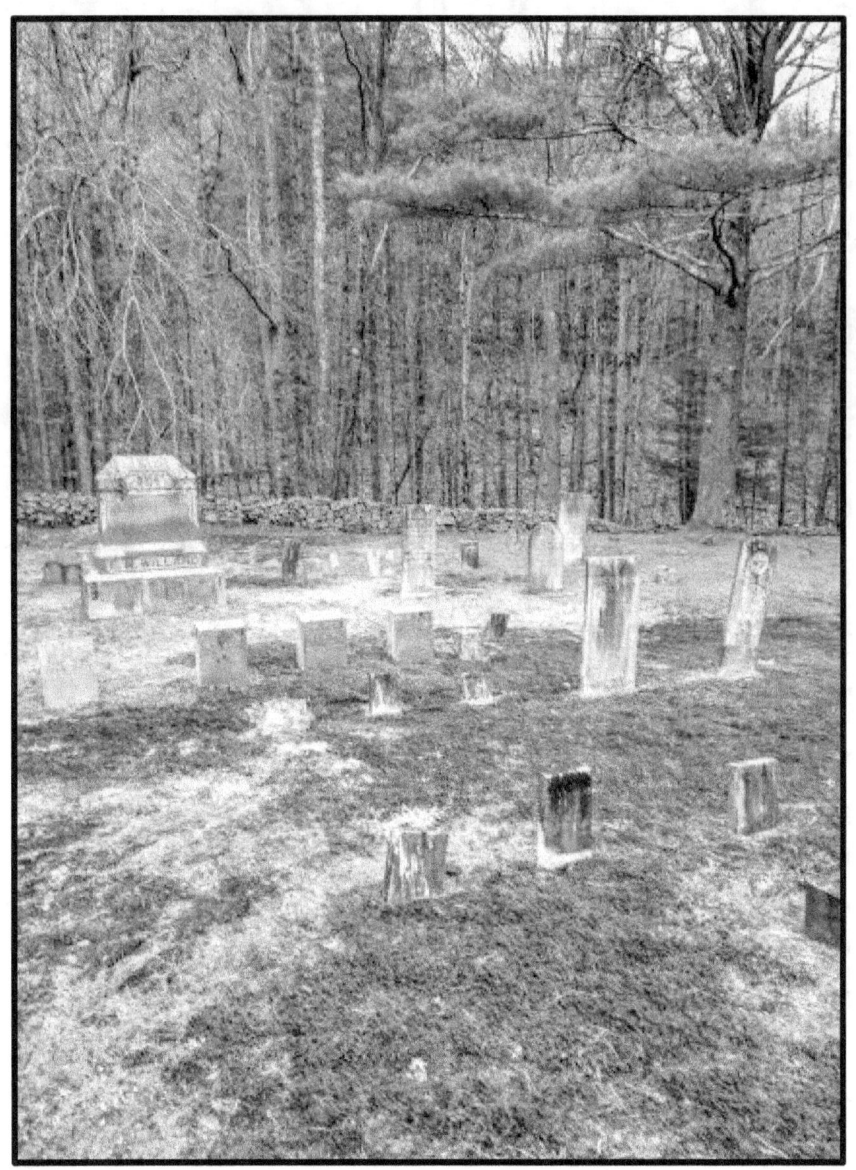

Hope Valley (Willard) Cemetery, Hope, NY

The chart on the next page shows who's buried in this cemetery but the very sad thing to me is how many young children died. And some died very, very young. It's sad. I highlighted the deaths of children in yellow.

Hope Valley (Willard) Cemetery, Hope, NY

Last Name	First Name	Birth	Death	Comments
Groff	Isaac J.		Dec 6, 1880	age 26 yrs. 10 mo 13 days s/o Eliphalet Groff and Martha J. Conklin Groff
Groff	Eliphalet	1826	1889	[s/o John P. Groff]
Groff	Martha J. Conklin	[Mar. 24, 1834]	Aug 8, 1877	[d/o Isaac Conklin and Polly Stone]
Groff	Laura M.		Jul. 9, 1864	age 4 yrs. 7 mo. 22 days d/o Eliphalet and Martha
Greene	Emily E.	1856	Dec 31, 1878	age 22 w/o Jackson Green Jr [d/o Eliphalet Groff]
Groff	Carrie	1874	1890	[d/o Eliphalet Groff]
Williams	Tunis	[1795 Vt.]	Mar. 8, 1883	age 87 yrs. 10 mo.
Williams	Gitty	1800	Dec. 23, 1888	w/o Tunis [d/o Isaac Conklin]
Williams	Elizabeth		Mar 28, 1854	age 23 yrs. 1 mo 22 days d/o Tunis and Gitty
Ostrander	Laura		Jan 5, 1887	age 15 yrs. 9 mo. 27 days d/o Alson and D. Ostrander
Bass	Delphene		Oct. 8 1890	age 39 yrs. 7 mo. 21 days w/o Alson P. Ostrander
Ostrander	Alson P.		Dec. 3, 1925	age 76 yrs. 2 mo 10 days
Lobdell	Lydia	Jun 30, 1811	Sep. 19, 1901	w/o Benjamin Scribner [d/o Jacob Elias Lobdell and Rachel Van Ness]
Scribner	Benjamin	1806	Sep. 28, 1889	[s/o Robert Scribner and Hannah Hewitt]

Surname	Given	Born	Died	Notes
Scribner	Charles	1879	1958	[s/o John D. Scribner and Laura Fountain]
Scribner	John D.	1842	1931	[s/o Benjamin Scribner and Lydia Lobdell]
Fountain	Laura	1844	1922	w/o John D. Scribner [d/o of David S. Fountain]
Robbs	Frank	1872	1931	
Dane	Mary	1876	1900	w/o Frank Robbs
Robbs	George	1899	1935	s/o Frank and Mary
Groff	Alice Evelyn	[Mar 3, 1902]	Jan. 4, 1921	[d/o Albert Groff and Carrie Carpenter]
Groff	Lee	[Nov 21, 1882]	Jan. 24, 1890	[s/o Albert Groff and Carrie Carpenter]
Groff	Crosby	[Oct 19, 1879]	Jan. 6, 1890	s/o Albert and Carrie
Groff	baby		Dec. 14, 1889	d/o Albert and Carrie age 2 mo. 6 days
Groff	Neal	[Aug 15, 1888]	May 14, 1892	s/o Albert and Carrie
Groff	Albert	Aug 14, 1855	6/12/40	[s/o Eliphalet Groff]
Carpenter	Carrie	May 5, 1862	5/20/28	w/o Albert Groff [d/o Adeline Sarah Kathan & Caleb Randolph Carpenter]
Groff	Nora	May 27, 1887	Sep. 14, 1921	w/o Frank Brown [w/o Thomas Masten] [d/o Albert Groff & Carrie]
Fitzgerald	David		Jun 29, 1891	age 49 25th Reg. NY Co. F.
Fitzgerald	Matilda		Mar. 18, 1917	age 78 w/o David
Harey	Hiram		Sep. 25, 1889	age 48 1st Reg. Penn. Vol. Co. C.
Harey	Millie		Jul. 21, 1868	age 25 days d/o H. & E. Harey
Harey	Alley		Dec. 15, 1869	age 11 weeks child of H. & E. Harey
Rider	John W.		Mar 9, 1882	"59 year of his age"
Rider	Huburt C.		Apr. 22, 1876	age 5 yrs. 8 mo. 11 days s/o John W. and H. Rider
Seaver	Louise		Aug 23, 1890	age 23 w/o Chauncy

Courtney

Surname	Given name	Birth	Death	Notes
McGinnis	Lydia	1863	1939	
McGinnis	Alwinnie	Jun 25, 1888	Dec. 31, 1914	
Ingraham	Electa L.		Jan. 27, 1864	age 37 yrs. 10 mos. w/o Clark
Ingraham	Oliver	Apr. 18, 1848	May 21, 1850	s/o Clark and Electa
Wooster	Olive	[Dec 29, 1852]	Dec 17, 1849	w/o John Wooster, Jr. [d/o Hatevil Roberts]
Groff	John	[Apr. 4, 1762]	Dec 5, 1846	age 84 yrs. 8 mo 1 days
Willard	Reuben		Mar 11, 1881	age 92 yrs. 8 days
Willard	Rachel	Aug 24, 1796	Dec 26, 1847	w/o Reuben [maiden name Washburn]
Willard	Elisha H. [larger stone]	Feb 20, 1824	Apr. 1, 1904	[s/o Reuben and Rachel]
Willard	Grace Ann Conklin	Dec 2, 1827	Apr. 5, 1909	w/o of Elisha Willard
Willard	Almira	Nov 29, 1846	May 5, 1847	[d/o Elisha and Grace Ann]
Willard	Elery B.	Dec 6, 1853	Mar 17, 1856	[s/o Elisha and Grace Ann]
Willard	James Wesley	Feb. 11, 1849	Mar 18, 1864	[s/o Elisha and Grace Ann]
Harris	John E.	Mar 24, 1841	Jan 7, 1874	
Harris	Ethalinda	Jul. 31, 1849	Jun 8, 1894	w/o of John E. Harris [d/o Elisha Willard]
Harris	Wesley	Dec. 17, 1869	May 2, 1870	s/o John E. and E. Harris
Bennett	Maggie		Dec. 2, 1891	16yrs 3mos 24days d/o John W. and Sarah
Bennett	John W.	1844	1921	Co. E NY Heavy Artillery
Bennett	Sarah M.	Nov.1851	1931	[maiden name Conklin]
Carpenter	Robert N.	[Aug 11, 1786]	Mar 12, 1876	[s/o Joseph Carpenter Sr.]
Carpenter	Betsey [Clark]	1791	Jan 22, 1876	w/o of Robert N. Carpenter
Dunn	Charles	1864	no date	[s/o William H. Dunn and Asenith Platt]
Dunn	Ella Carpenter	1869	1905	w/o Charles Dunn [d/o Adeline Kathan

Surname	Given Name	Born	Died	Notes
				and Caleb Randolph Capenter]
Carpenter	Caleb Randolph	Nov 14, 1834	Aug. 29, 1896	s/o Robert N. Carpenter and Betsey Clark
Carpenter	Adeline Sarah Kathan	Nov 28, 1839	Oct. 2, 1923	w/o C. R. Carpenter [d/o Rennselear Kathan and Sarah Thayer]
Carpenter	Fred R. [second stone]	Nov 21, 1878	Jan 3, 1890	s/o C. R. and A. S. Carpenter
Carpenter	Maud L. [second stone]	Mar 31, 1881	Jan 3, 1890	d/o C. R. and A. S. Carpenter
Carpenter	Jennie	Oct 31, 1873	Mar 7, 1874	d/o C. R. and A. S. Carpenter
Groff	Elizabeth		Apr. 6, 1841	age 1 yr. 21 days [d/o William Henry Groff and Esther Ingraham]
Groff	Laura		Aug. 7, 1846	age 7 days d/o William and Esther
Groff	Olive Eliza		Sep. 23, 1848	age 11 months 11 days [d/o William Henry Groff and Esther Ingraham]
Groff	Paul		Oct 3, 1852	age 1 yr. 8 mo. 18 days s/o William and Esther
Conklin	John	Nov. 5, 1785	Jul. 1, 1846	age 60 yrs. 7 mo. 25 days [hus. of Barbara Abbott]
Groff	Olive	1790	Jan. 30, 1865	w/o John P. Groff [d/o John Wooster Jr. and Olive Roberts]
Groff	Mathew		Apr. 15, 1849	age 25 years 21 days s/o John P. and Olive Groff
Scribner	Russell E.	1889	no date	[s/o John d. Scribner and Laura B. Fountain]
Scribner	Amy Slack	1885	1949	w/o Russell Scribner [d/o Lyman Holmes Slack and Inez Anna Wilbur]

Surname	Given	Born	Died	Notes
Willard	John H.	Jan 22, 1852	July 25, 1876	
Willard	Norman J.	Aug 6, 1820	Feb. 26, 1864	44th Reg. NY Vol. Co. C. Art.
Thomas	Jane M.	Nov. 22, 1820	no date	w/o Norman J. Willard
Willard	Rachel	no dates		d/o N.J and J.M. Willard
Willard	Charlie	no dates		s/o N.J and J.M. Willard
Willard	Mary J.	no dates		d/o N.J and J.M. Willard
Willard	Lydia	May 6, 1856	Sep. 20, 1877	d/o N.J and J.M. Willard
Stickney	Almira		Oct 20, 1841	age 2 yrs. 1 mo. 18 days d/o D. and L. Stickney
Eglin	Synthia		Oct 19, 1837	age 43 w/o Peter D.
Bodine	Hannah		Sep. 20, 1854	age 78 w/o Albert
Bodine	Albert		Mar 1, 1846	age 71
Van Husen	Cornelius		Feb. 27, 1858	age 29 yrs. 10 mo. 11 days
Stanclift	Ann Eliza		Apr. 22, 1859	age 34 yrs. 4 mo 18 days w/o William
Stickney	Alida		Oct 10, 1883	age 66 yrs. 8 mo 6 days w/o David
Stickney	David	Feb. 27, 1807	June 14, 1893	
Stickney	Mary	Jan 31, 1852	Oct 12, 1890	
Stickney	John	Aug 8, 1854	Dec. 31, 1910	
Groff	Fred	1871	1896	[s/o Eliphalet and Martha J.
Letson	William H.	Jan 20, 1857	Jun 9, 1898	[s/o Charles Letson and Margaret Courtney]
Letson	Charlotte		Jul. 19, 1883	age 21 w/o William Letson [d/o Eliphalet Groff]
Lobdell	Lydia	Jun 30, 1814	Sept 18, 1900	
Scribner	Russell E.		1968	
Olsen	Mable S.	1914		
Olsen	Arne Niles	1903	1998	
Patterson	George A.	1951	1995	

Patterson	Robert E. [second stone]	Nov 8, 1916	Oct 20, 1981	Tec4 US Army WWII
Patterson	Virginia R.	1921		wife of Robert E.
Peters	Hugh R.	1930		
Peters	Beatrice VanAvery	1932	1996	m. Nov. 24, 1956
Craig	Scott	1903	1985	
Craig	Dorothy Mosher	1912	2003	His Wife [w/o Scott Craig]
King	Thomas M.	1919	2001	US Navy WWII
King	Rozella G.	Dec 28, 1923	Apr 13, 2002	
Christensen	Lillian M.	Sept 5, 1913 Montreal Canada	Sept 19, 1996 Hope NY	
Christensen	Carl E.	June 14, 1905 Ribe, Denmark	Nov 2, 1982 Hope NY	
Mundell	Melony Susan			age 5mos.
Courtney	Florence	June 4, 1889	Jan. 16, 1970	

(http://www.hamilton.nygenweb.net/cemeteries/willard.html)

This cemetery is peaceful. My team will go back and visit the children and the others because they are deserving to not be forgotten.

Sammons Private Cemetery
Fonda, NY
Montgomery County

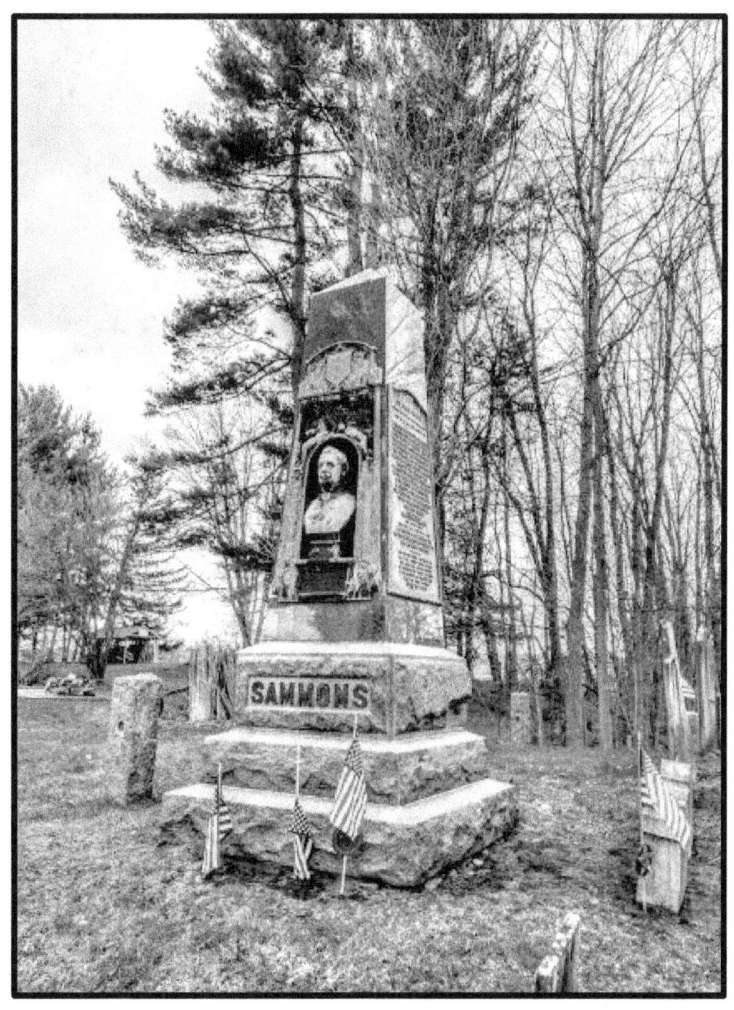

This is a private cemetery owned by the Sammons family. However, for historical sake, we found this cemetery quite interesting. It was also an honor to visit. The cemetery is located on Old Trail Road just off Route 30 about 2 miles south of Johnstown, in the town of Mohawk.

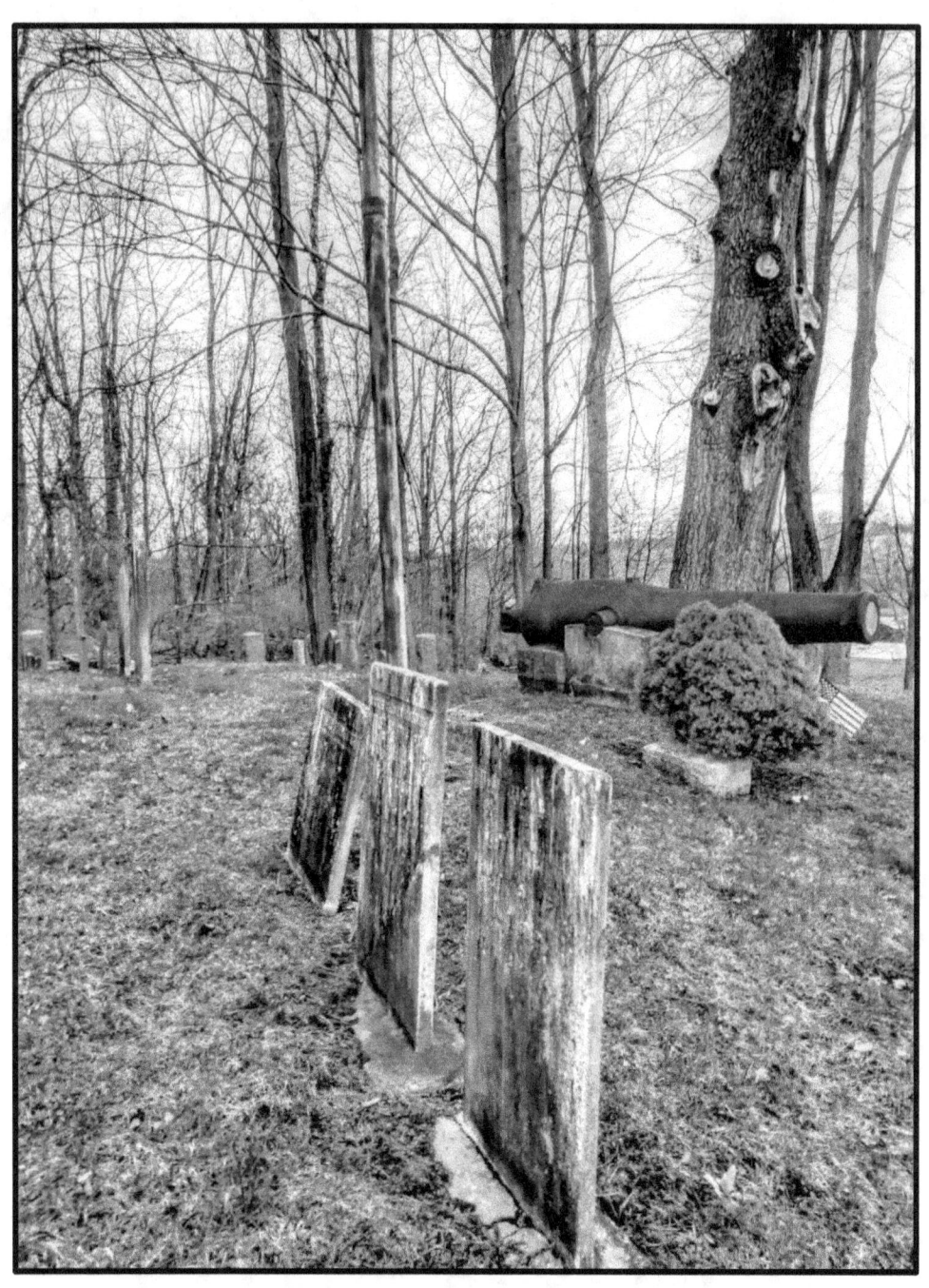

Sammons Private Cemetery

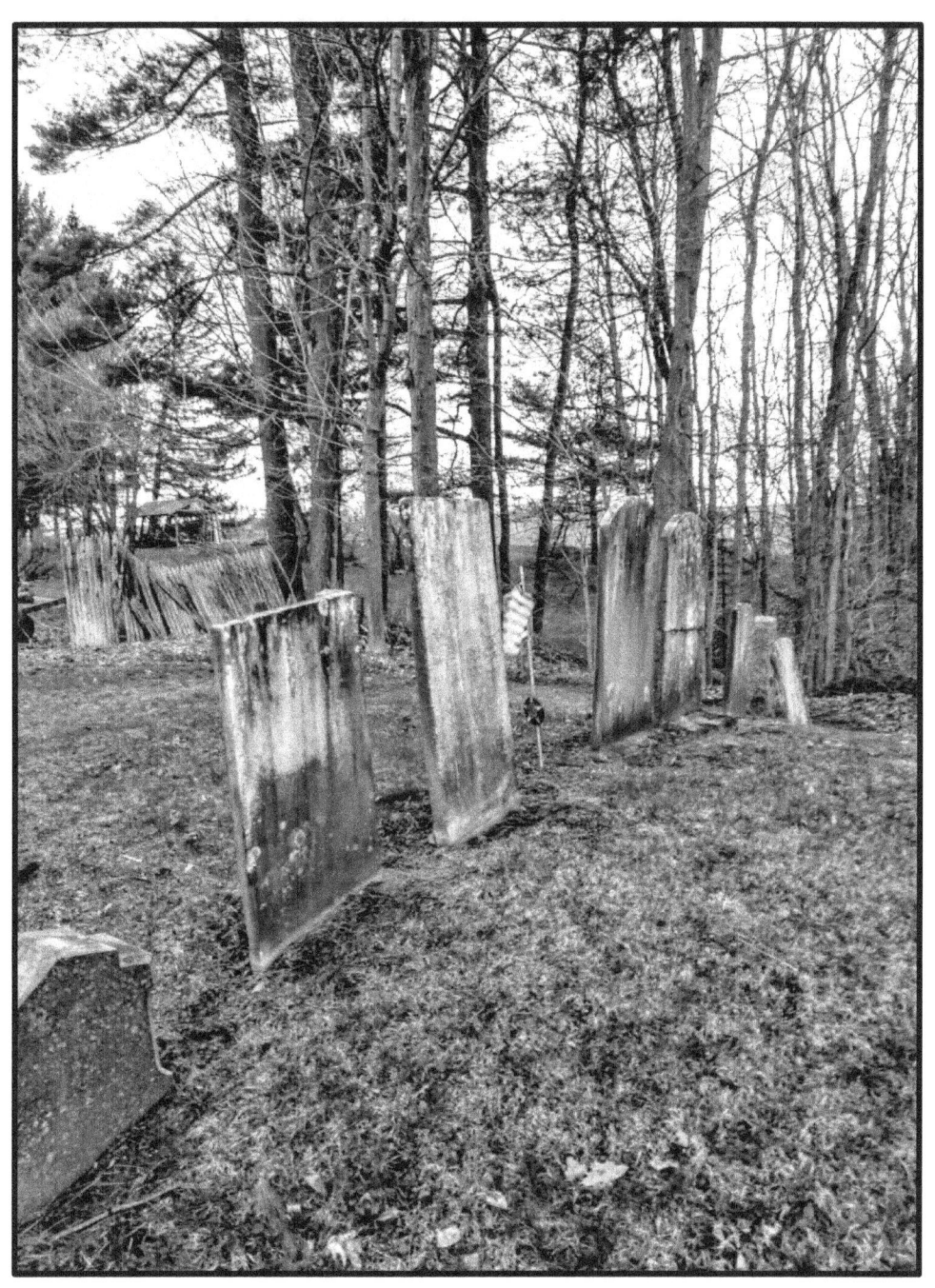

Sammons Private Cemetery

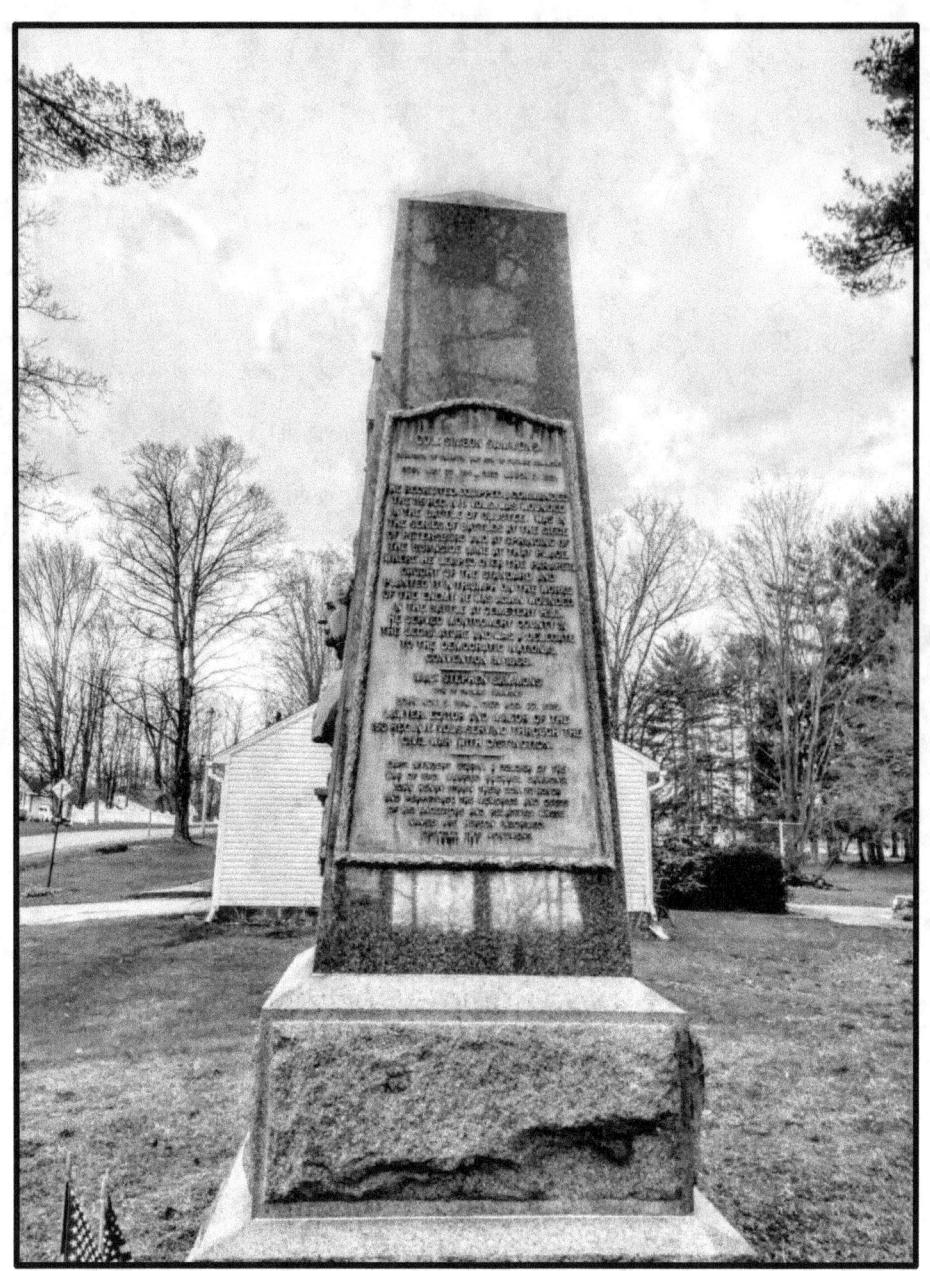

Sammons Private Cemetery

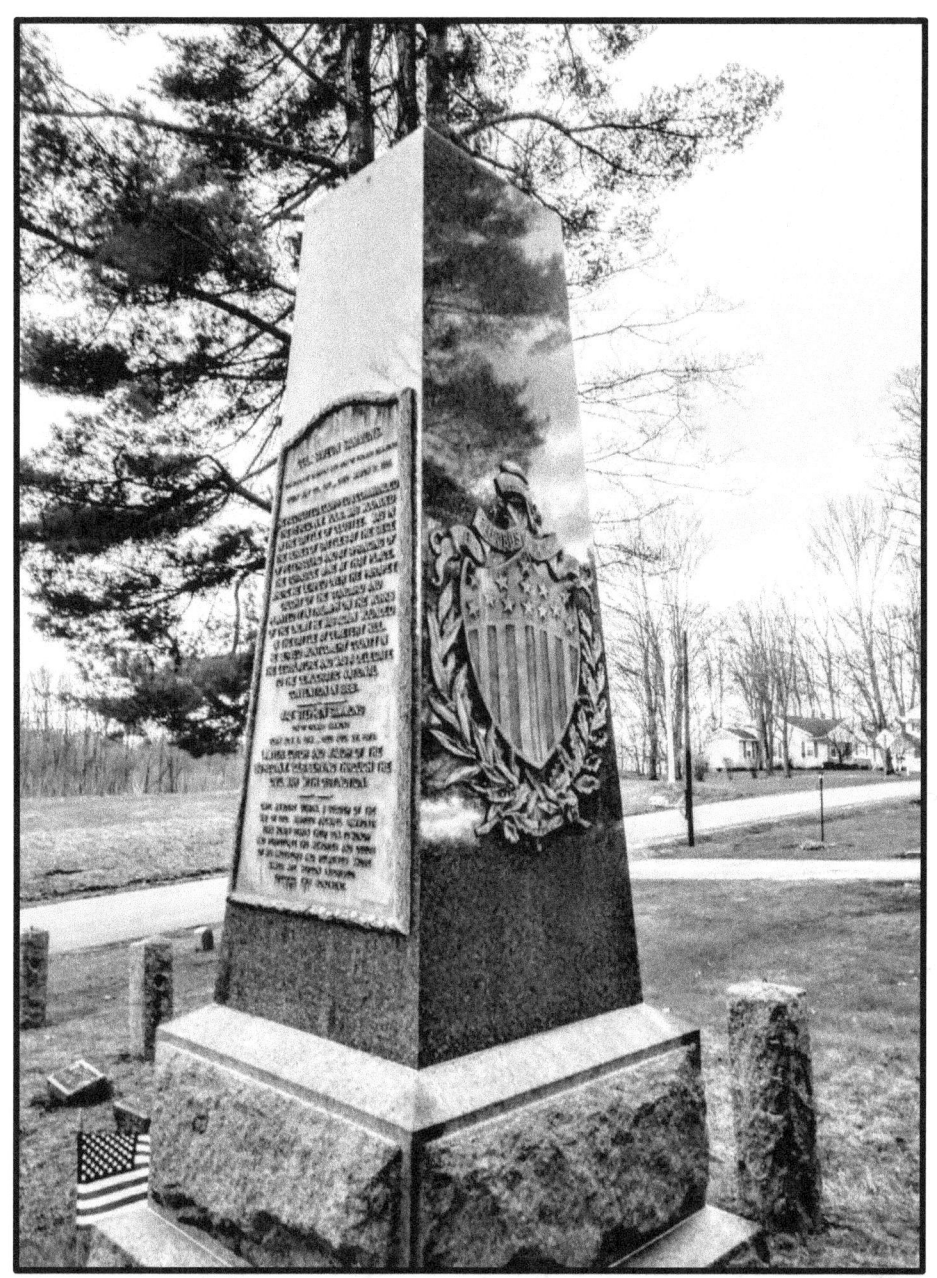

Sammons Private Cemetery

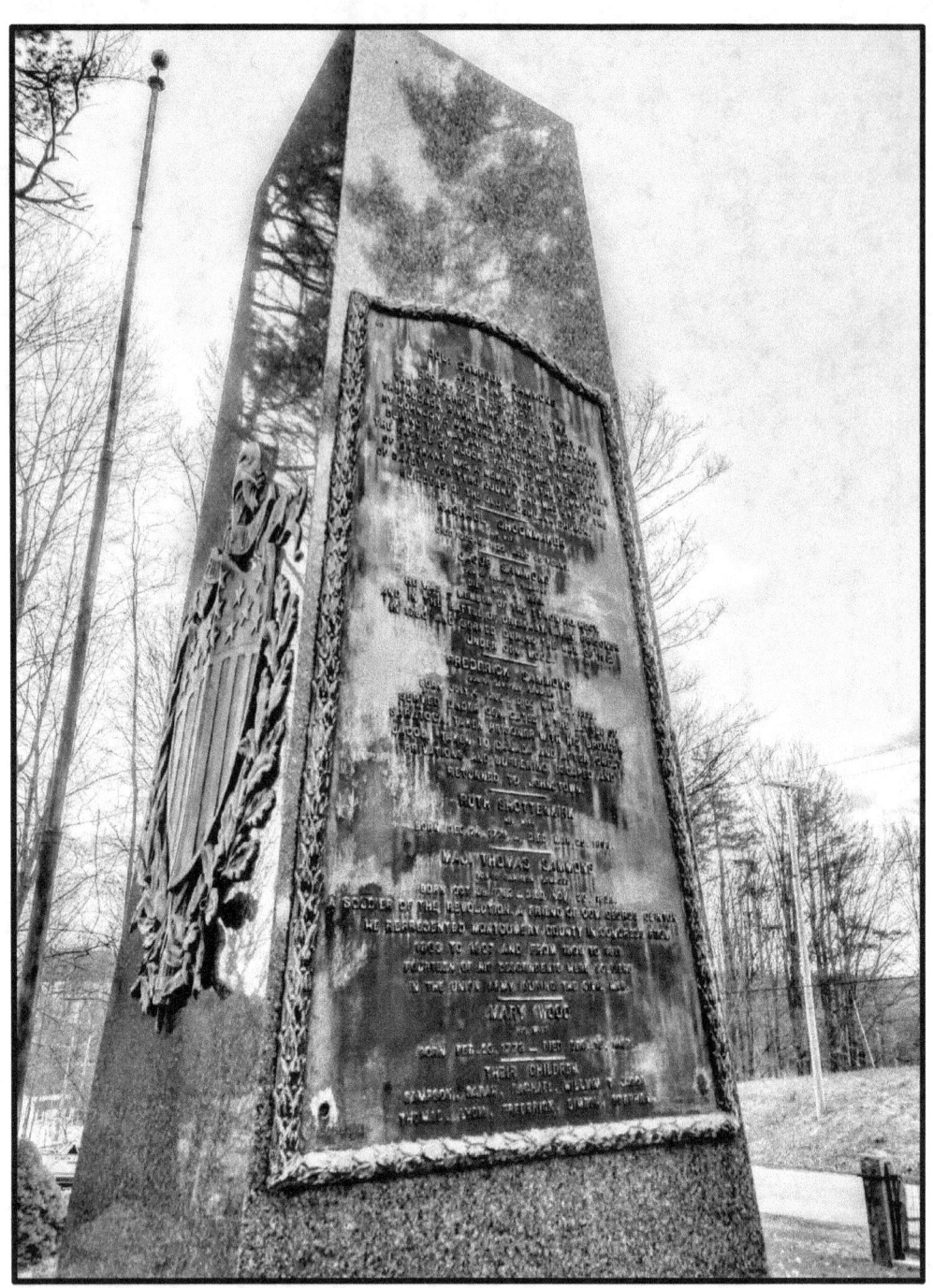

Sammons Private Cemetery

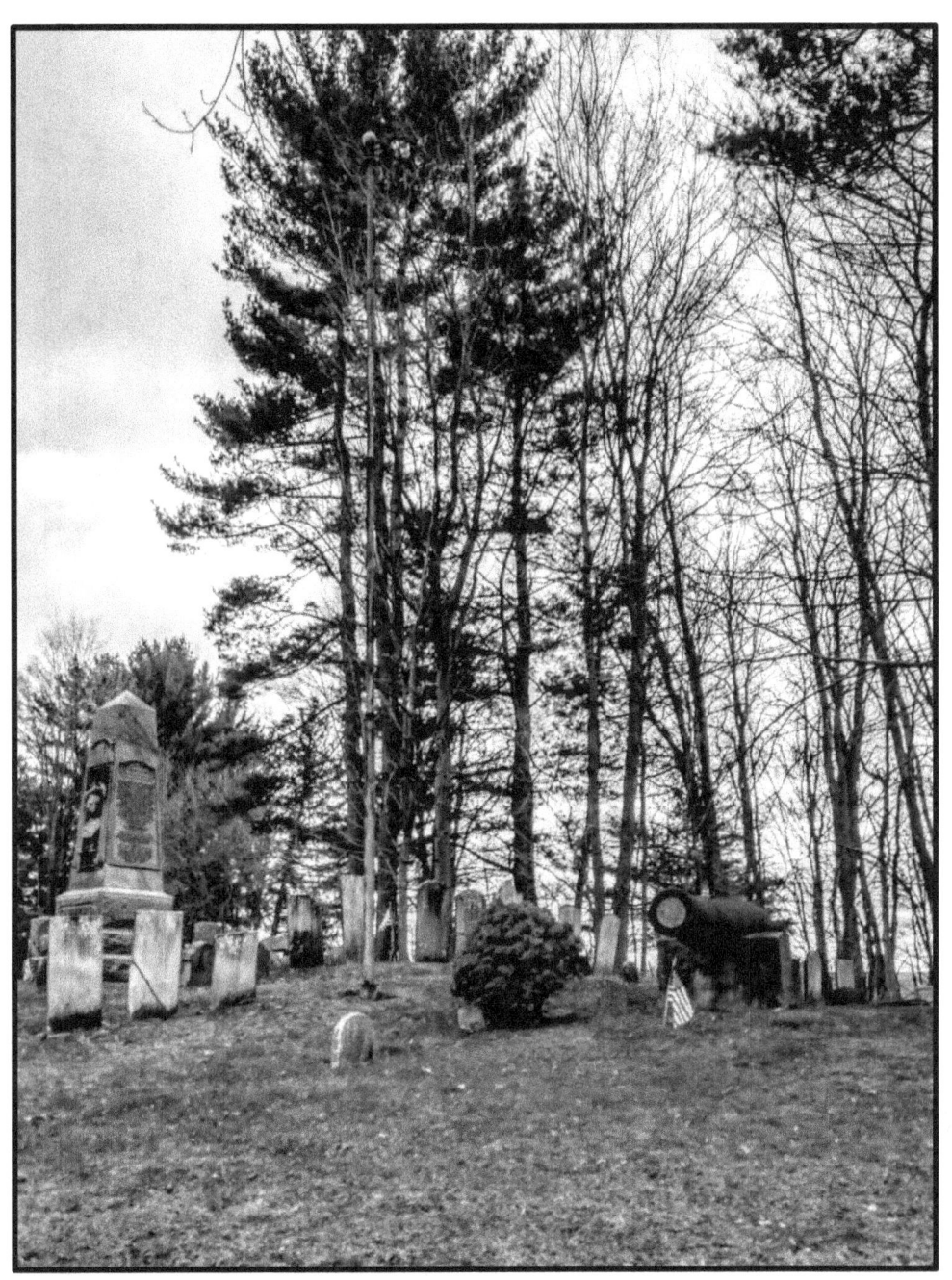

Sammons Private Cemetery

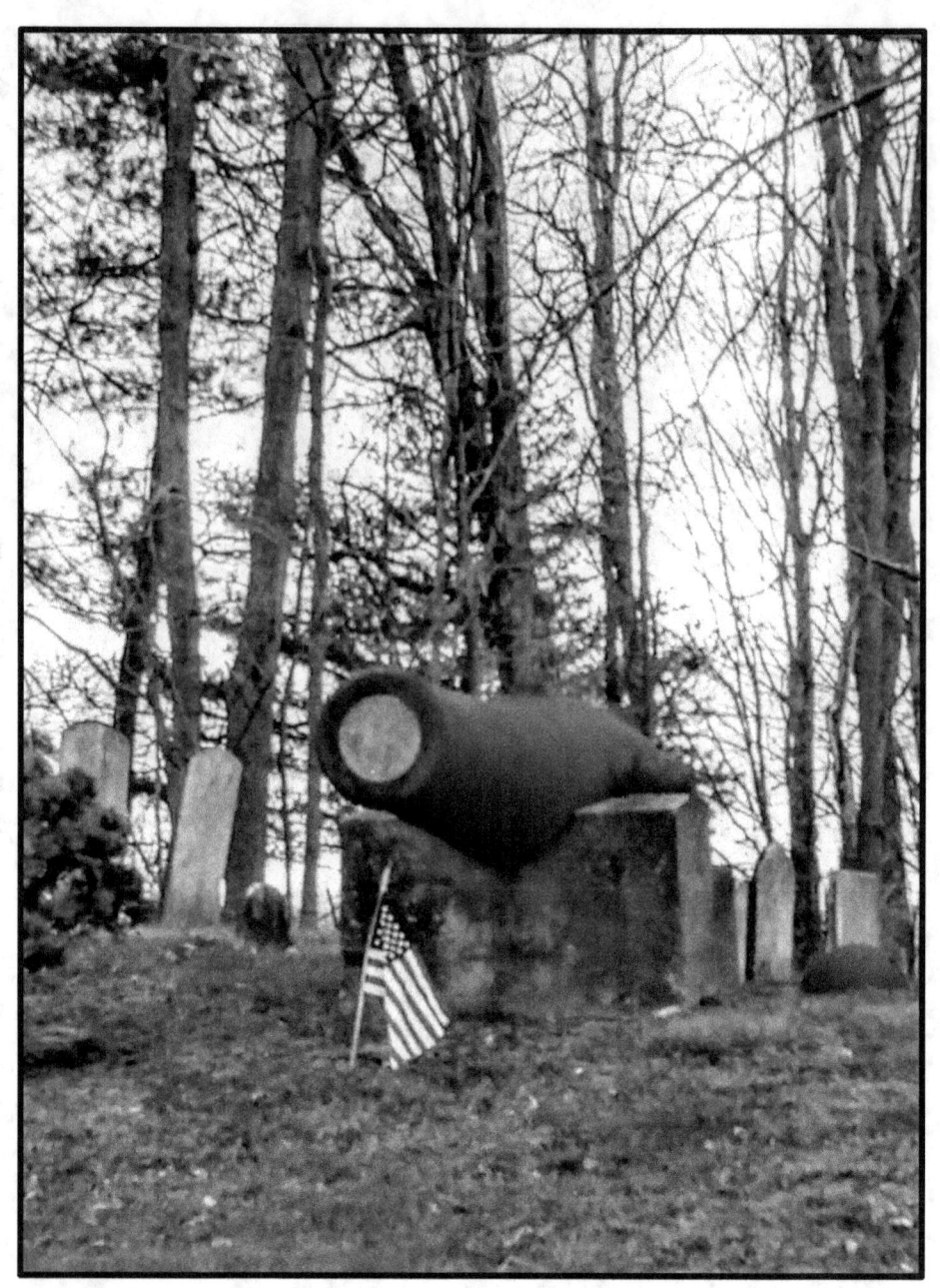

Sammons Private Cemetery

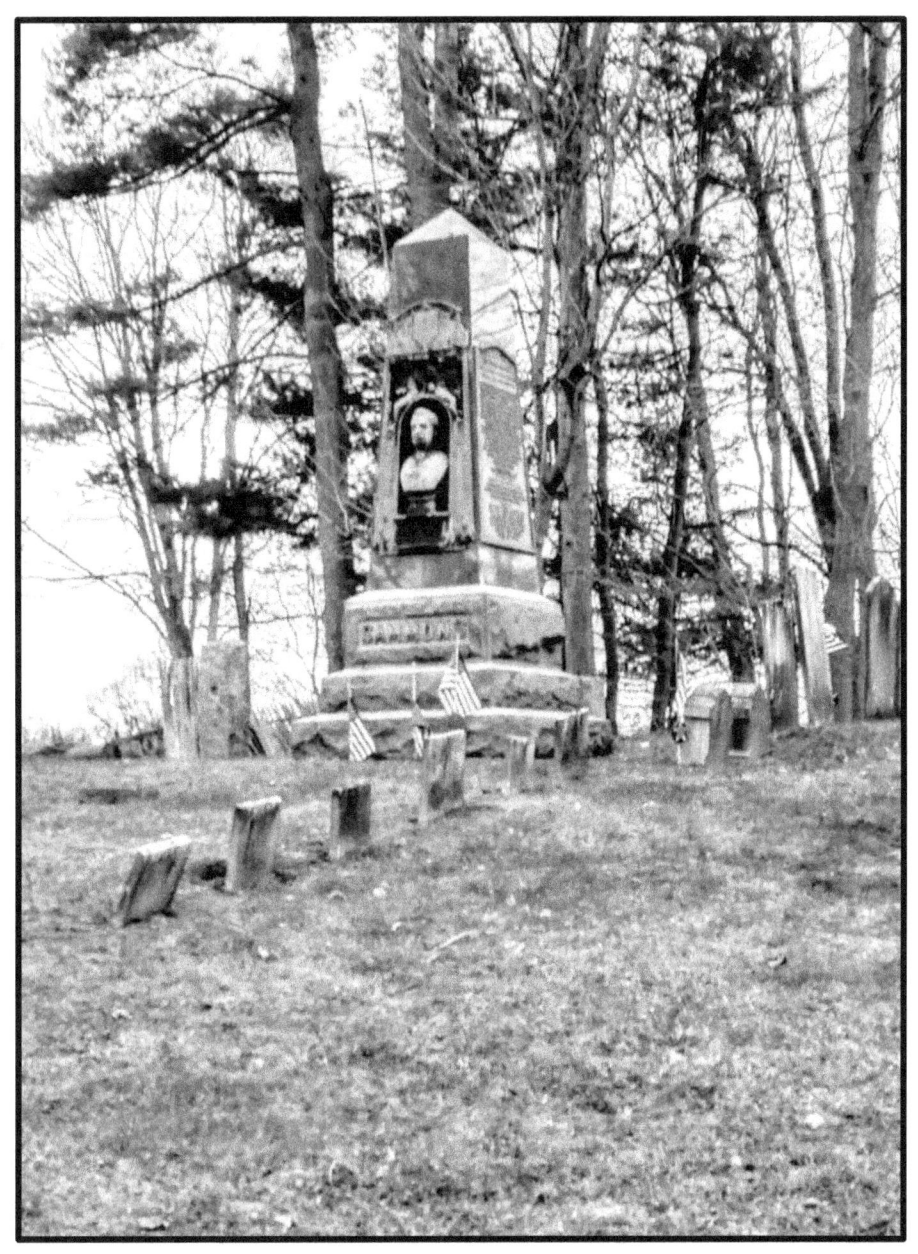

Sammons Private Cemetery

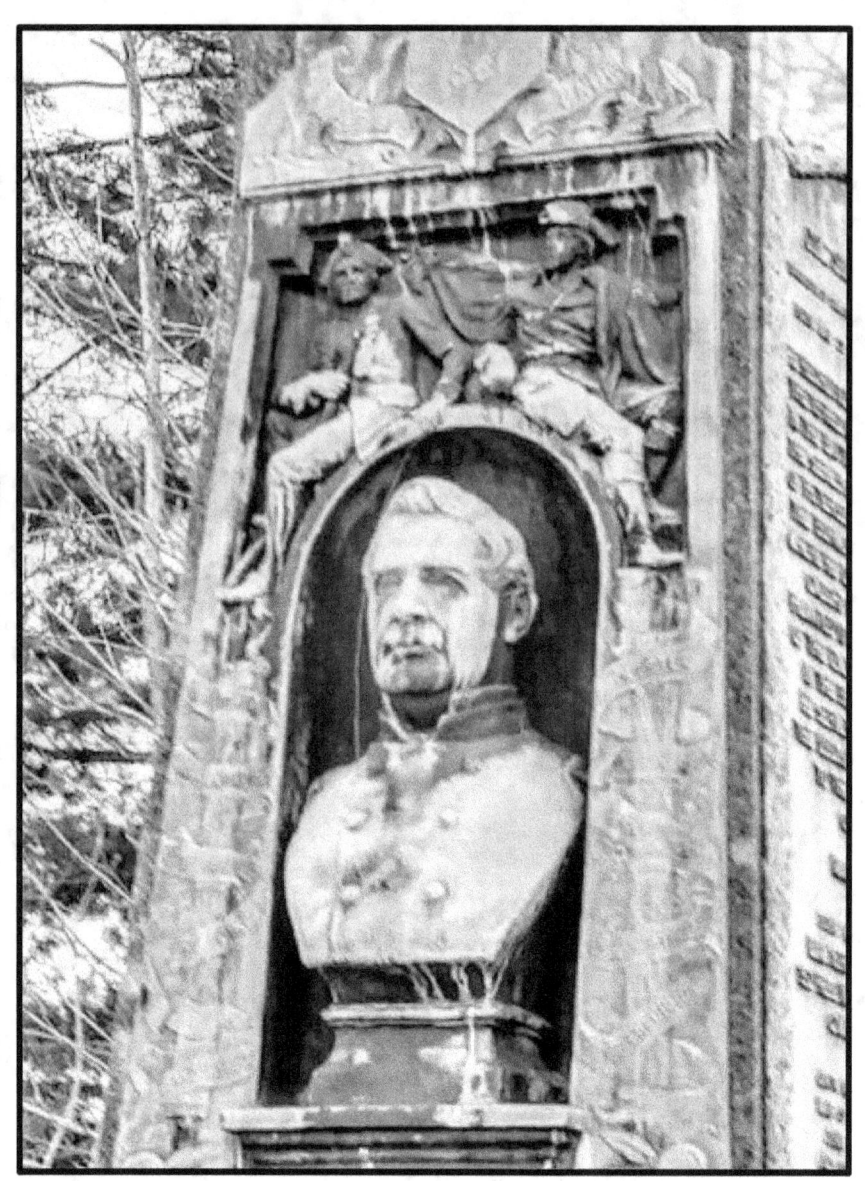

Sammons Private Cemetery

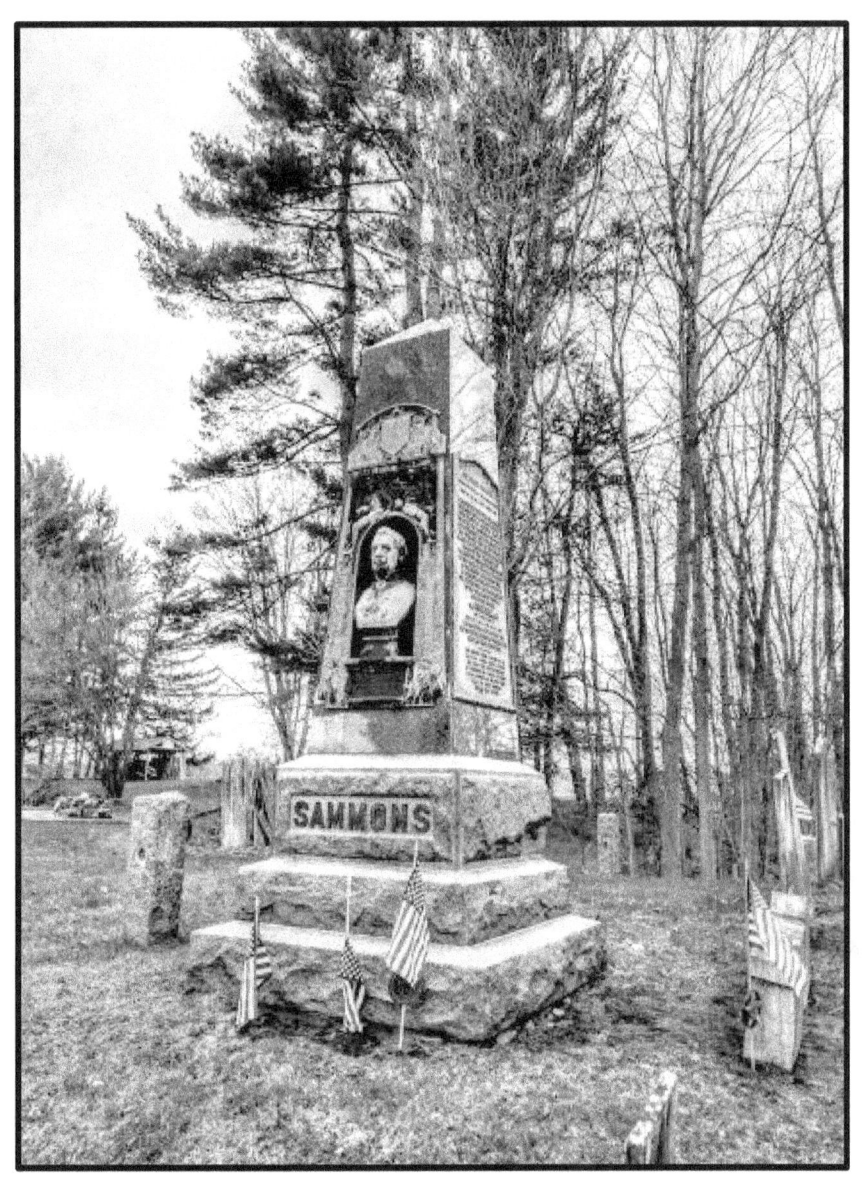

Sammons Private Cemetery

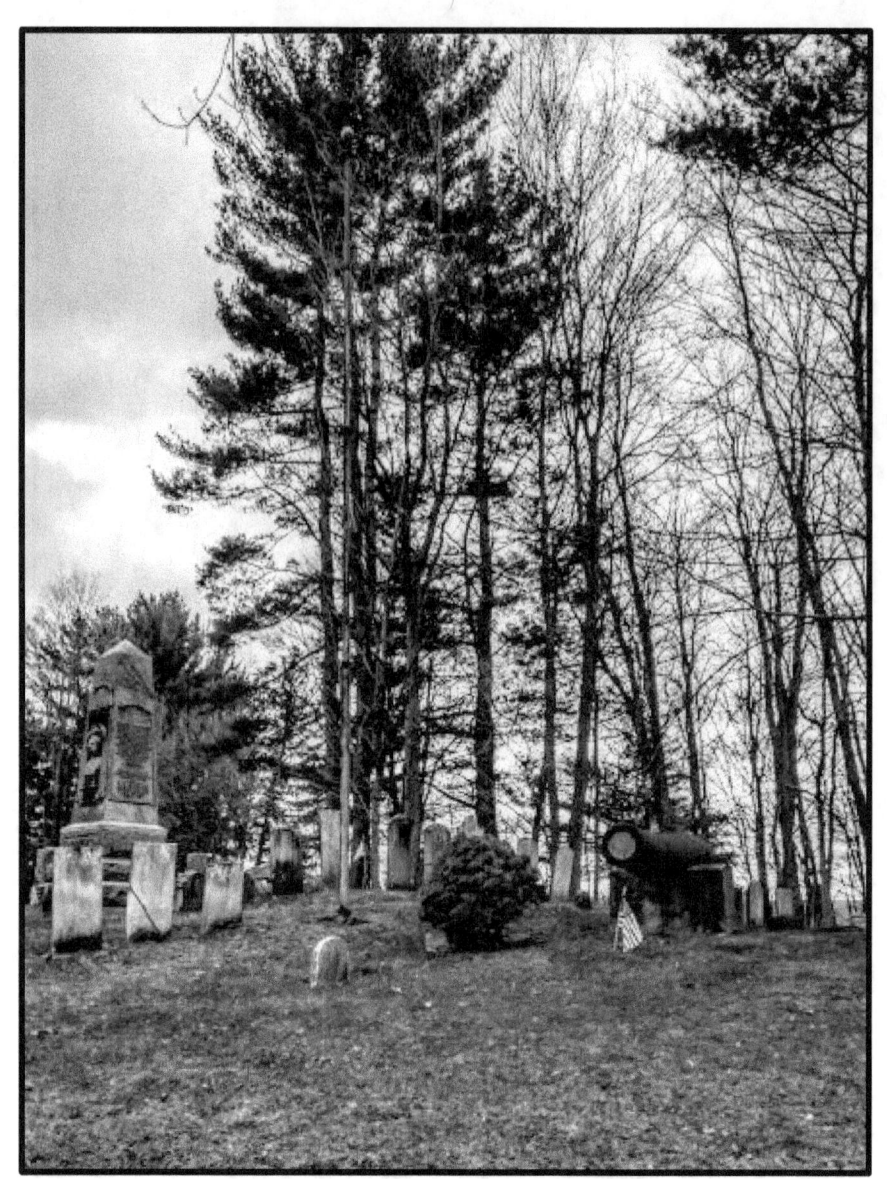

Sammons Private Cemetery

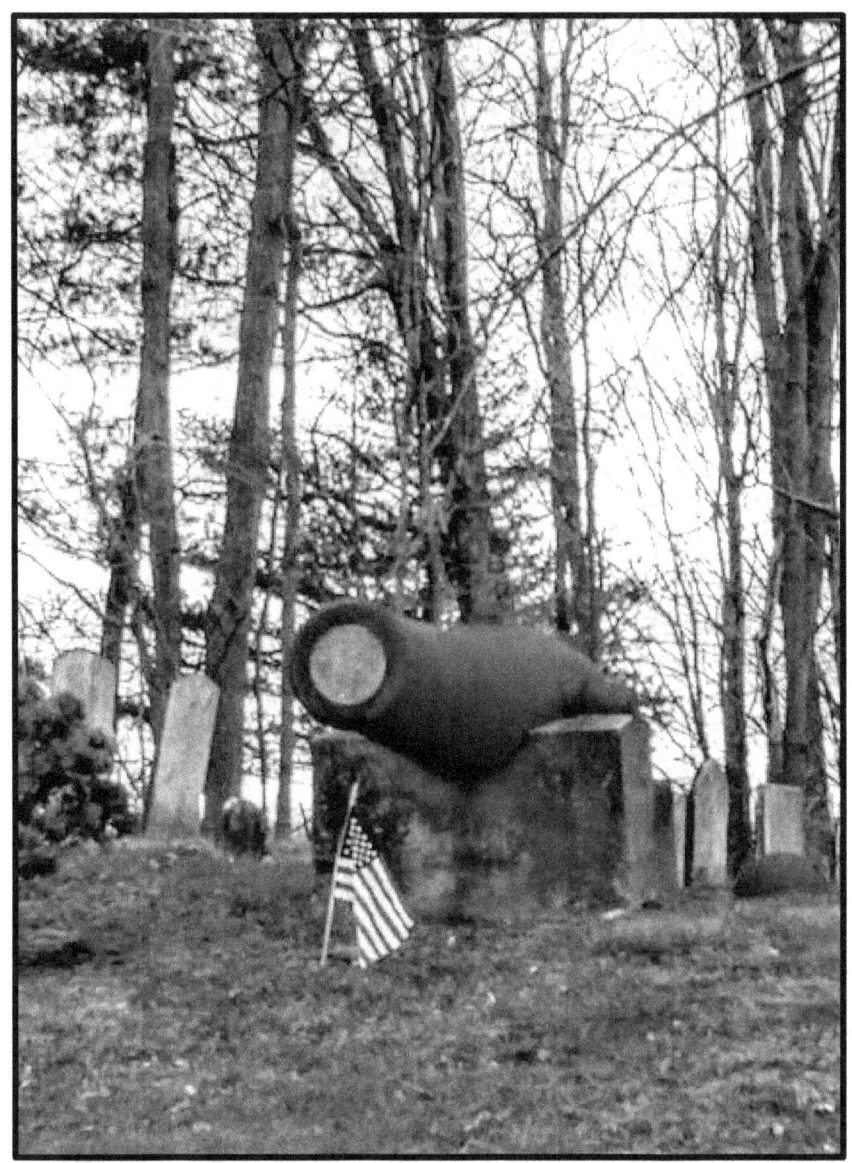

Sammons Private Cemetery

What I most enjoyed about this cemetery was the historical information on the statue stone and seeing the actual cannon. Cannons generally hold a lot of energy paranormally speaking. We often can get good readings off of them. Although we didn't do that here out of respect of the family as it's a privately owned cemetery.

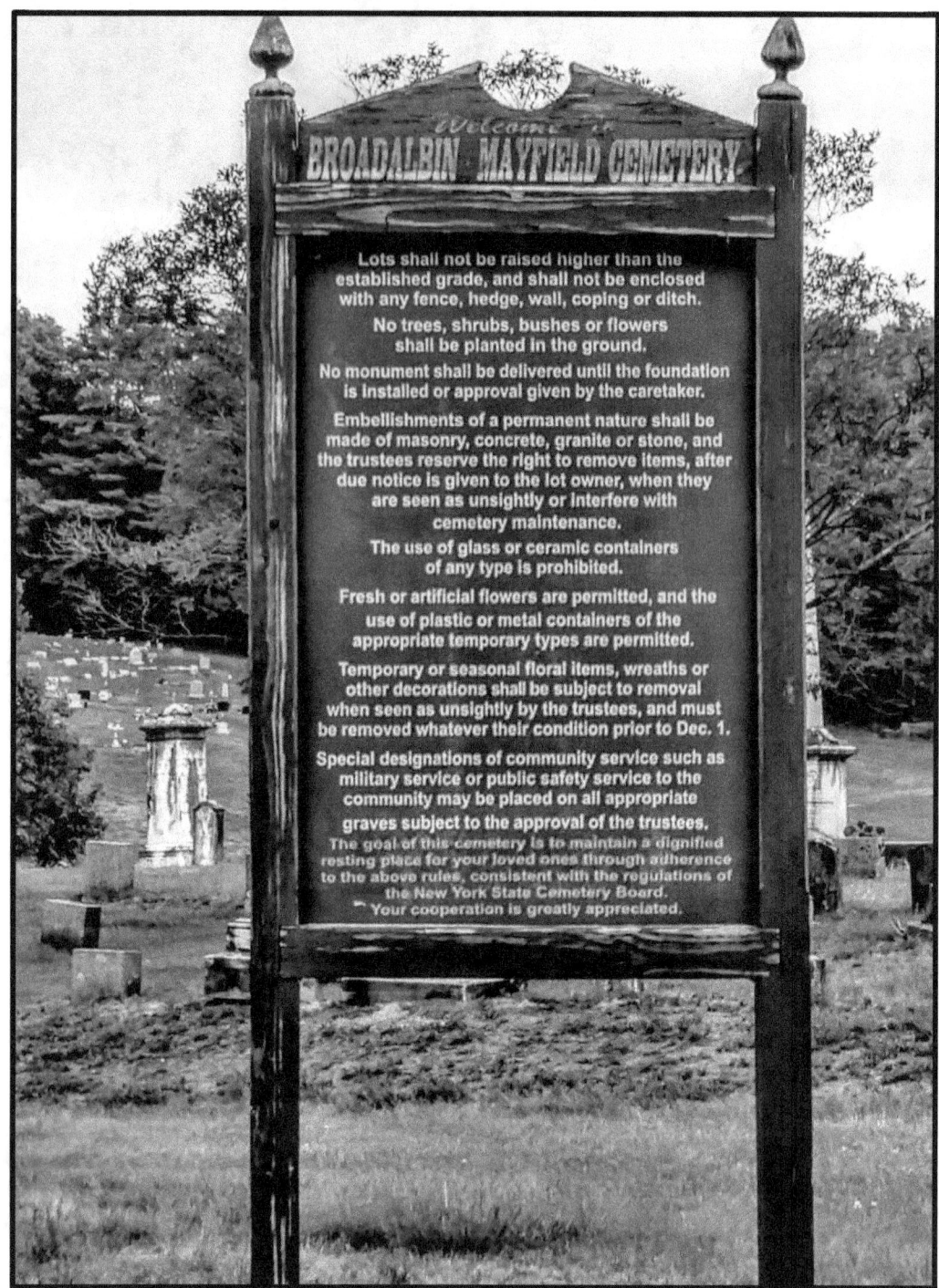

Broadalbin Mayfield Cemetery

There is a section map posted in the center of the cemetery. Many early graves were moved from small family cemeteries, with the earliest death date being about 1810.

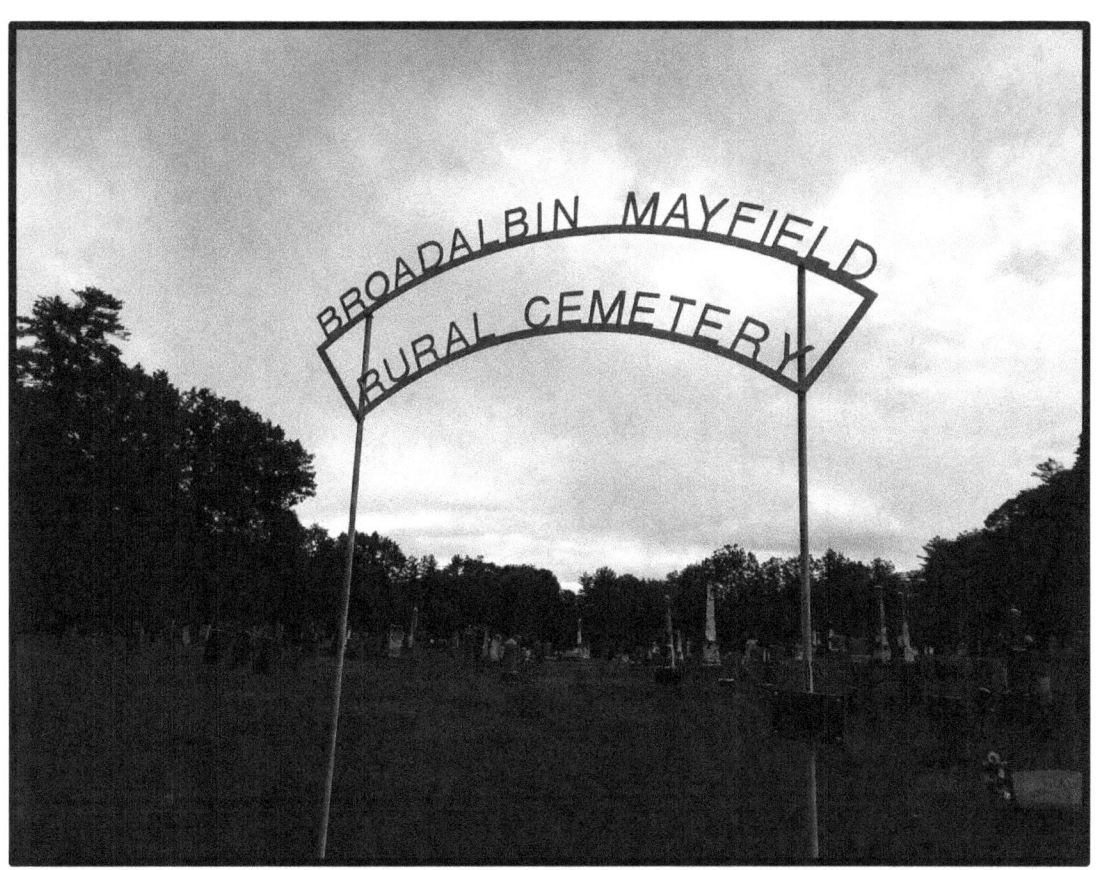

Broadalbin Mayfield Cemetery

Located in Mayfield approx. 0.1 miles west of the Broadalbin town line on Broadalbin's North Main Street Extension. (Also known as Broadalbin Cemetery Road). The proper name for this cemetery is Broadalbin-Mayfield Rural Cemetery. Sections are numbered from 1 on the right side faced from the road through 7 at the far left, with 8 also tucked in on the left and 9 at the far right rear.

This was a large cemetery as it has stones tucked in around to the left hand side, way up on a hill. It's quite nice in there and seemed to be calm as far as spirit activity.

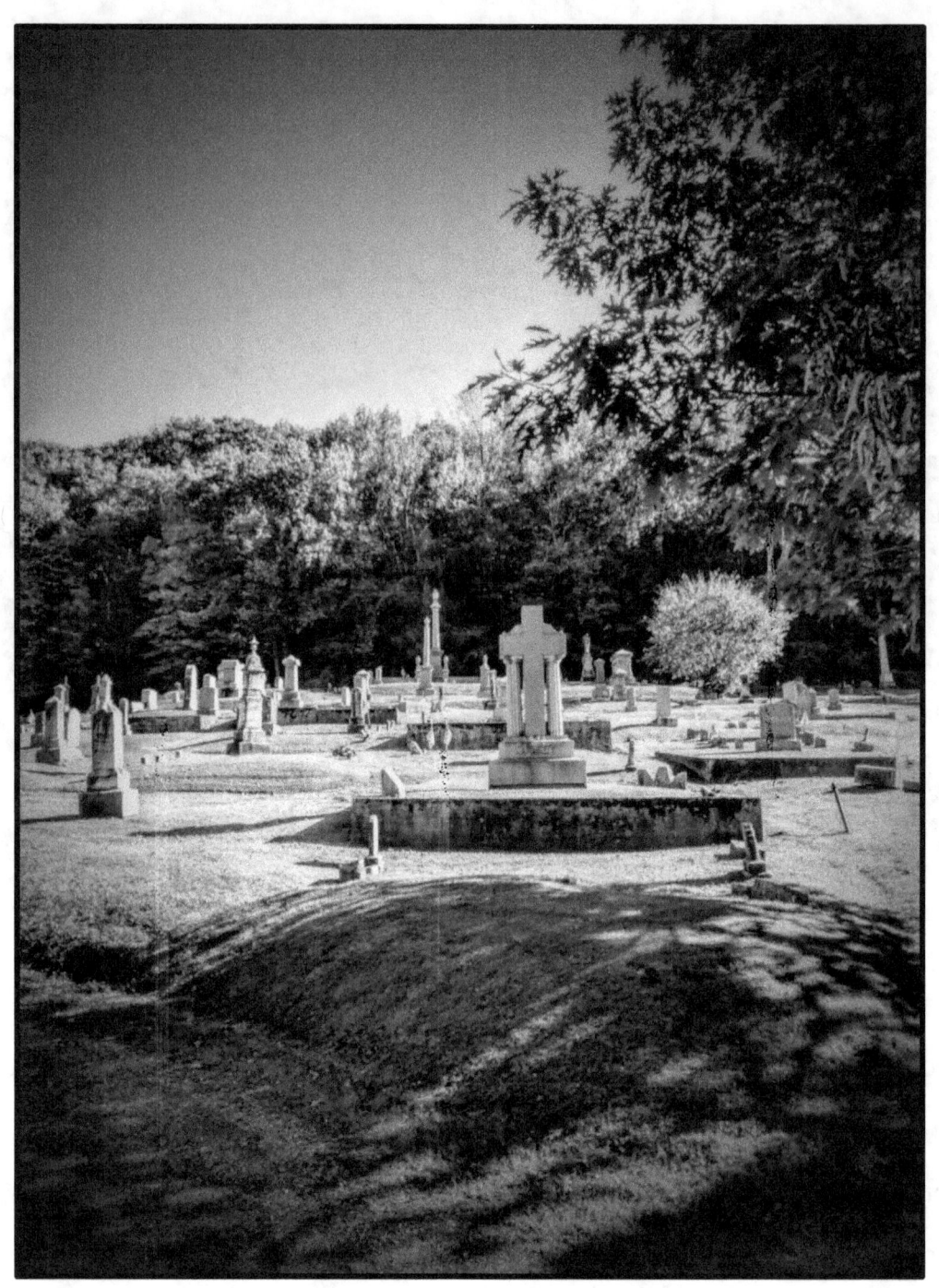

Broadalbin Mayfield Cemetery

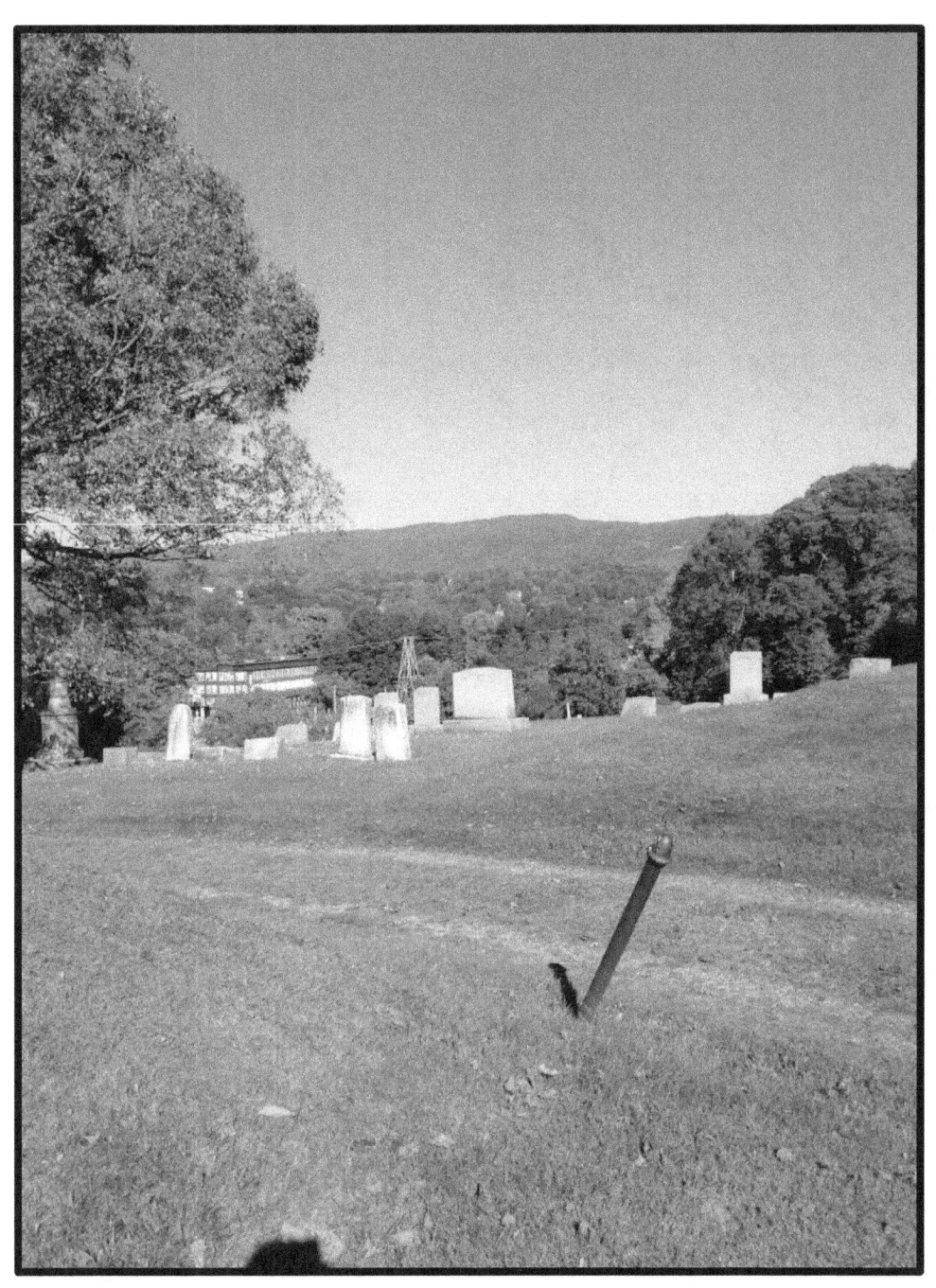

Broadalbin Mayfield Cemetery

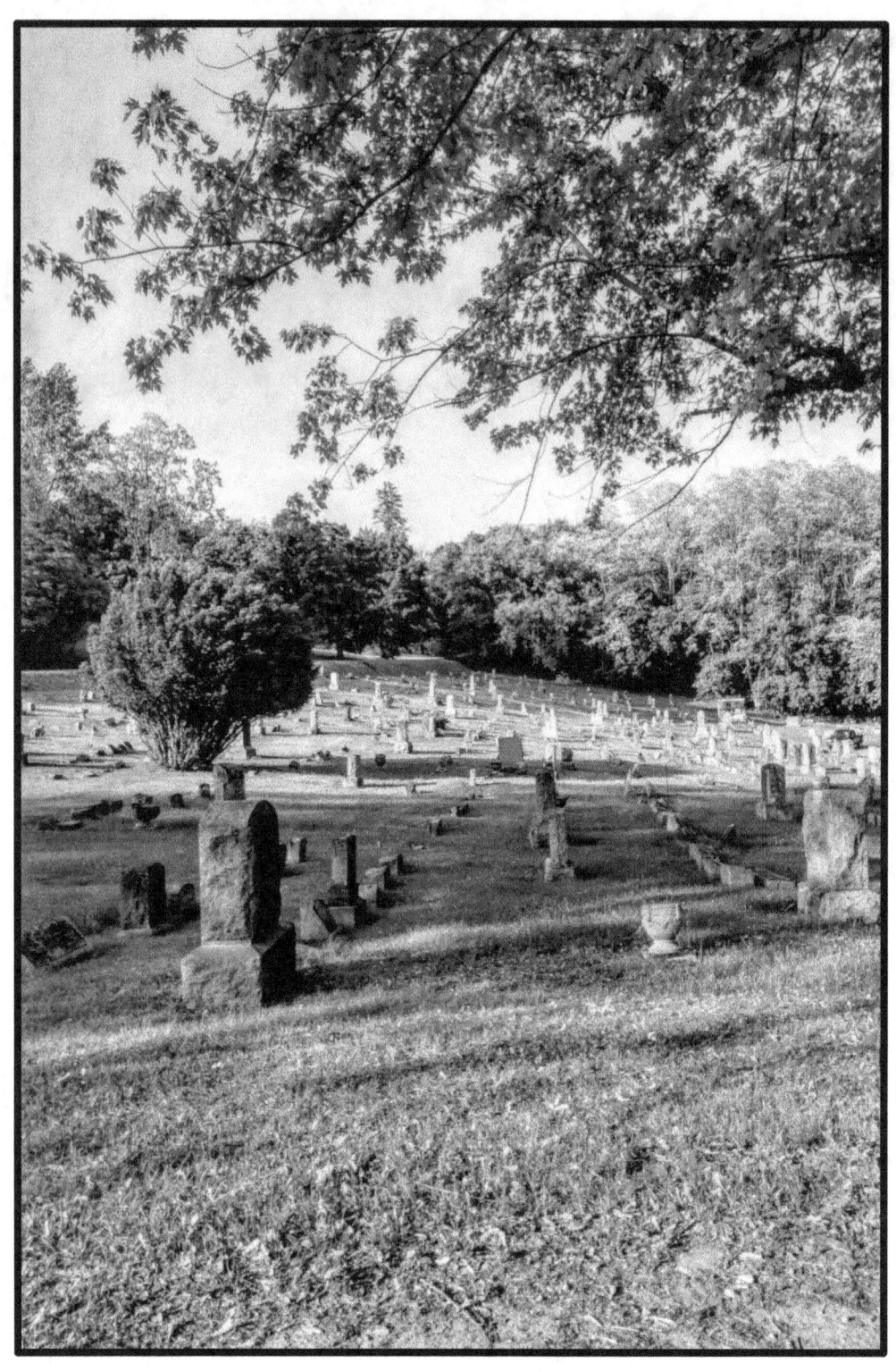

Broadalbin Mayfield Cemetery

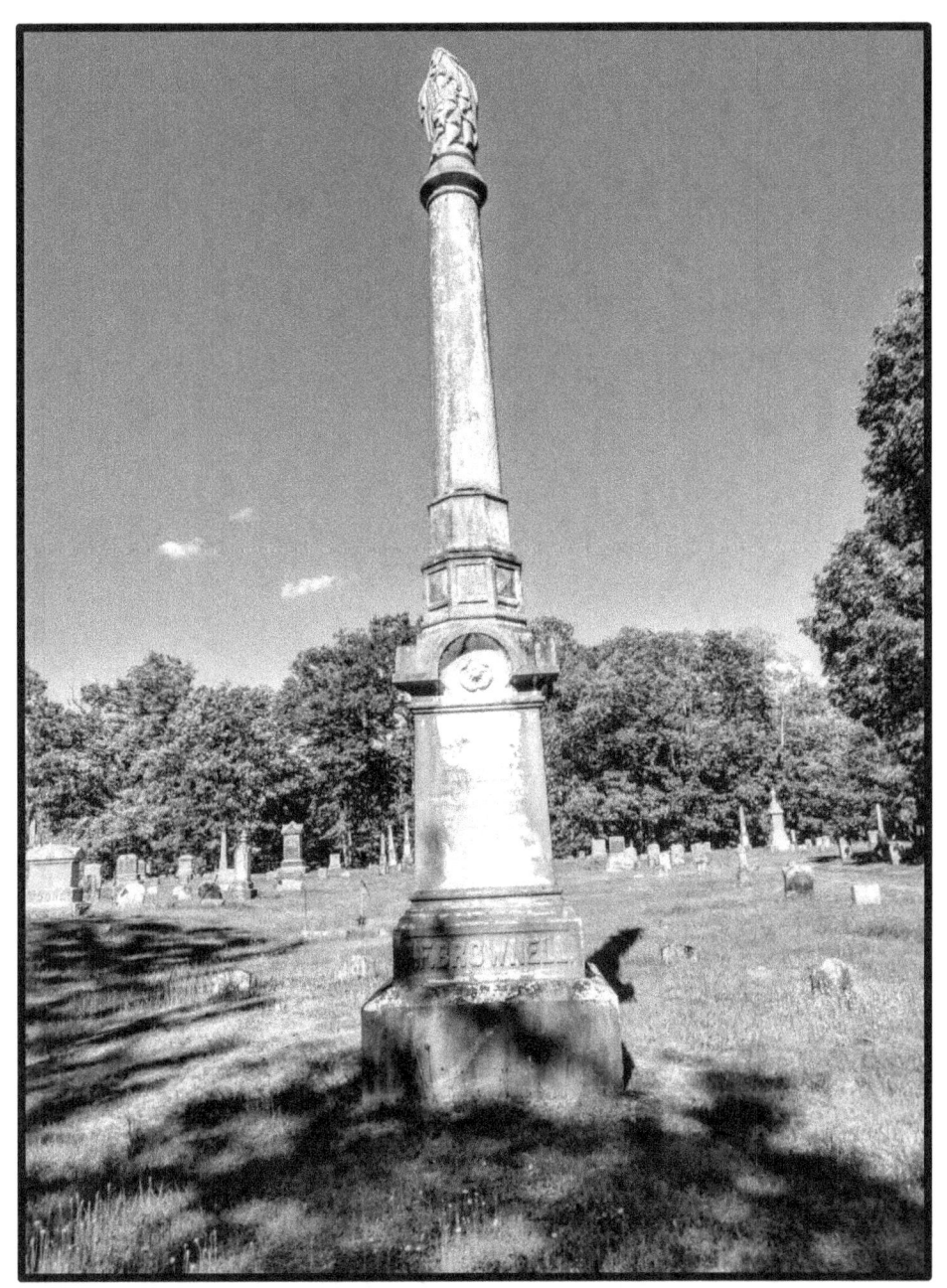

Broadalbin Mayfield Cemetery

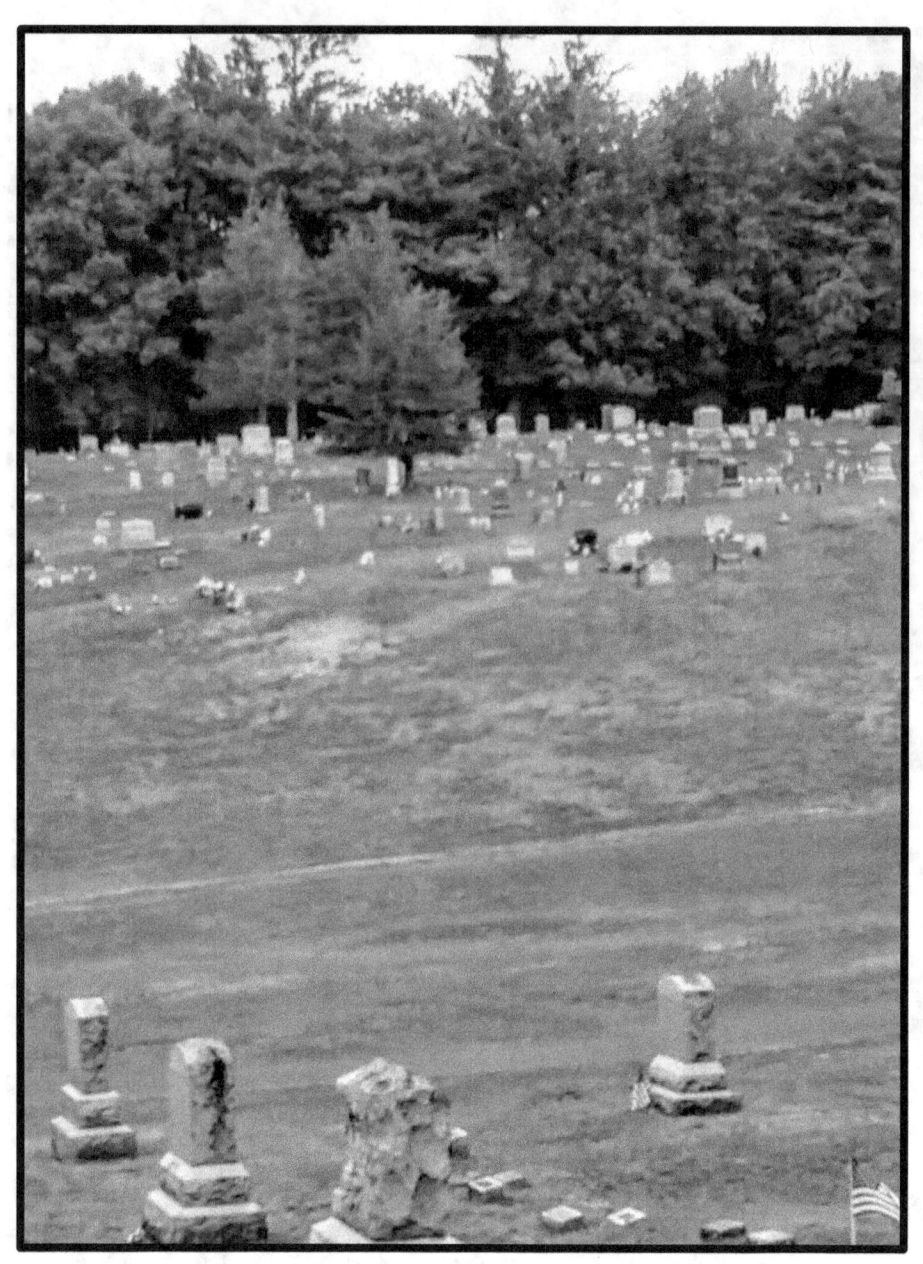

Broadalbin Mayfield Cemetery

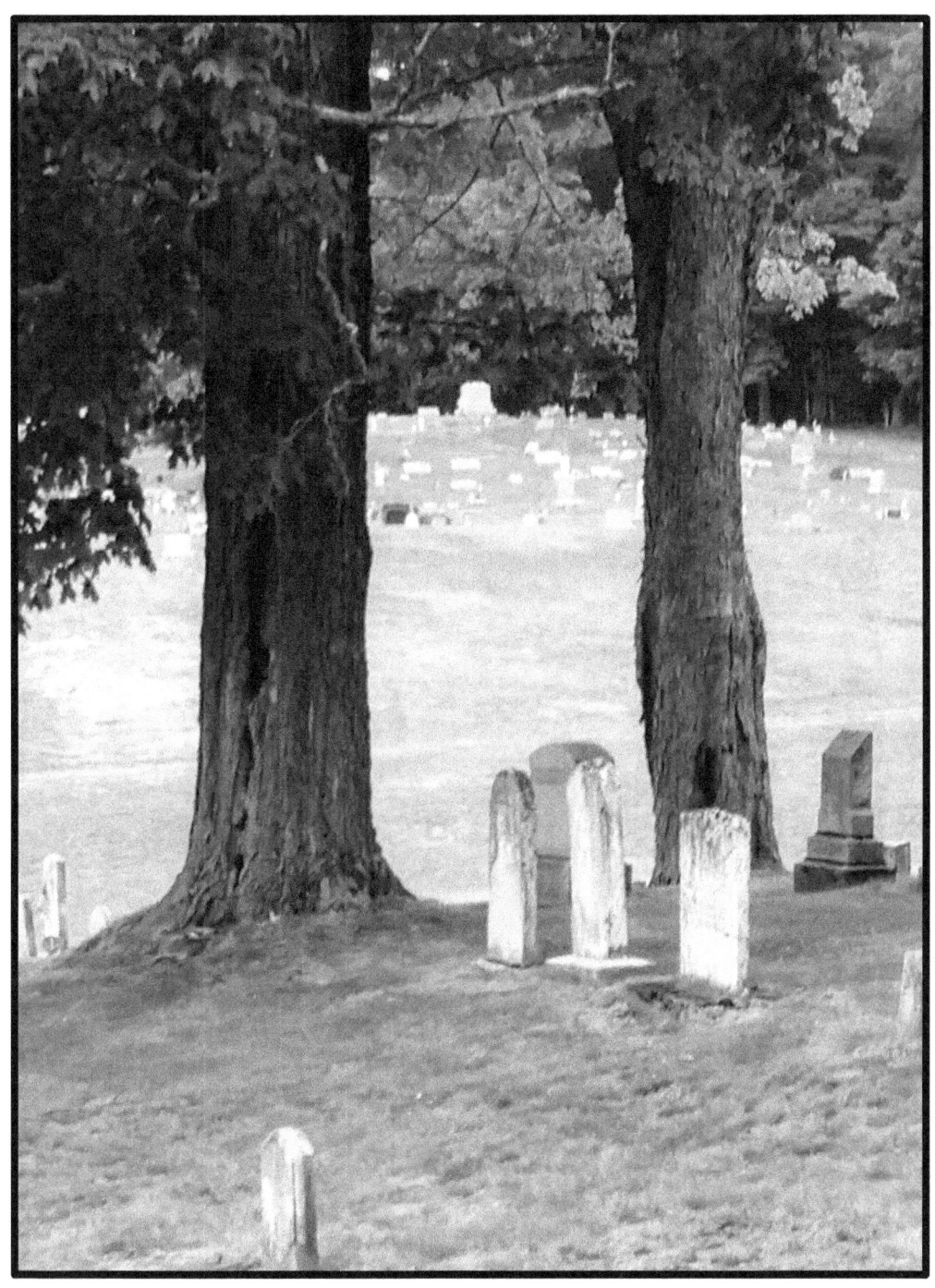

Broadalbin Mayfield Cemetery

I think a black and white picture shows a certain beauty too. This cemetery, no matter where I drove, felt quiet. I was surprised how far up and in and around the corner I could drive.

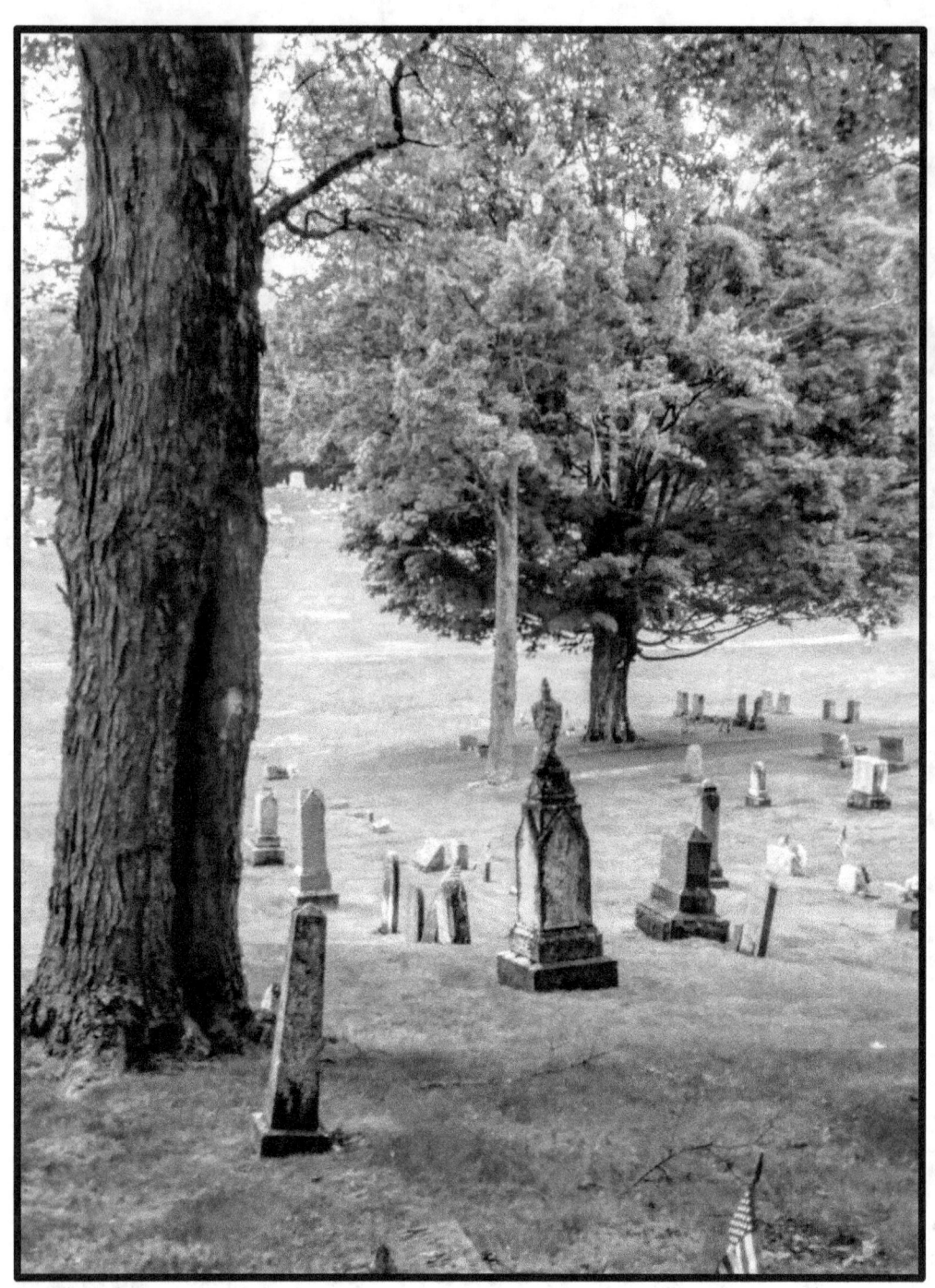

Broadalbin Mayfield Cemetery

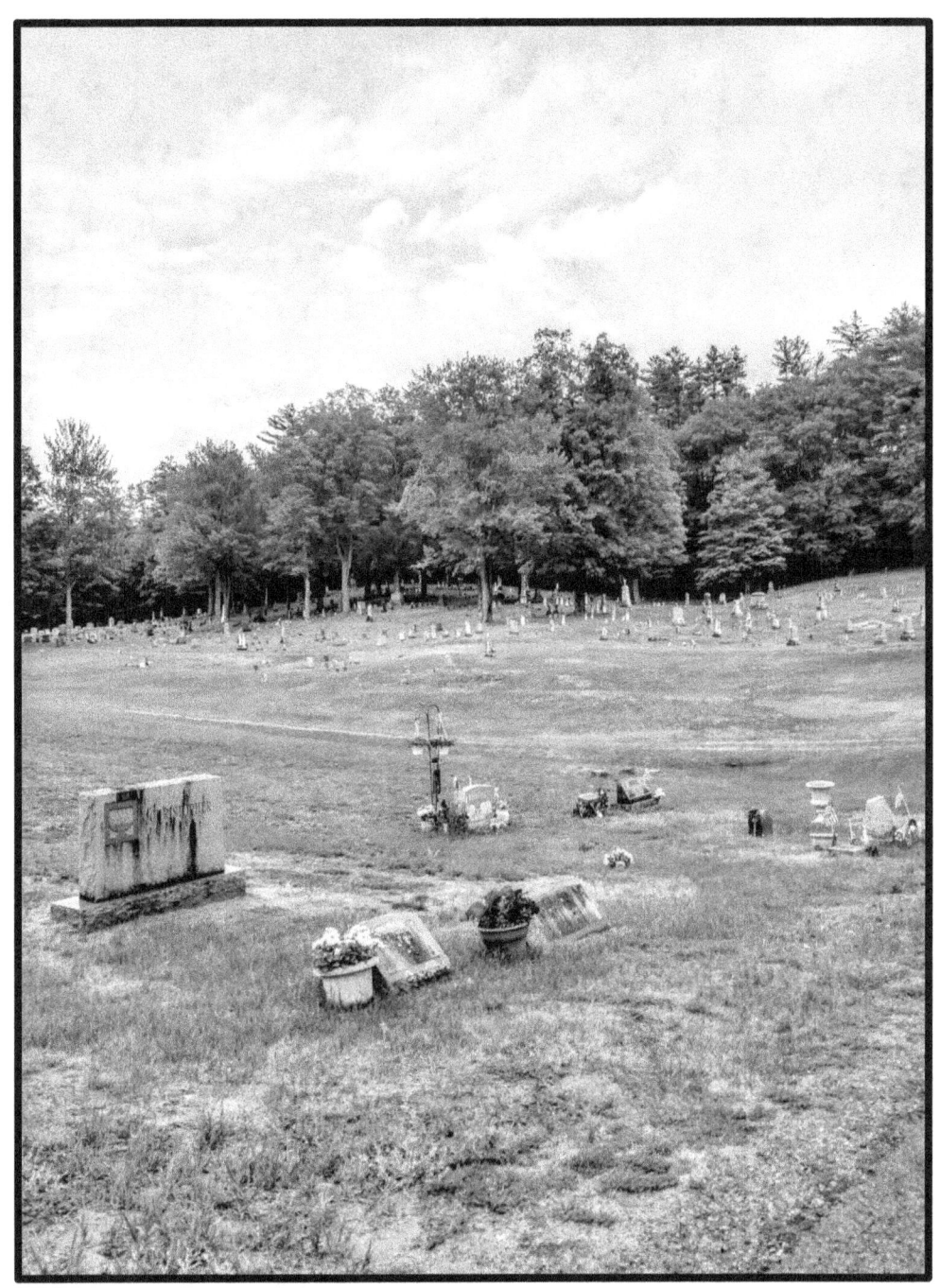

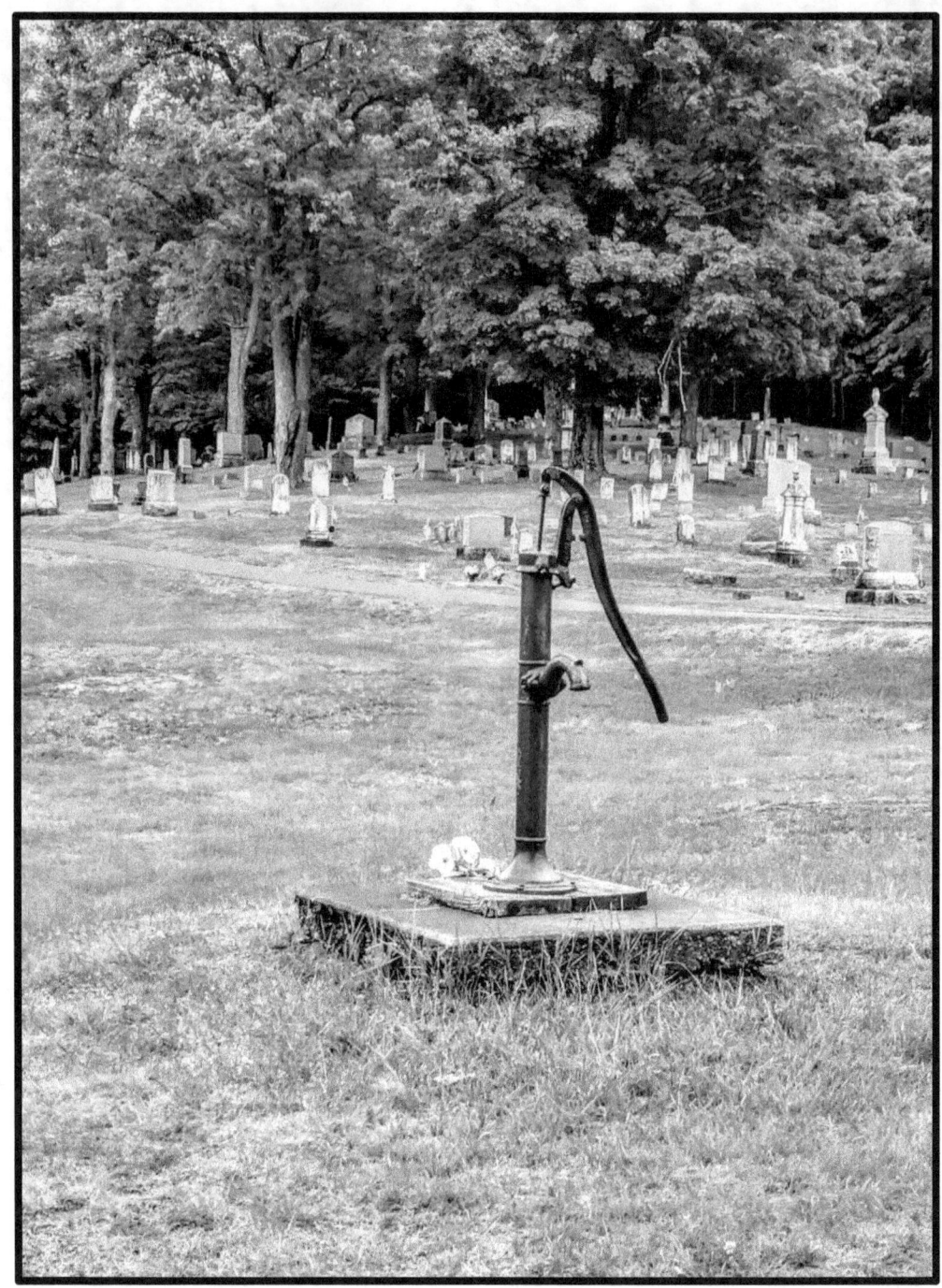

Broadalbin Mayfield Cemetery

I enjoy seeing these old fashioned water pumps.

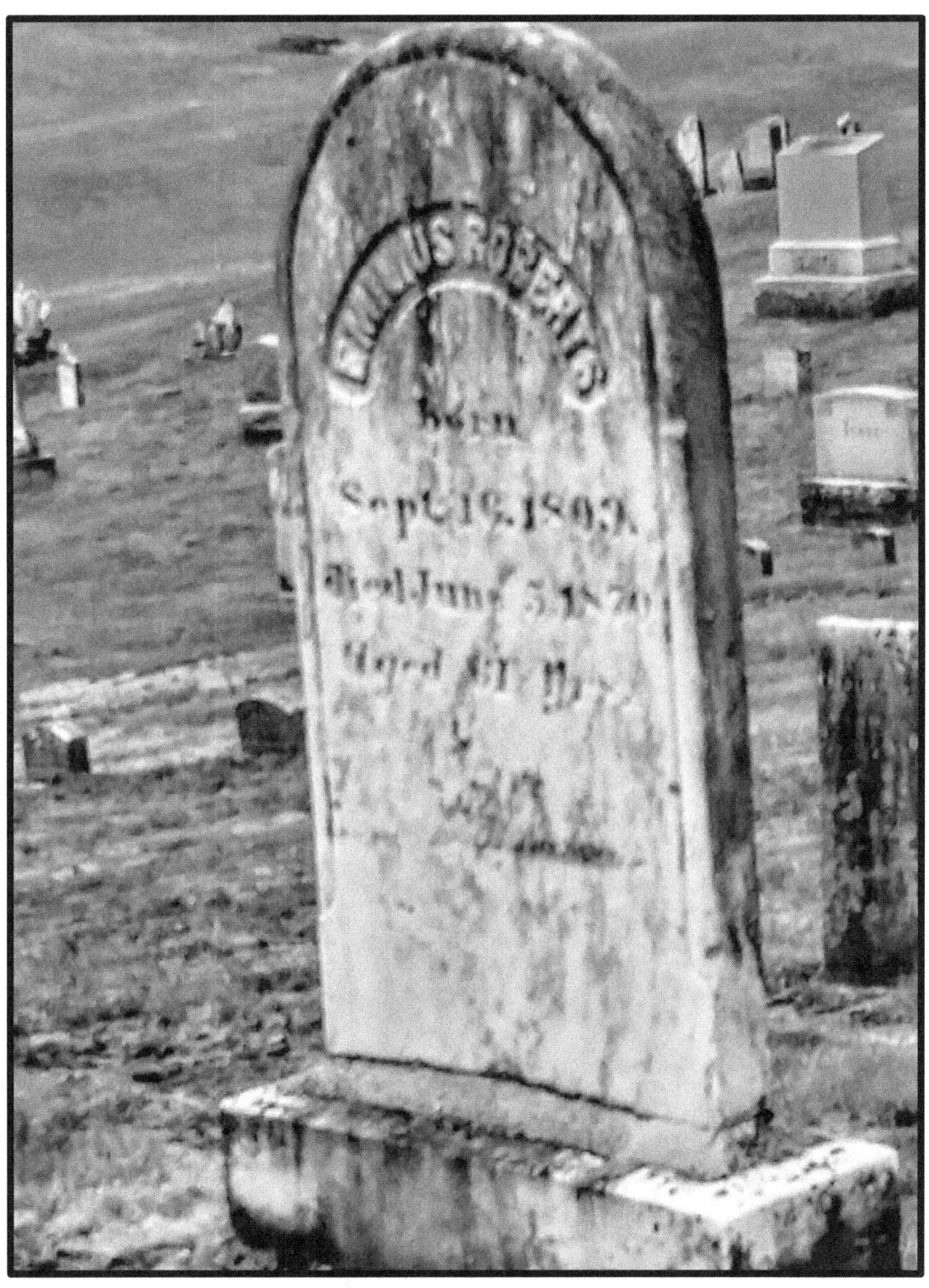

Broadalbin Mayfield Cemetery

Some of these really old stones are so tall. There is a lot of history in this cemetery.

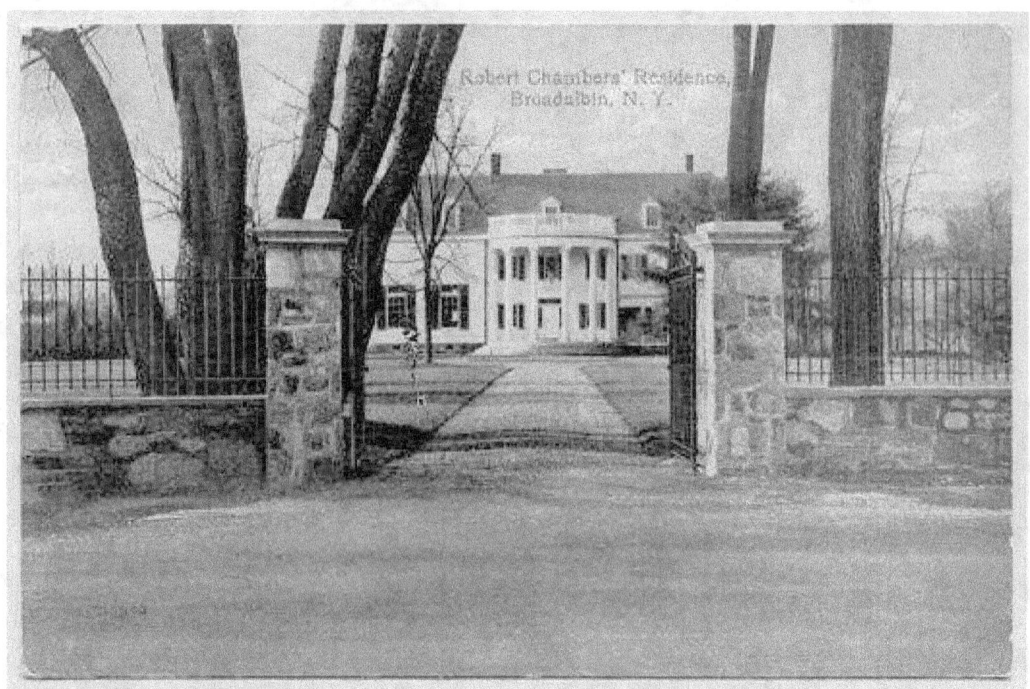
tony-baulos.squarespace.com

Robert W. Chambers, Author

One of those stones of particular interest was the Robert Chambers gravesite. I wanted to see this because he was a writer like myself, only much better than me. He has published many, many books with some turning into a movie.

The Robert William Chambers home at one time comprised an 800 acre wooded estate, which stretched from North Main St. all the way to lands now covered by the Great Sacandaga Lake. Chambers was a very successful author whose works were published from 1894-1938. He is noted for writing over 100 novels. His earliest works were of the horror/sci-fi genre, and his most well-known, The King in Yellow (1895), was featured in season one of the HBO original series True Detective.

This resulted in a revived popularity of that particular title. In his later years, Chambers focused on historical fiction, using Fulton County history as his backdrop. One of his novels, Cardigan, was made into a film in 1922. He also wrote poetry and children's books. Chambers was an illustrator and amateur entomologist. He died in 1933 and the estate was purchased by the Albany Catholic Diocese in 1955.

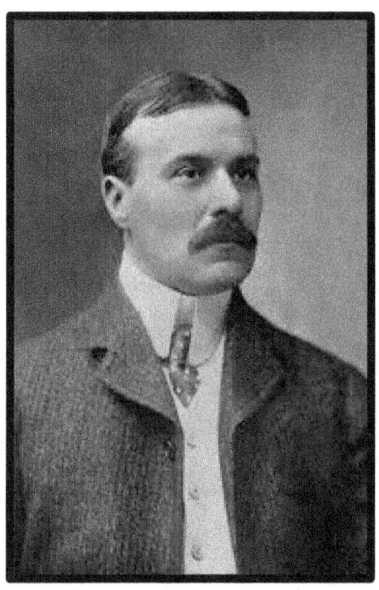 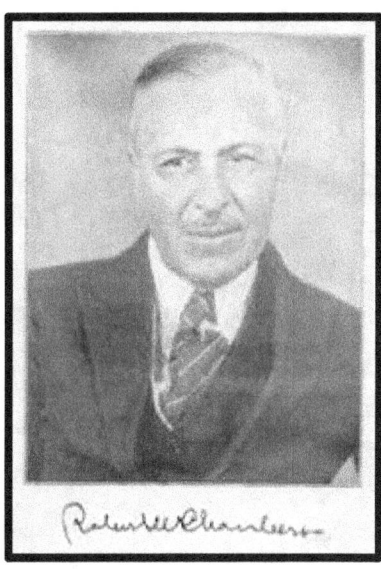

The younger version and elder version of Robert W. Chambers.

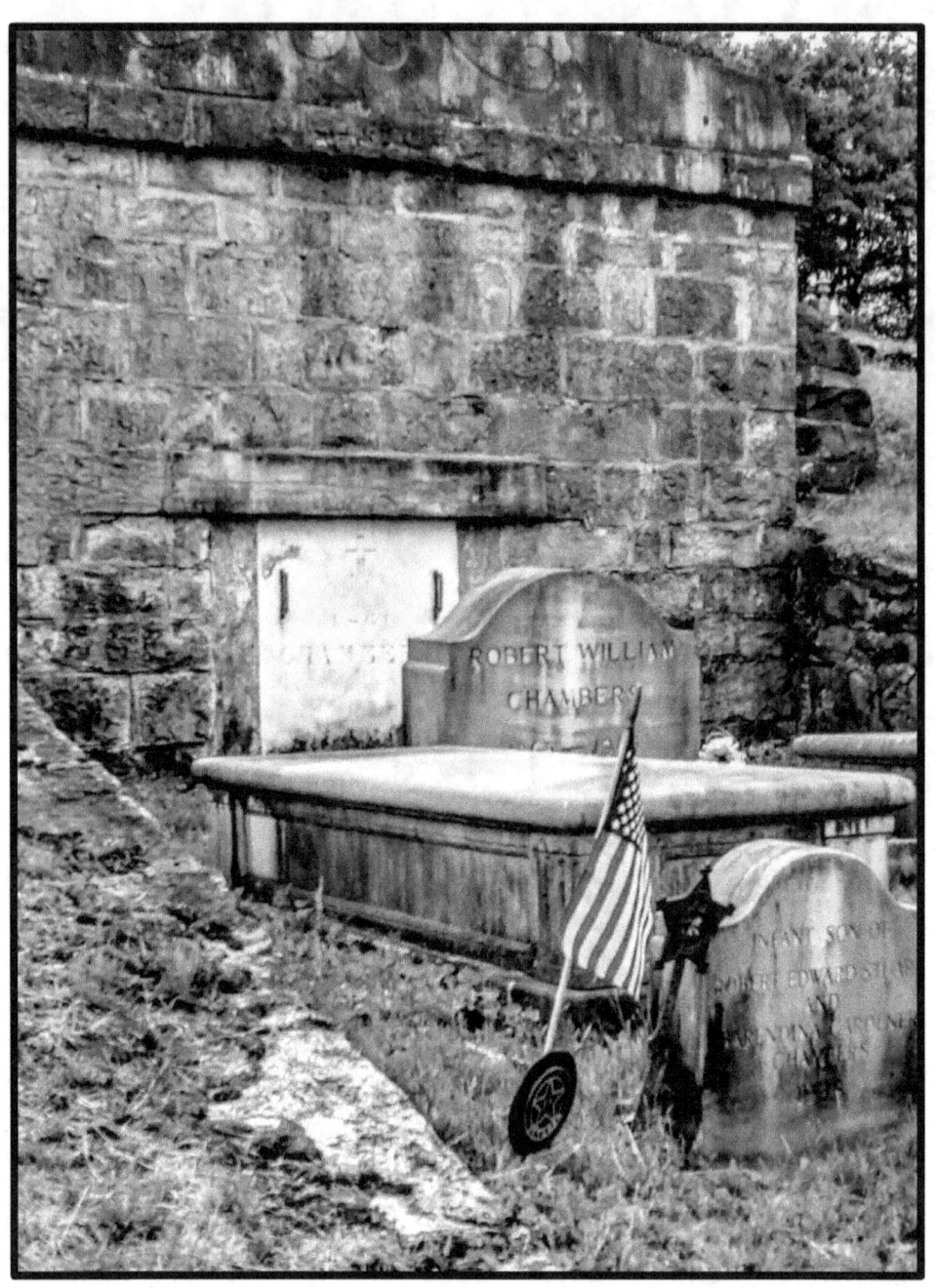

Broadalbin Mayfield Cemetery

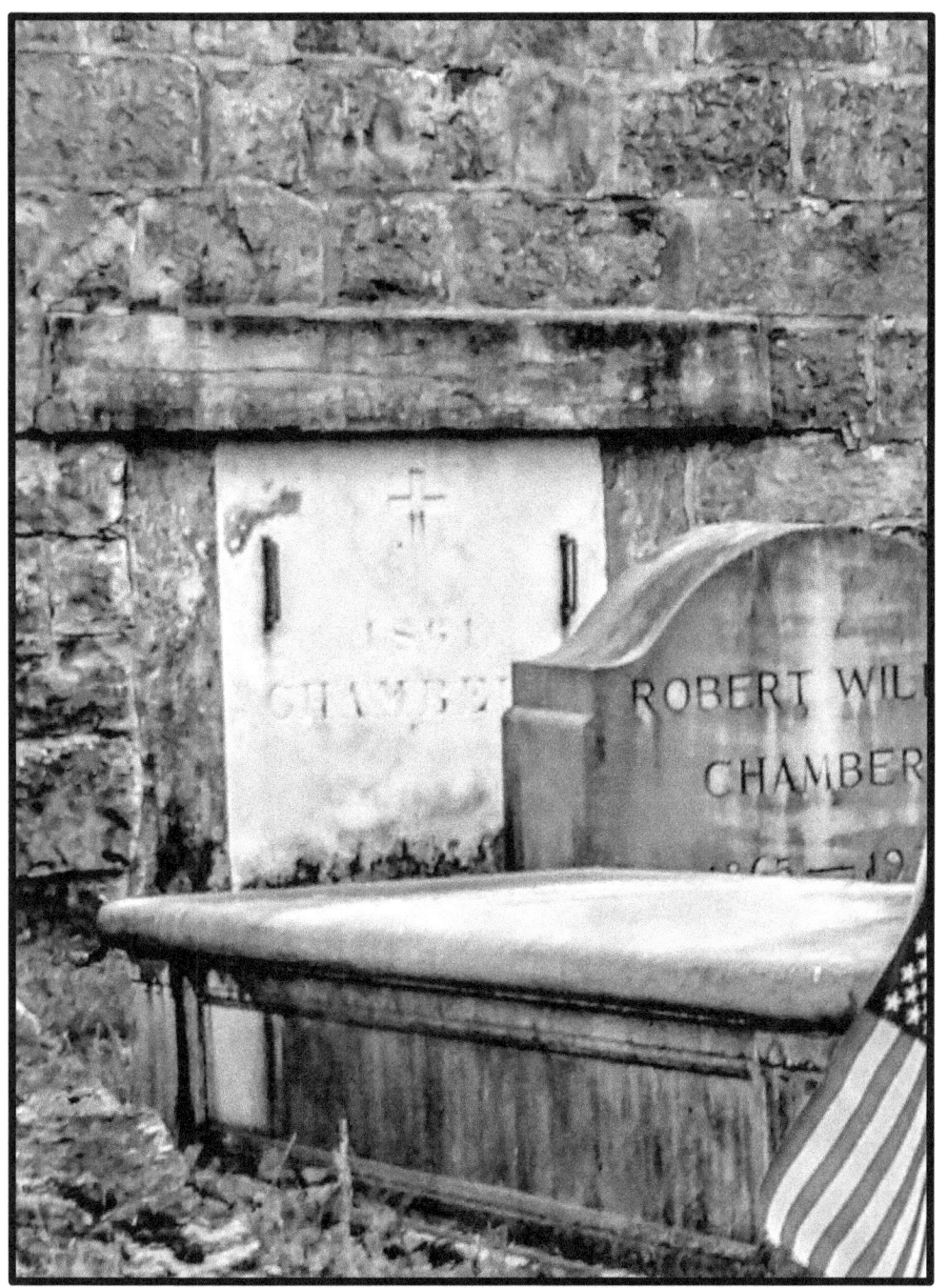

Broadalbin Mayfield Cemetery

My paranormal team did try to get some EVP's from this particular area. I don't think they picked up anything spectacular that needed to said. We often try to see if the deceased have any messages to share. This area however did show spirit energy around the stones. I think that is understandably so as the whole family is buried here.

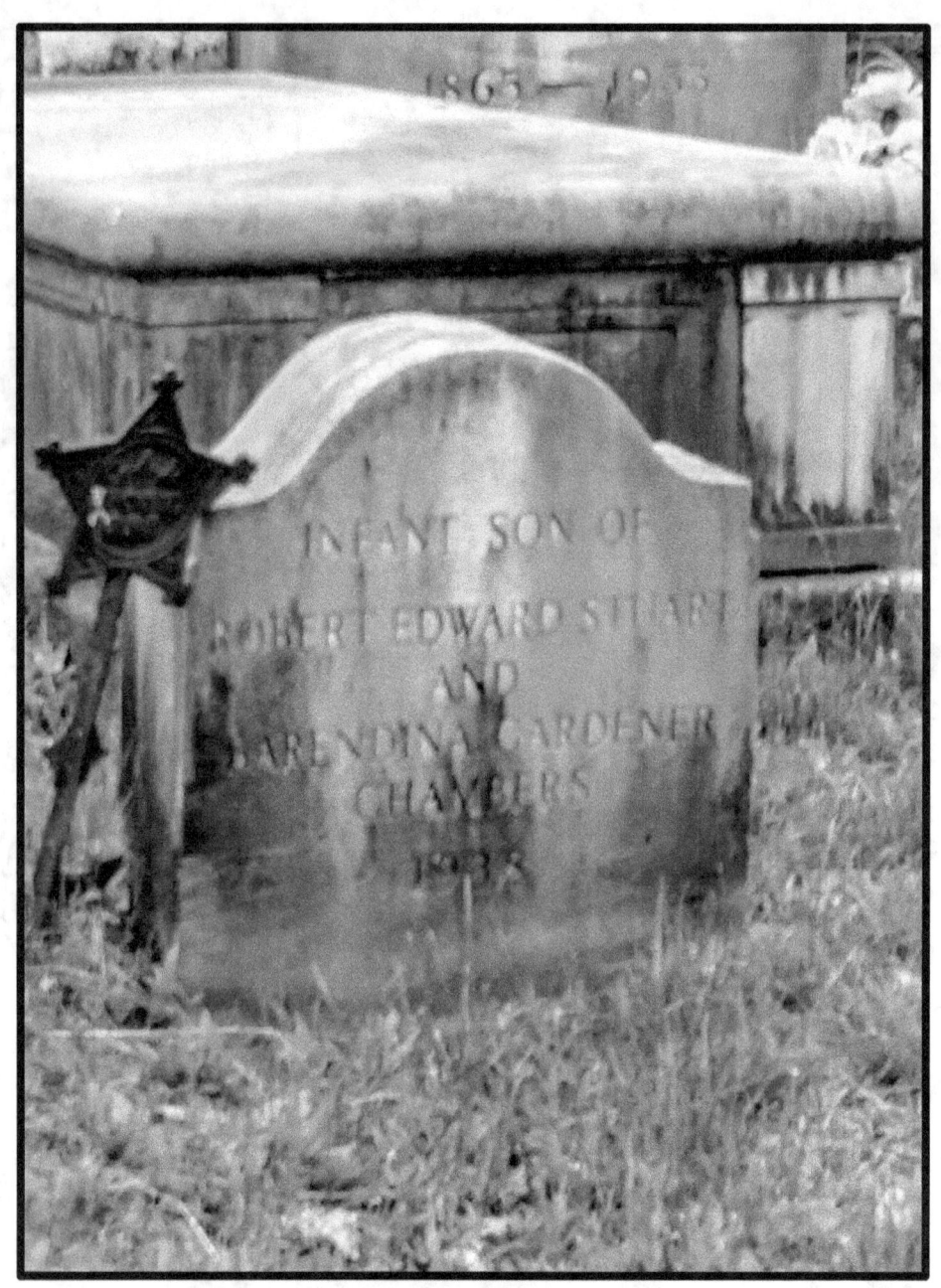

Broadalbin Mayfield Cemetery

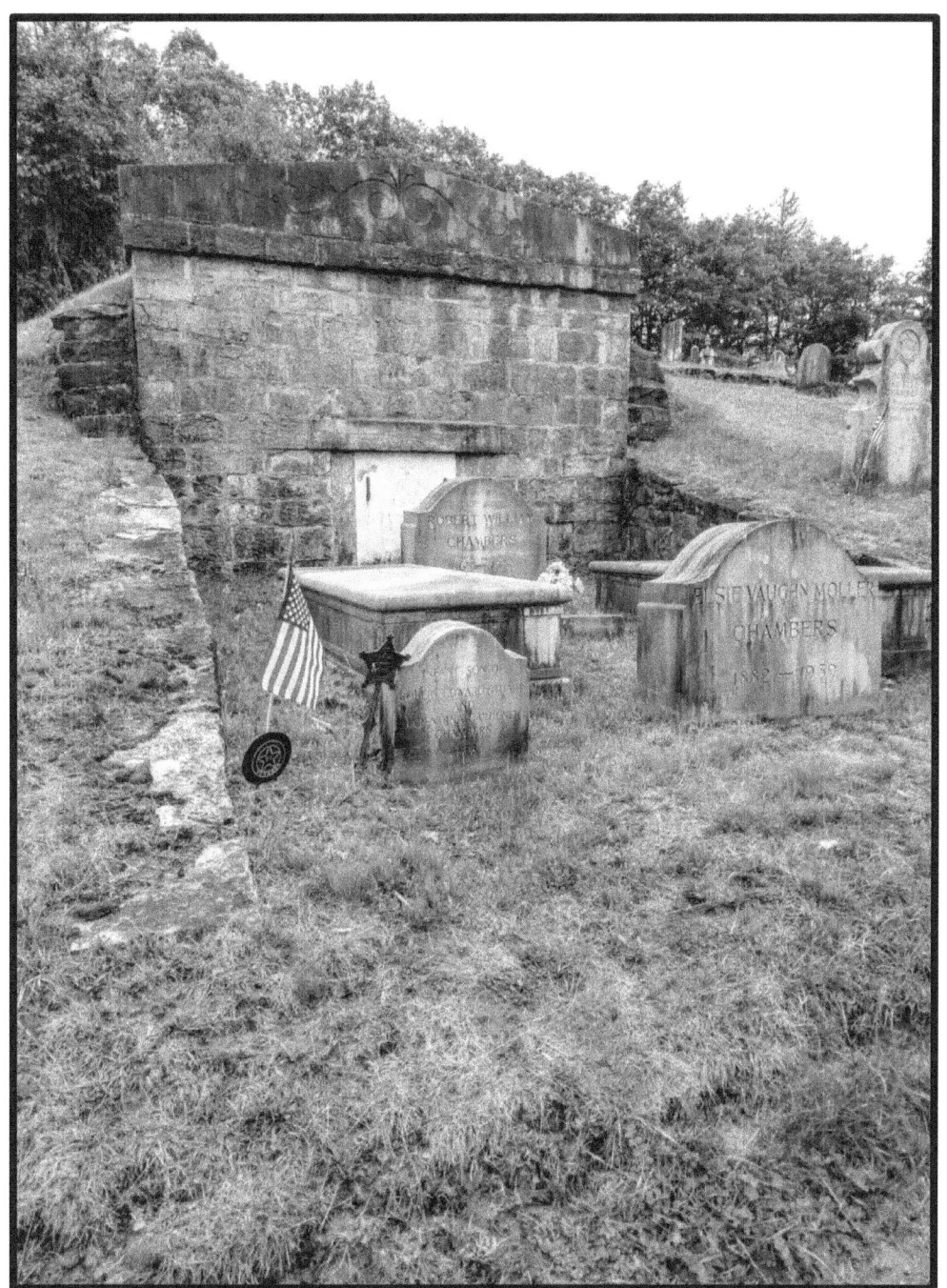

(Data as regards burial plot of Chambers' family in Broadalbin - Mayfield Cemetery http://yellowking.fortunecity.ws/rwc-his.html)

Inscribed on vault door, Chambers 1861.

Elder members of the Chambers family, including the Grandfather, and Great Grandfather of the author Robert W. Chambers, and immediate families buried in vault as recorded in early Broadalbin history.

Buried in front center of vault Robert William Chambers, the author (1865 - 1933) born May 26, 1895.

Left in front of vault William P. Chambers (1827 - 1911) (father of the author) (a lawyer practiced in New York City)

In front right his [William P.'s] wife Caroline Boughton Chambers (1842 -1913)

In center, outer part of lot, Elsie Vaughn Moller Chambers (1882 -1939) [wife of the author, some sources say 1938]

Right front of lot Margaret Gale Chambers (1941) [who, sister, aunt, daughter? RWC dedicates The Firing Line (1908) to Margery Chambers, is this the same person?]

Left front of lot, infant son of Robert Edward Stuart and Berendina Chambers (1938) [I know from other sources that Broadalbin House was left abandon with all of RWC's papers, books, and paintings. Also have rumours that RWC's son was in an institution at one time. The death of an infant son in the same year as the death of the author's wife, Robert Husted's mother, may have had something to do with this abandonment]

Buried on plot, right above is stone reading Robert Husted Chambers, Captain United States Army (1889 - 1955) Robert a veteran of World Wars I and II.

Some records of the author's son Robert, reveal that fact he used two names from time of confirmation to date of death, as follows, Robert Edward Stuart Chambers, and Robert Husted Chambers.

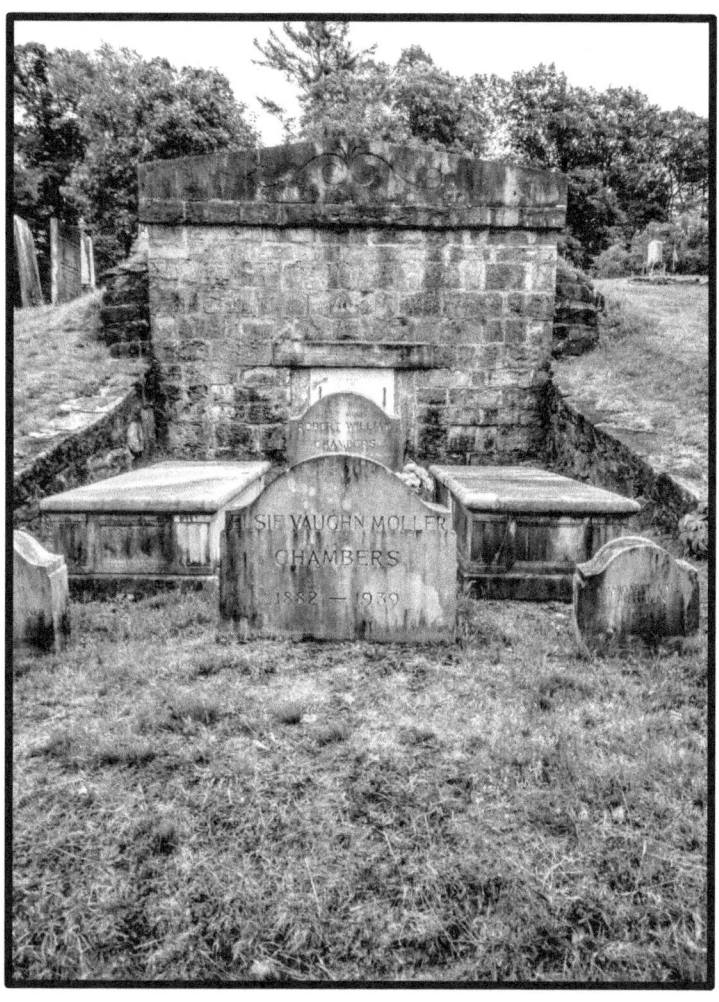

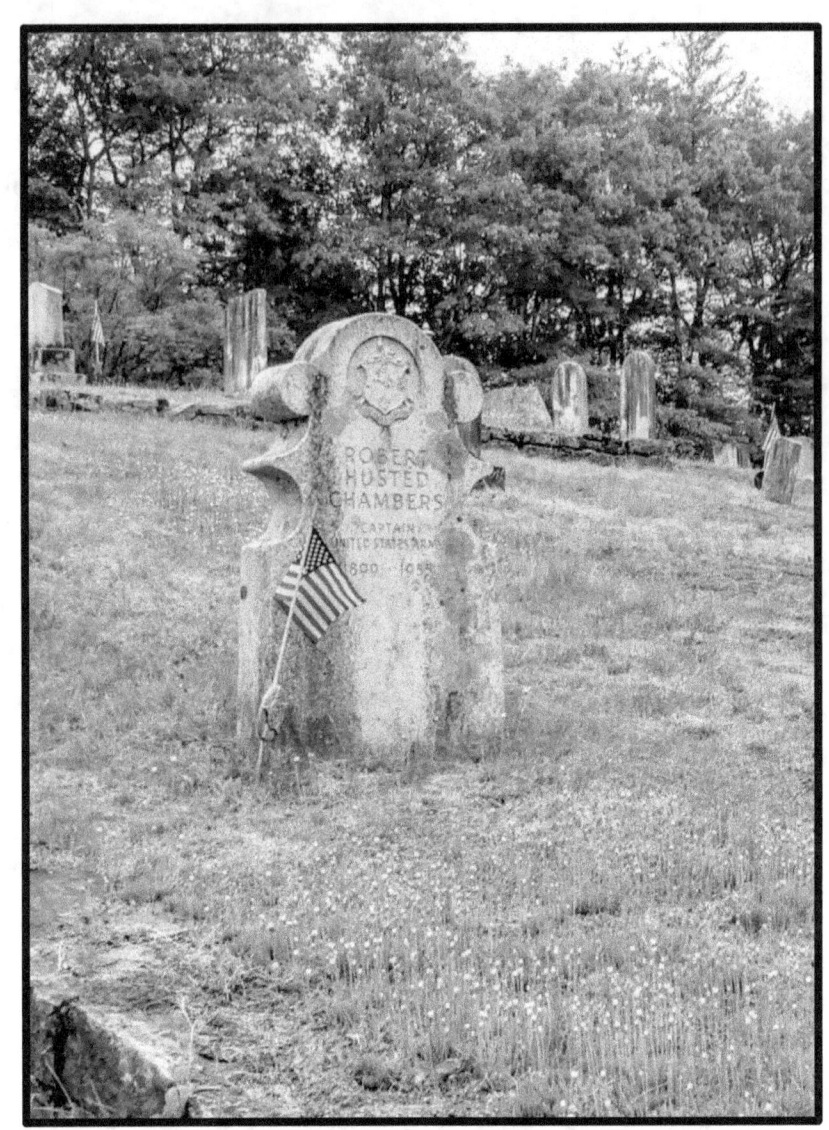
Broadalbin Mayfield Cemetery

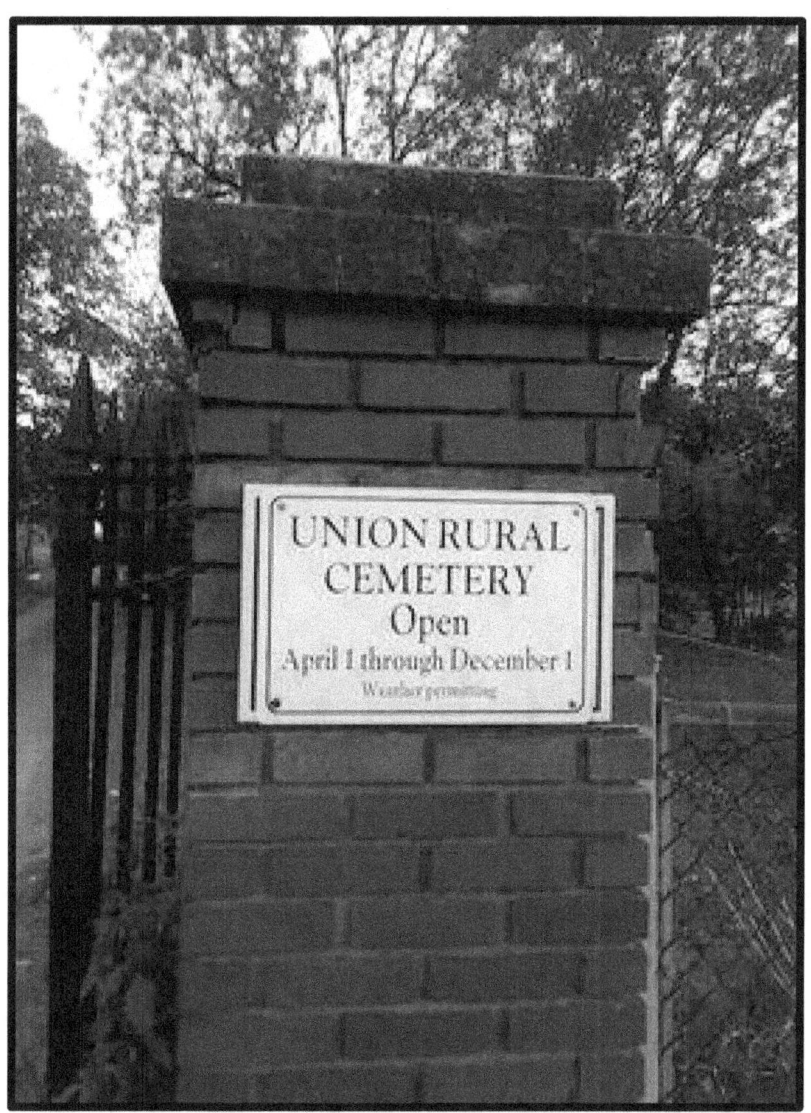

Union Rural Cemetery, Mayfield, NY

We took a couple trainees to this cemetery in Mayfield, across from the Mayfield Central High School, which is where I graduated from. This cemetery seemed especially nice because it felt peaceful. We could see people walking through or some with their dogs for walks. My team member, a paranormal investigator in training, noted that she herself walks through on occasion. What I noted quite a bit were the gravestones that seemed to have the artistic flare to them. These would be what I sought out. Following this page are a few that caught my attention.

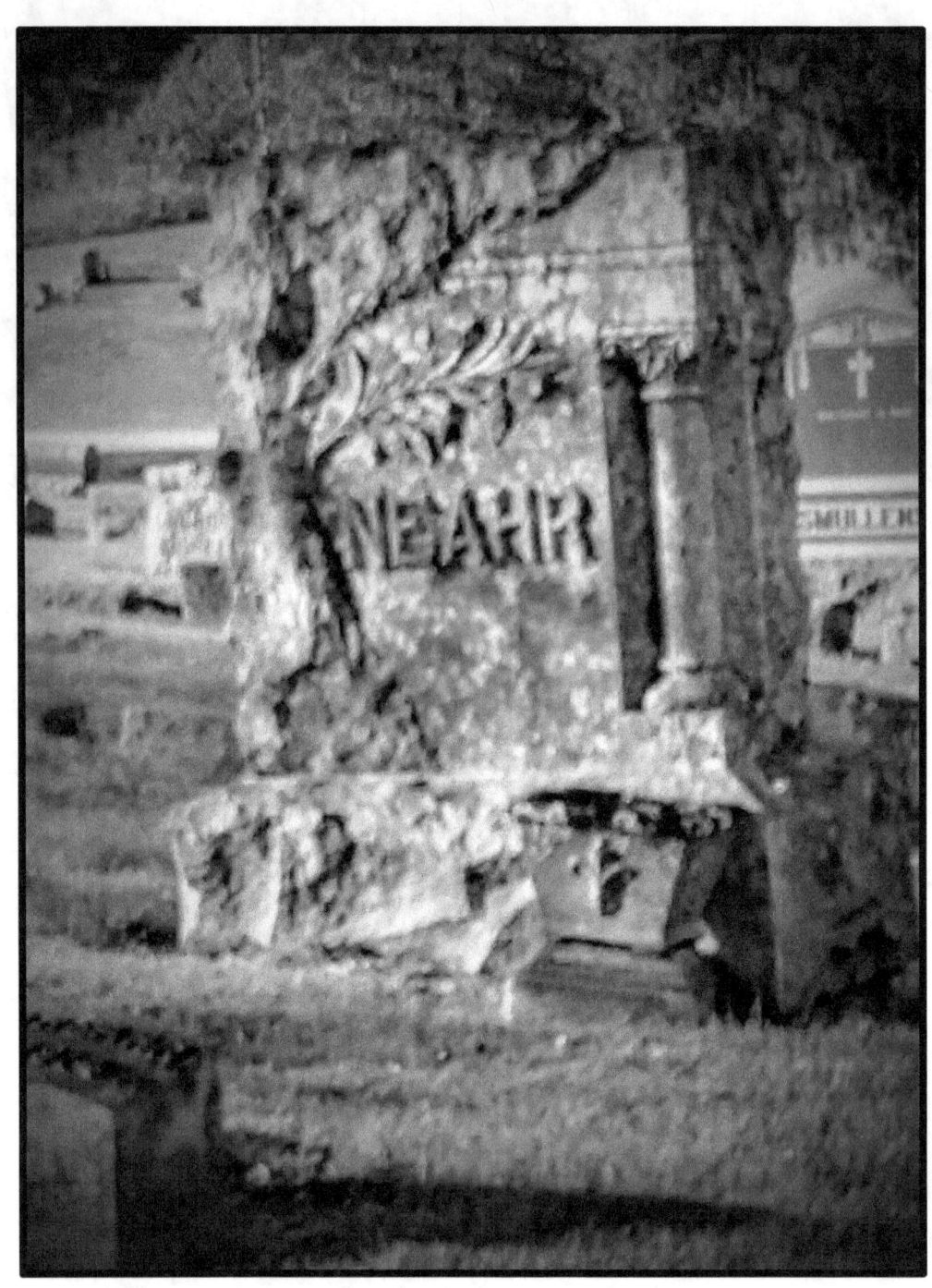

Union Rural Cemetery, Mayfield, NY

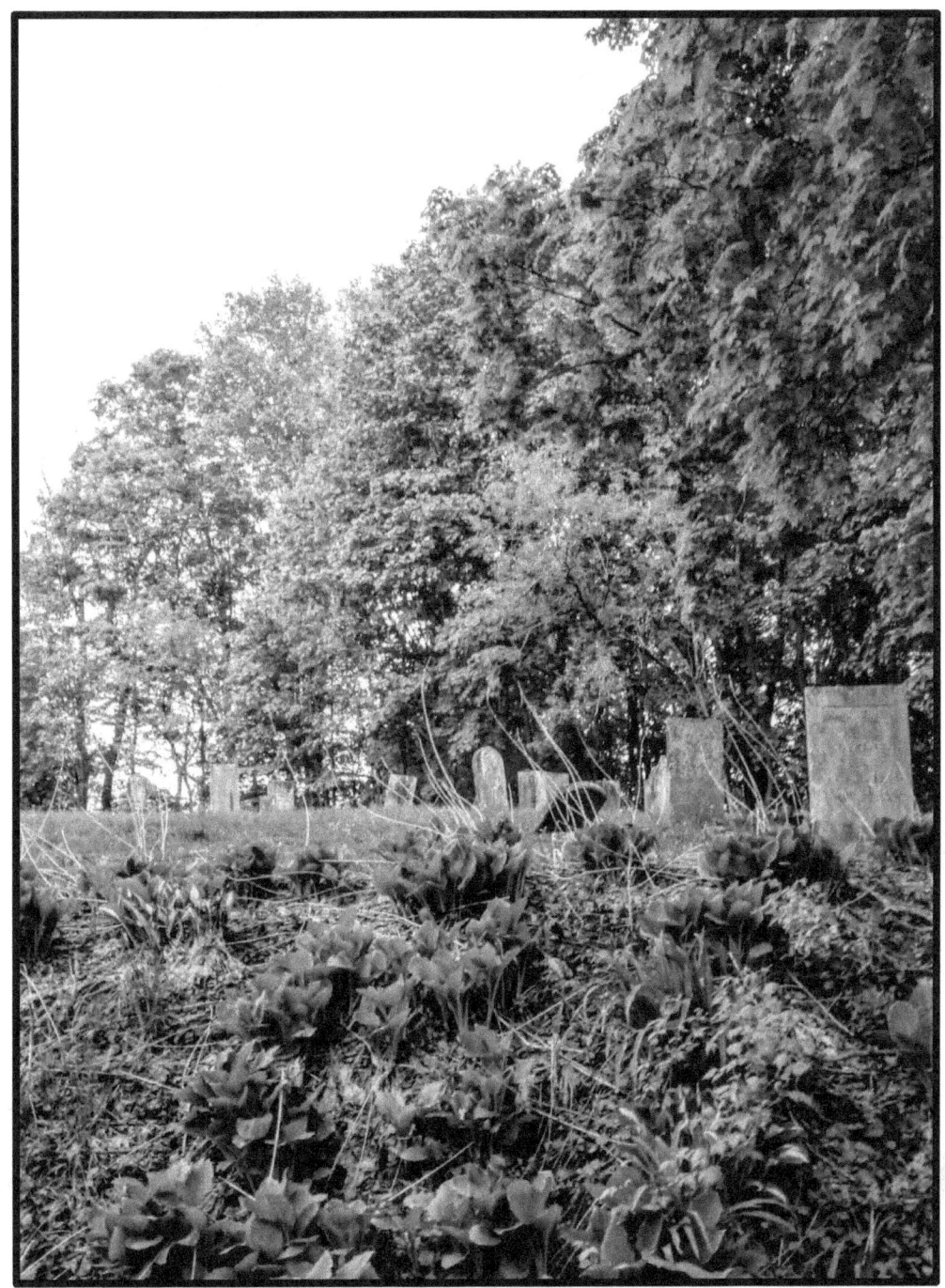

Union Rural Cemetery, Mayfield, NY

These gravestones were very, very old. They stood at the front of the cemetery but up on a steep hill and gated. I couldn't climb up there but from below I took this picture.

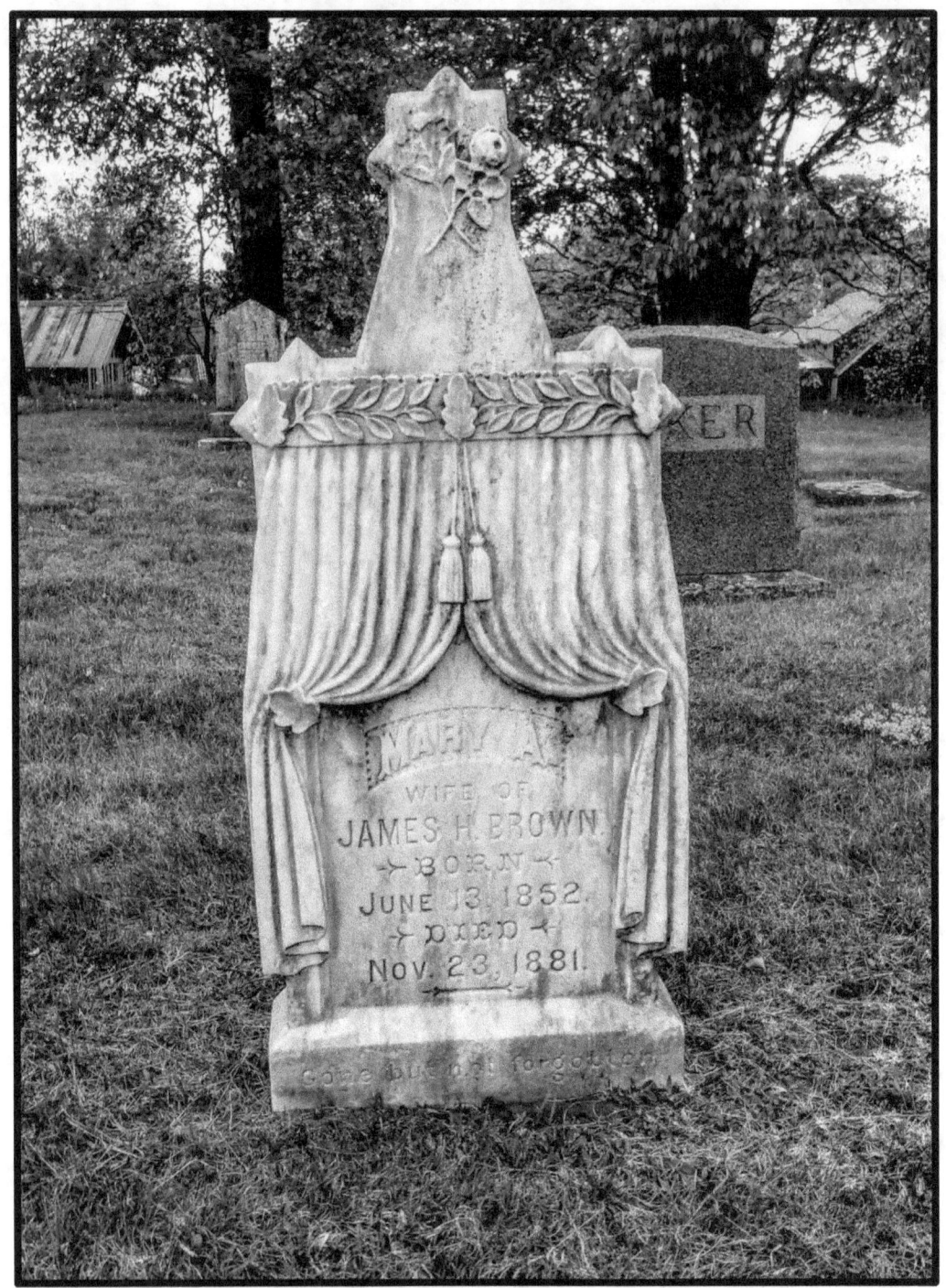

Union Rural Cemetery, Mayfield, NY

This gravestone to me looks like a stage curtain. I wonder what the history was behind this stone? If not that then another type of curtain but it definately stood out.

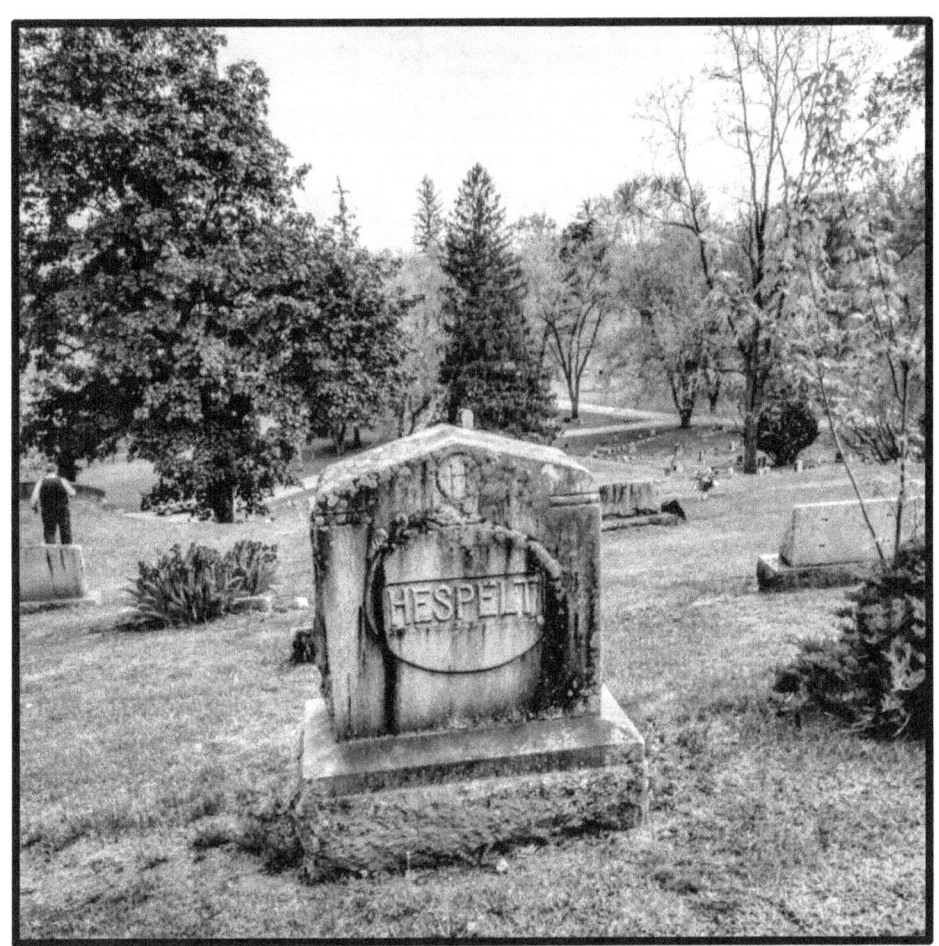

Union Rural Cemetery, Mayfield, NY

Again, this stone has some design on it.

Ferndale Cemetery, Johnstown, NY

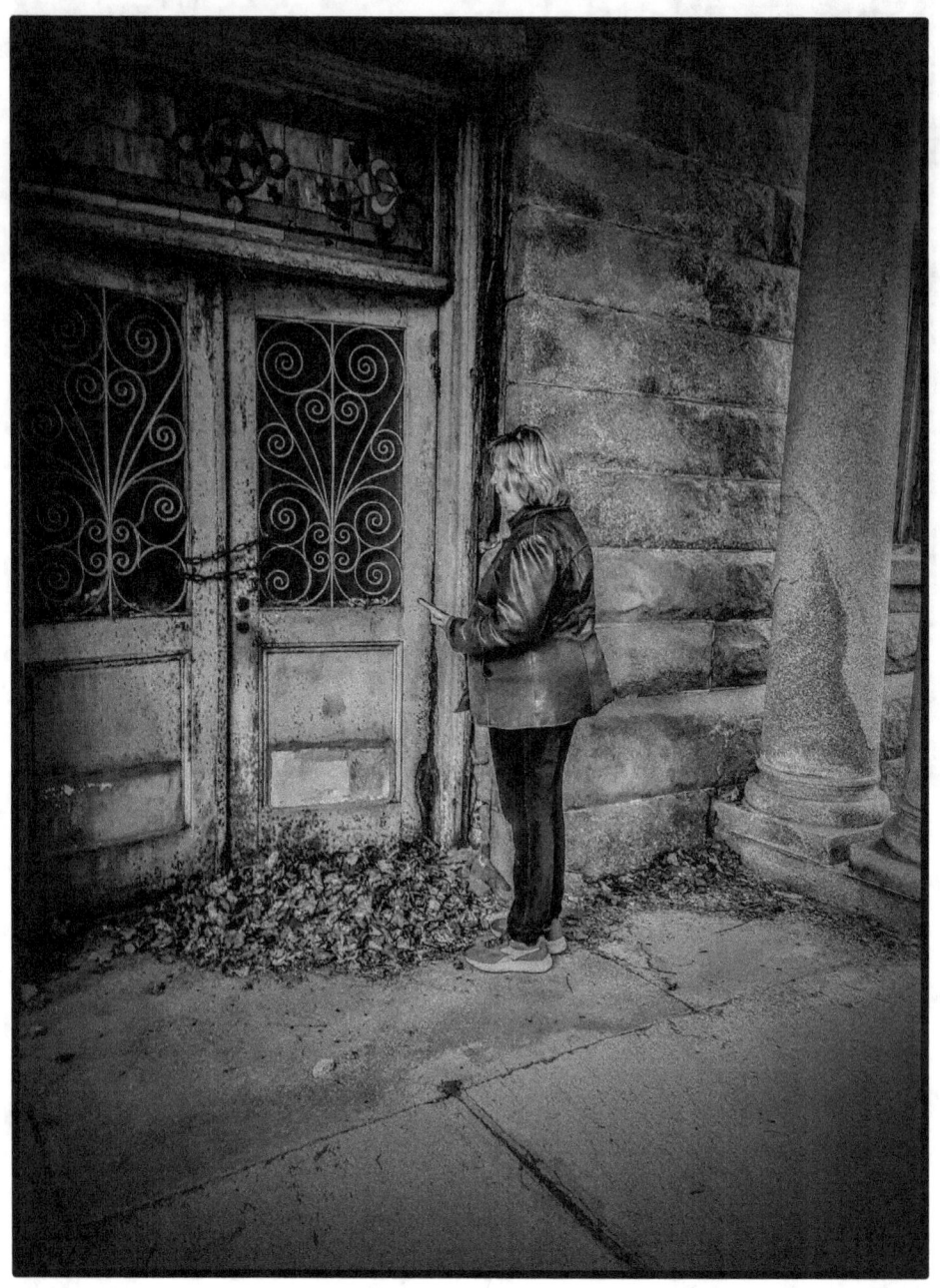

This is the cover of myself in this book which was taken at Ferndale Cemetery in Johnstown, NY. I often take my paranormal team here to test our equipment and see what we receive. We have received quite a bit actually. EVP's, pictures, spirit box word generator and more.

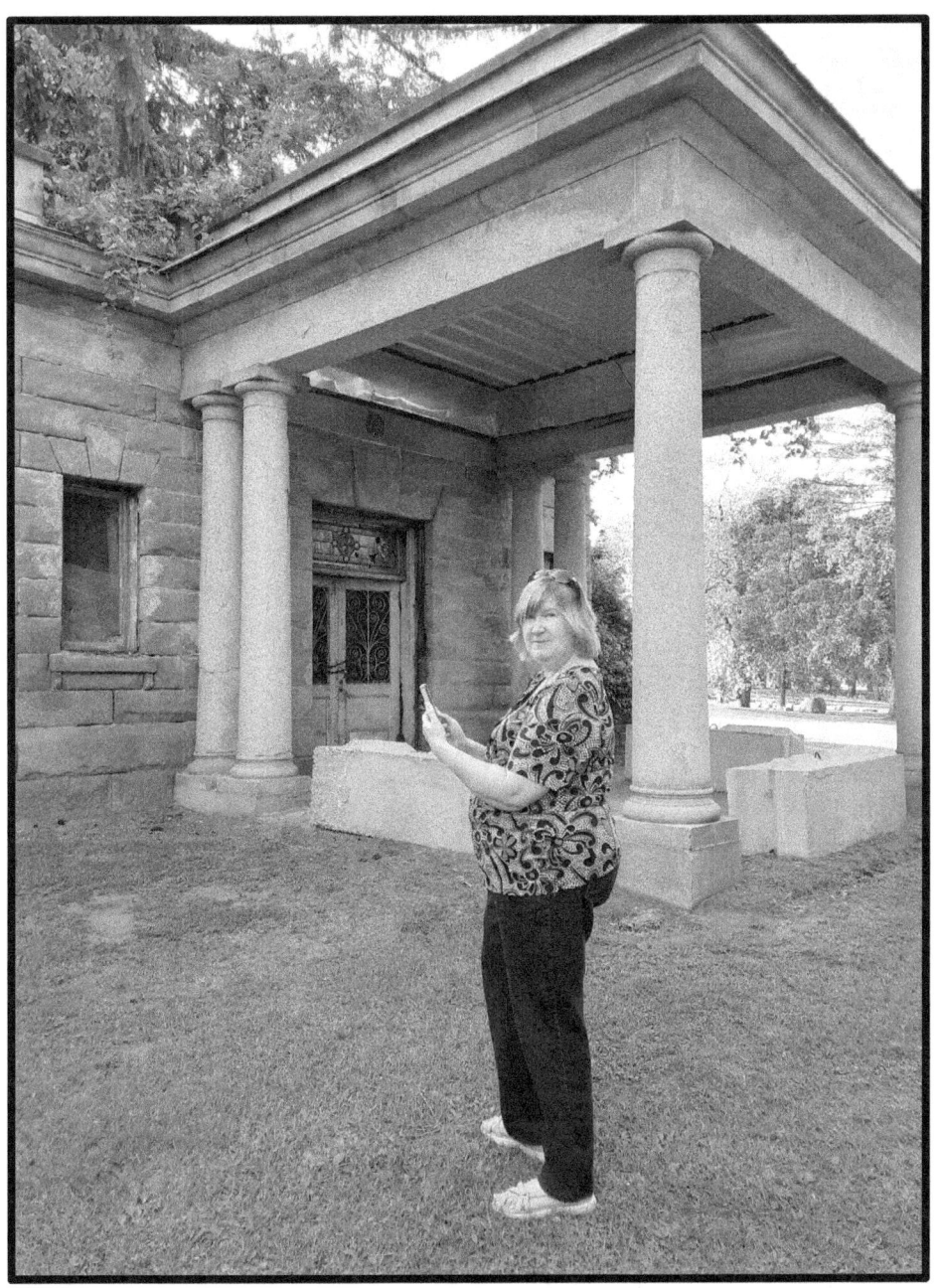

Ferndale Cemetery, Johnstown, NY

This is one of the creepiest places I have visited. Don't get me wrong, it's a beautiful cemetery but you have to admit there are a lot of souls here. My own family members are buried here. Above is a mausoleum and as you can see it's so old and not taken care of that they chained the doors together. However, you can see inside. I never saw inside one before and really didn't want to but I said to myself, "Face your fears," and I tried to. I made my team members look inside with me.

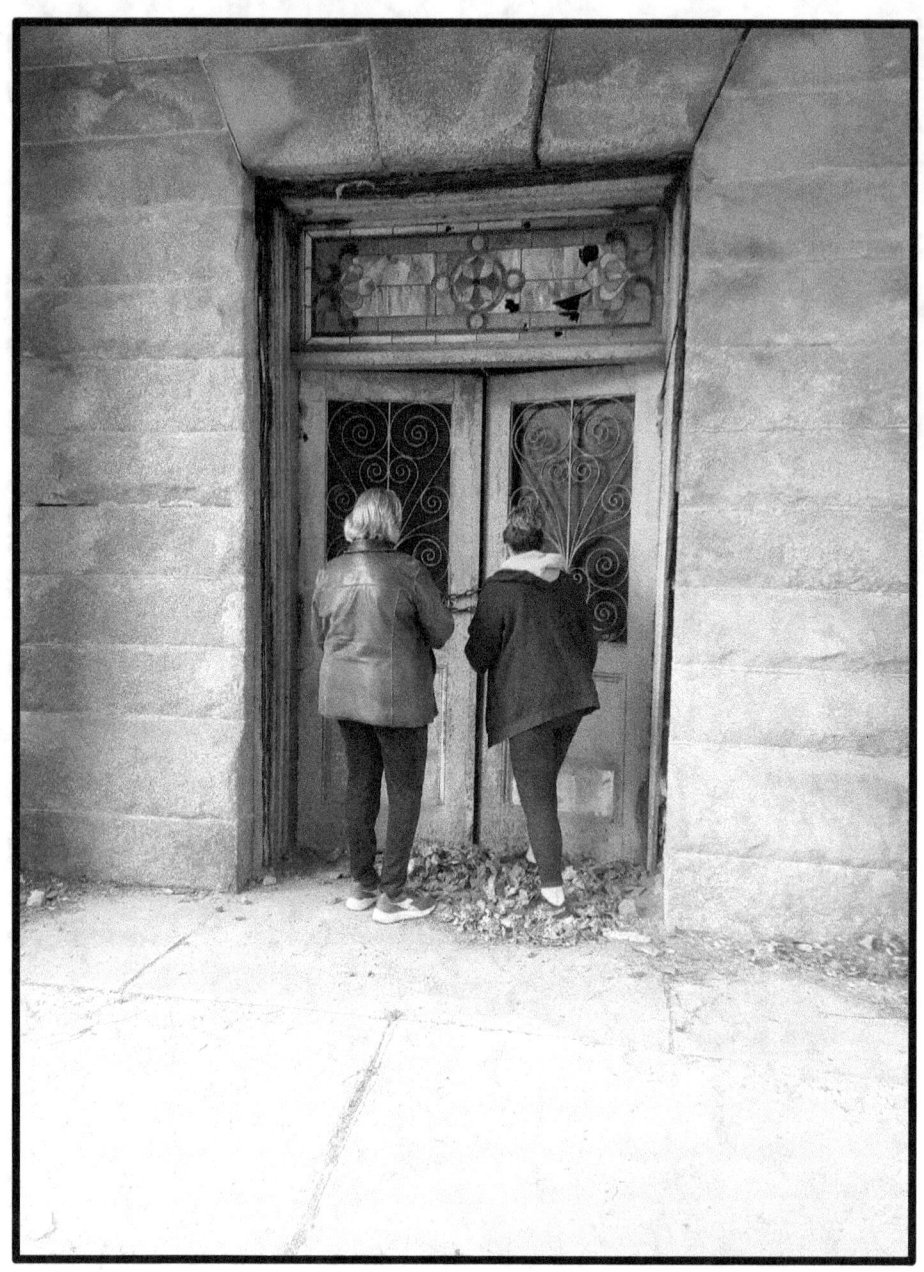

Ferndale Cemetery, Johnstown, NY

Here myself and team member, Sue Petoff, are peering in. I tried to tell myself to focus on the beauty that is left to this structure but the energy within was strong. When there is spirit energy attached to something I can actually *"feel"* it. I feel it by my nerves becoming heightened. My stomach starts to *"buzz."* It's just an uncomfortable feeling much like what fear feels like.

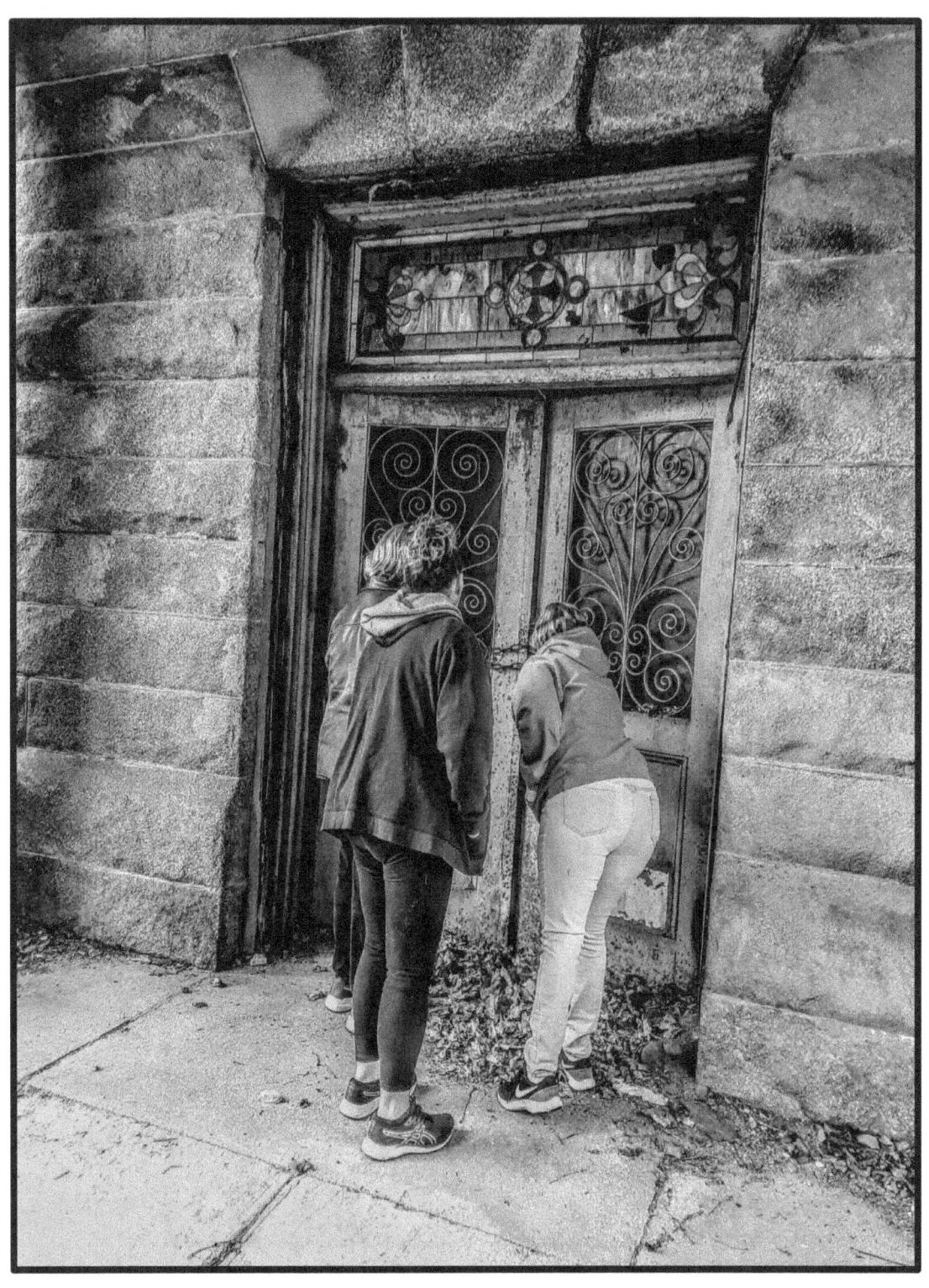

Ferndale Cemetery, Johnstown, NY

Here we are looking inside. Do you think you know what we were really looking at? It wasn't quite like I thought I would see in there. I really didn't know what to expect. Visiting cemeteries is educational. There's so much to see and experience. We saw these "cubby holes" that were long like where a casket would slide in to it. There were several "cubby holes" here. Each section for one deceased person to rest. I think I like the thought of being "together" with your family but personally I felt strange about it. Again, not knowing much about mausoleums…

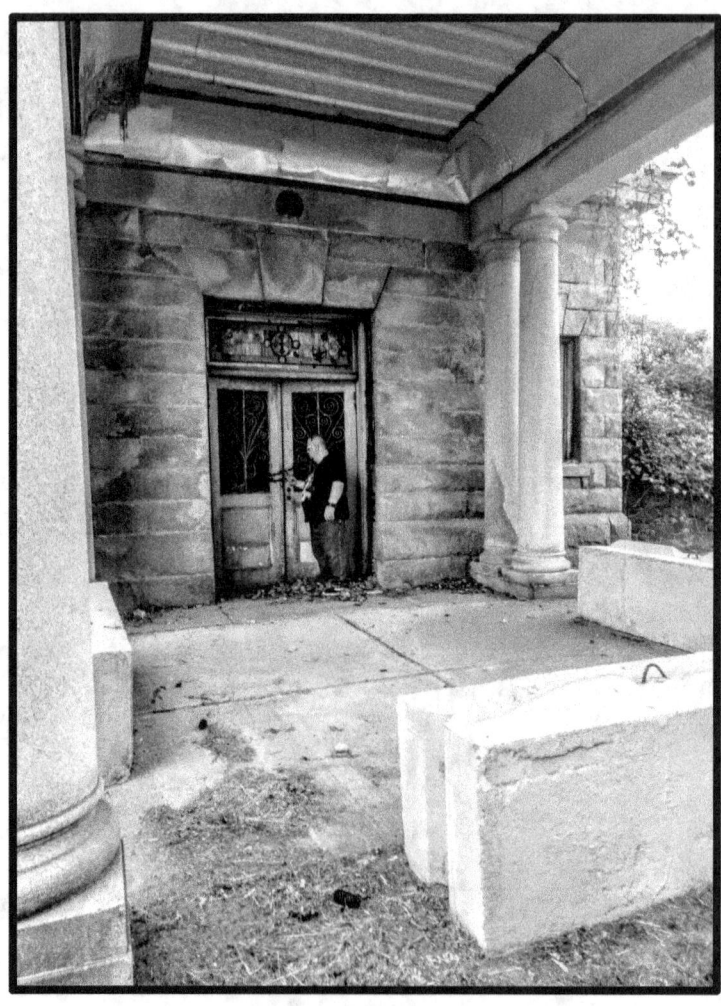

This is my team member, Eric Perry, Expert Paranormal Investigator.

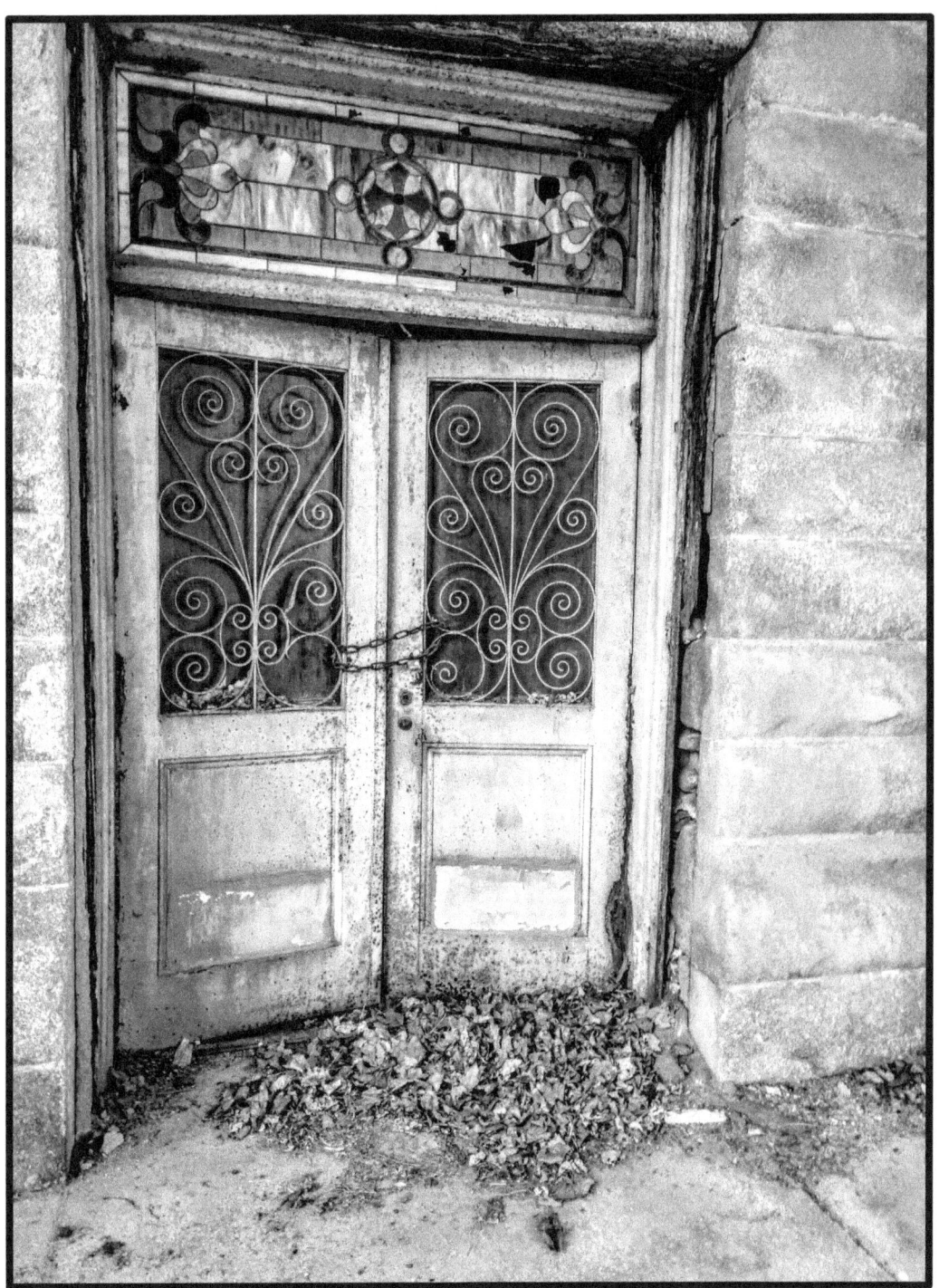

Ferndale Cemetery, Johnstown, NY

Structurely speaking this mausoleum has some natural beauty to it and I am sure when it was first put in it must have really been a site to see. From the stained glass work to the scrolling iron door window plates, there is beauty here.

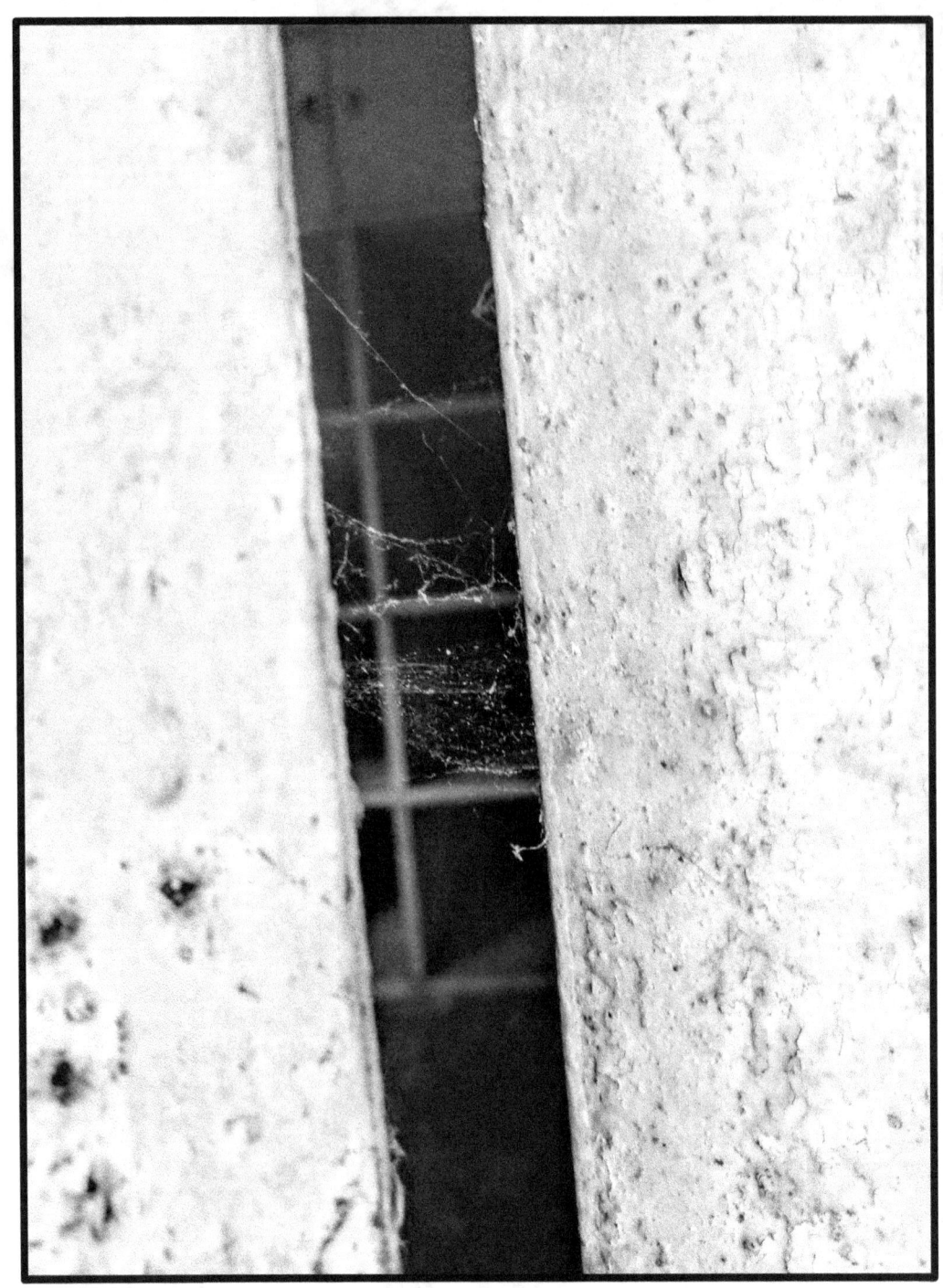

Ferndale Cemetery, Johnstown, NY

This is just creepy to me. This is inside the mausoleum. It's dark and dank. It's a shame that it's not kept up. See the areas in which a coffin could fill that spaces?

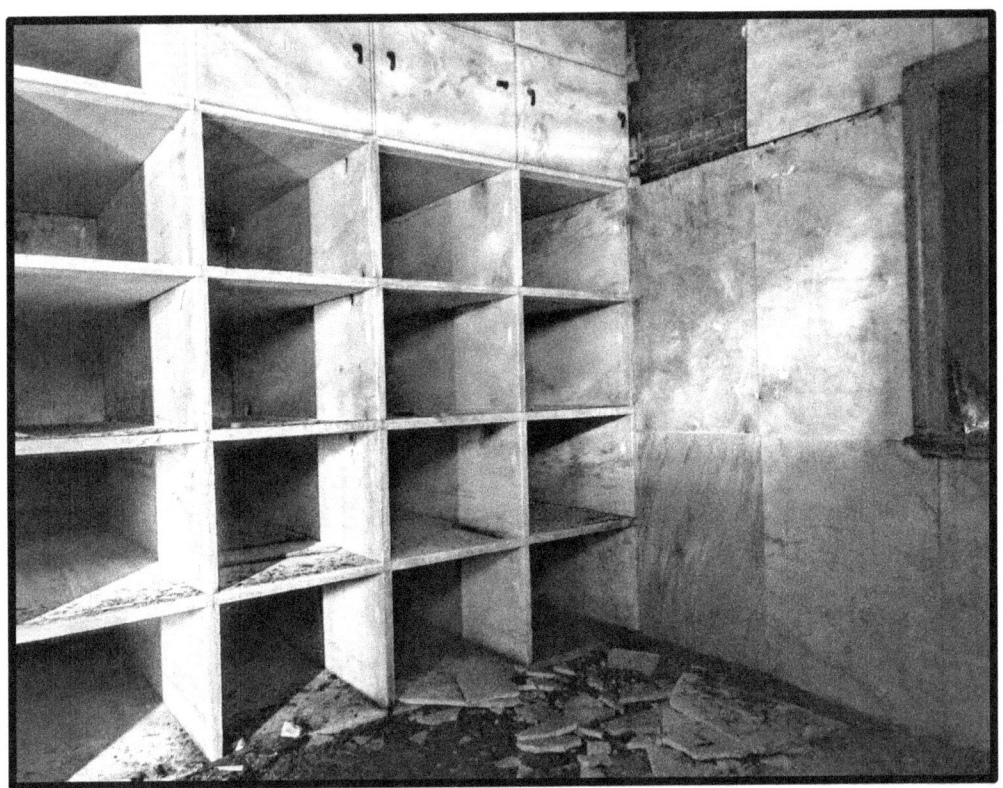

Ferndale Cemetery, Johnstown, NY

Here there are many slots to fill and perhaps this is a general holding spot before someone is buried in the ground. I wonder how they get the ones up on the top row down? However, you can see the disarray with the broken marble slabs on the floor. It's old. I get that but does it have to look like this?

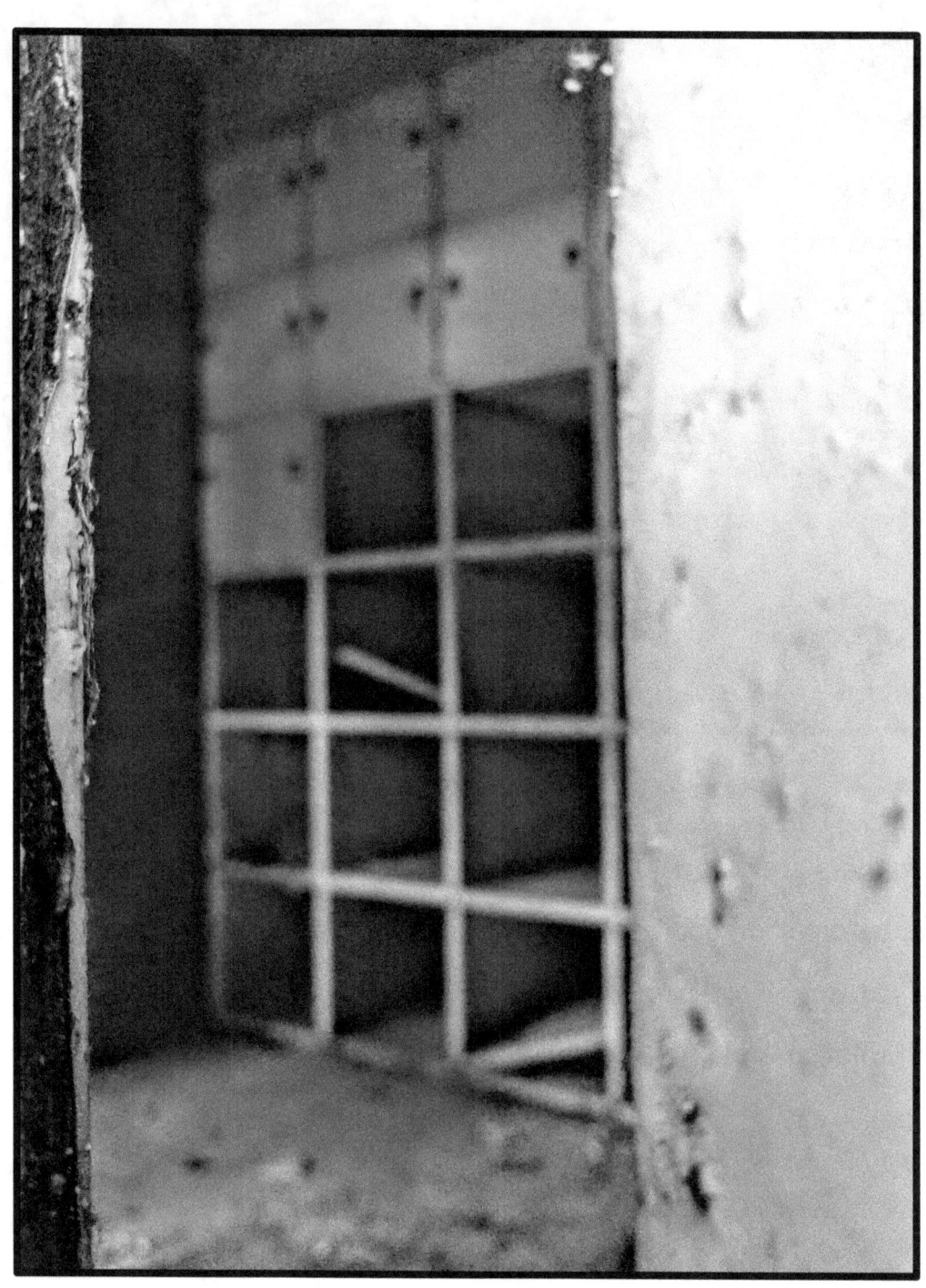

Ferndale Cemetery, Johnstown, NY

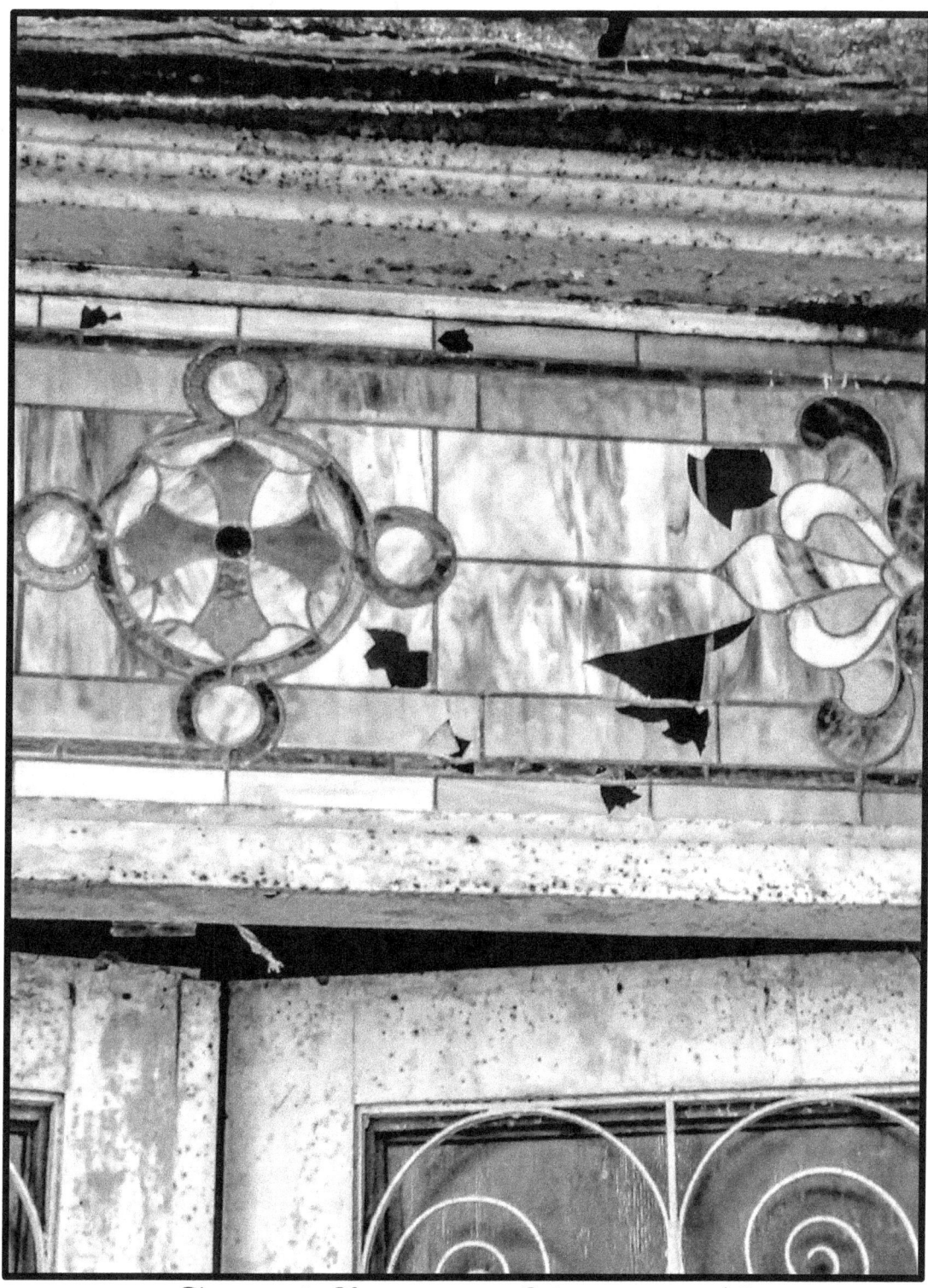

Ferndale Cemetery, Johnstown, NY

Once upon a time this was lovely stained glass work.

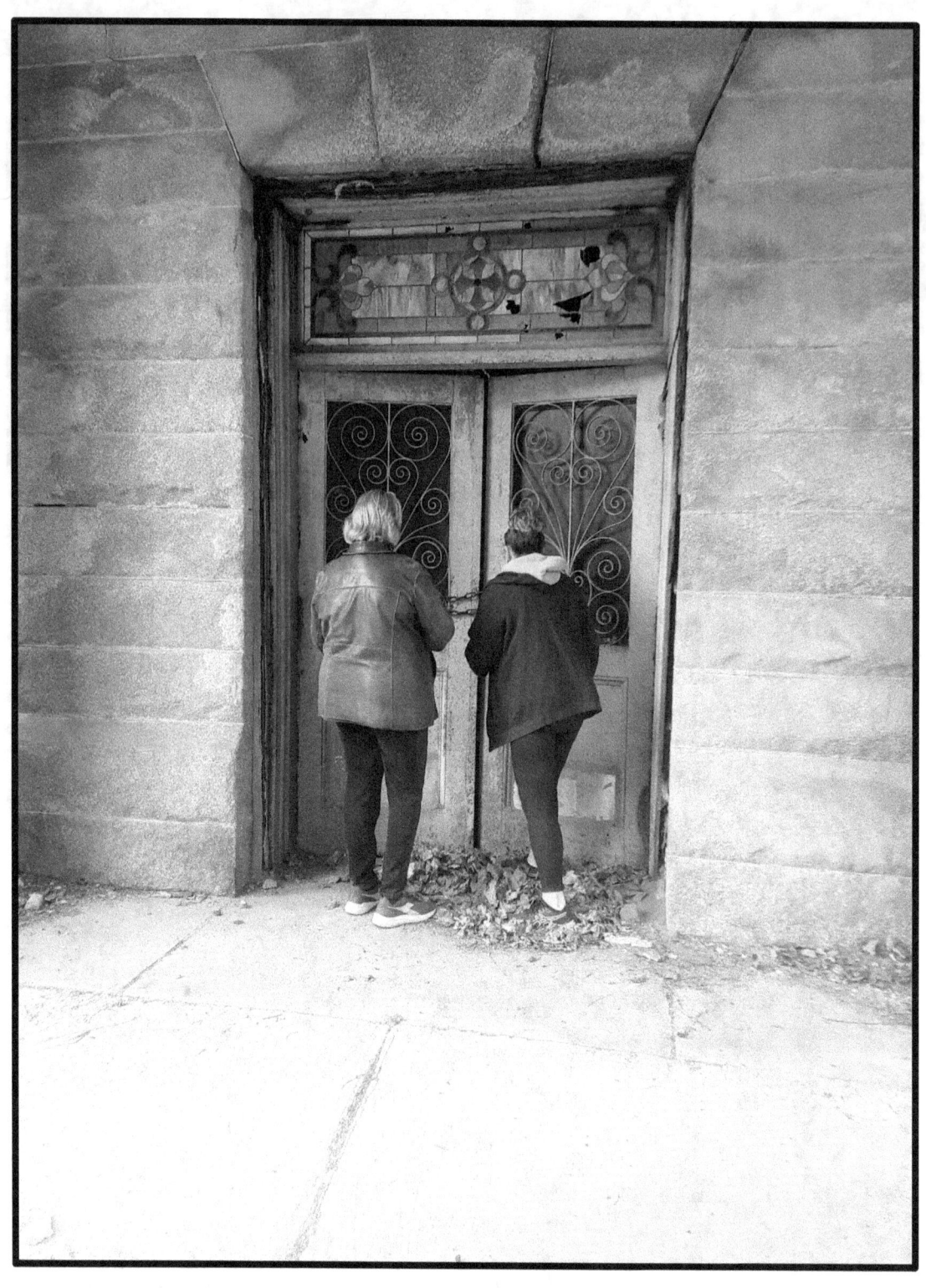

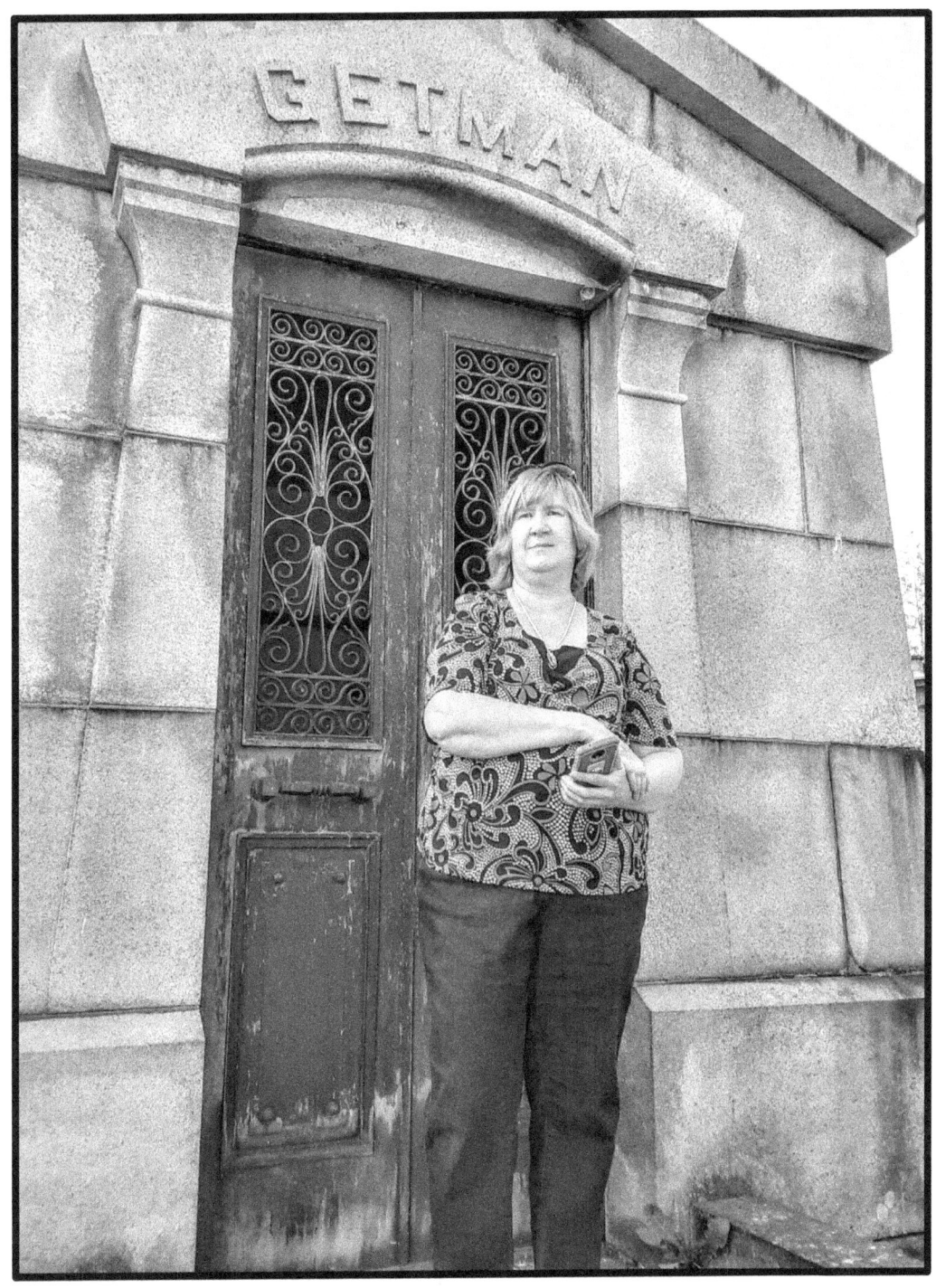

Ferndale Cemetery, Johnstown, NY

This is me, your Author, Shelley Brienza and I'm on an investigation at Ferndale. This is a different mausoleum. If we were able to, we would take pictures of the inside. In my hand is my phone which has several apps on it for paranormal work. Growing up and having my roots in Gloversville and Mayfield areas, the Getman name is a well known name.

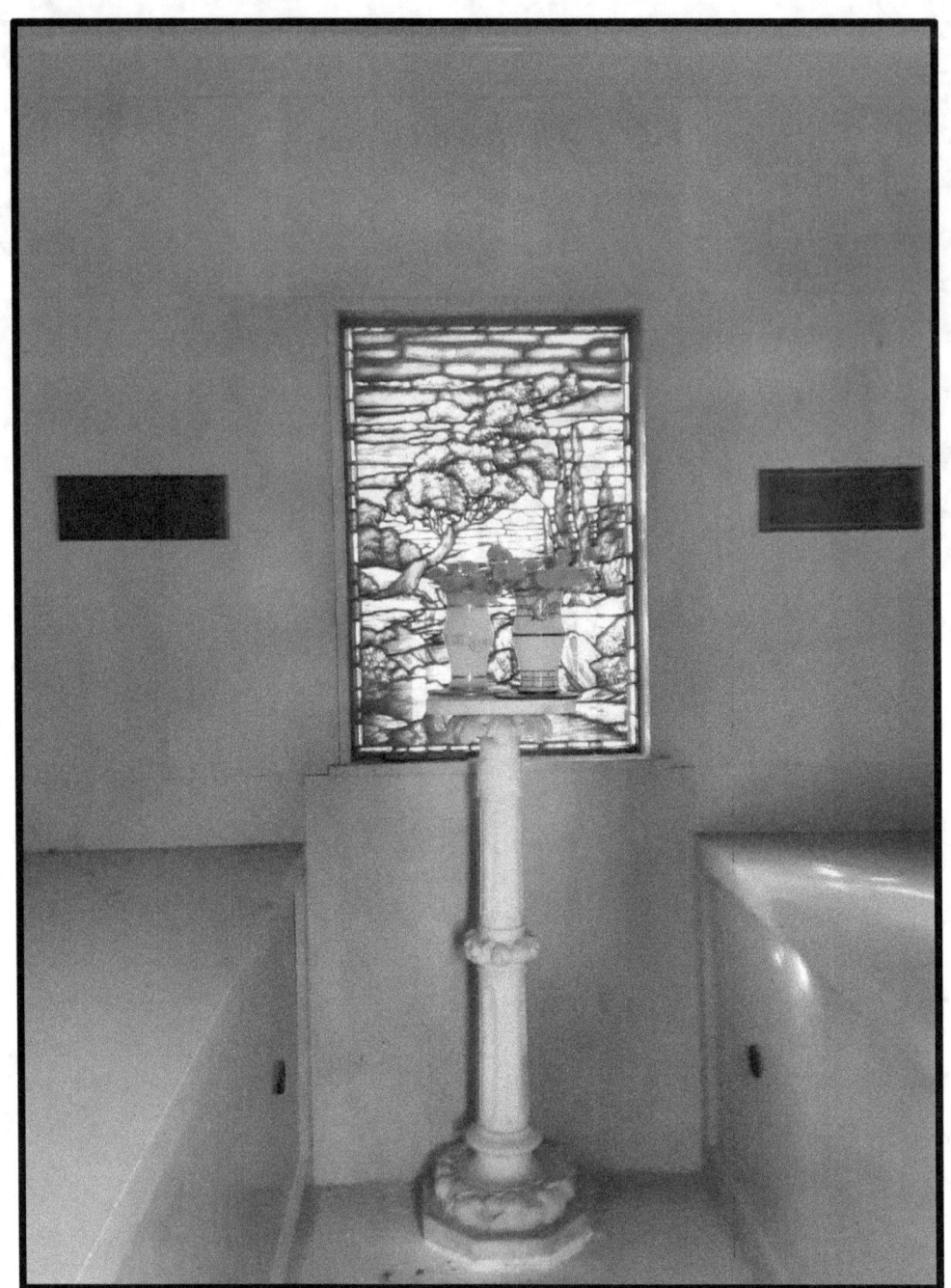

Ferndale Cemetery, Johnstown, NY

This is the inside view of one of the mausoleums we visited. This seems much more taken care of and peaceful inside.

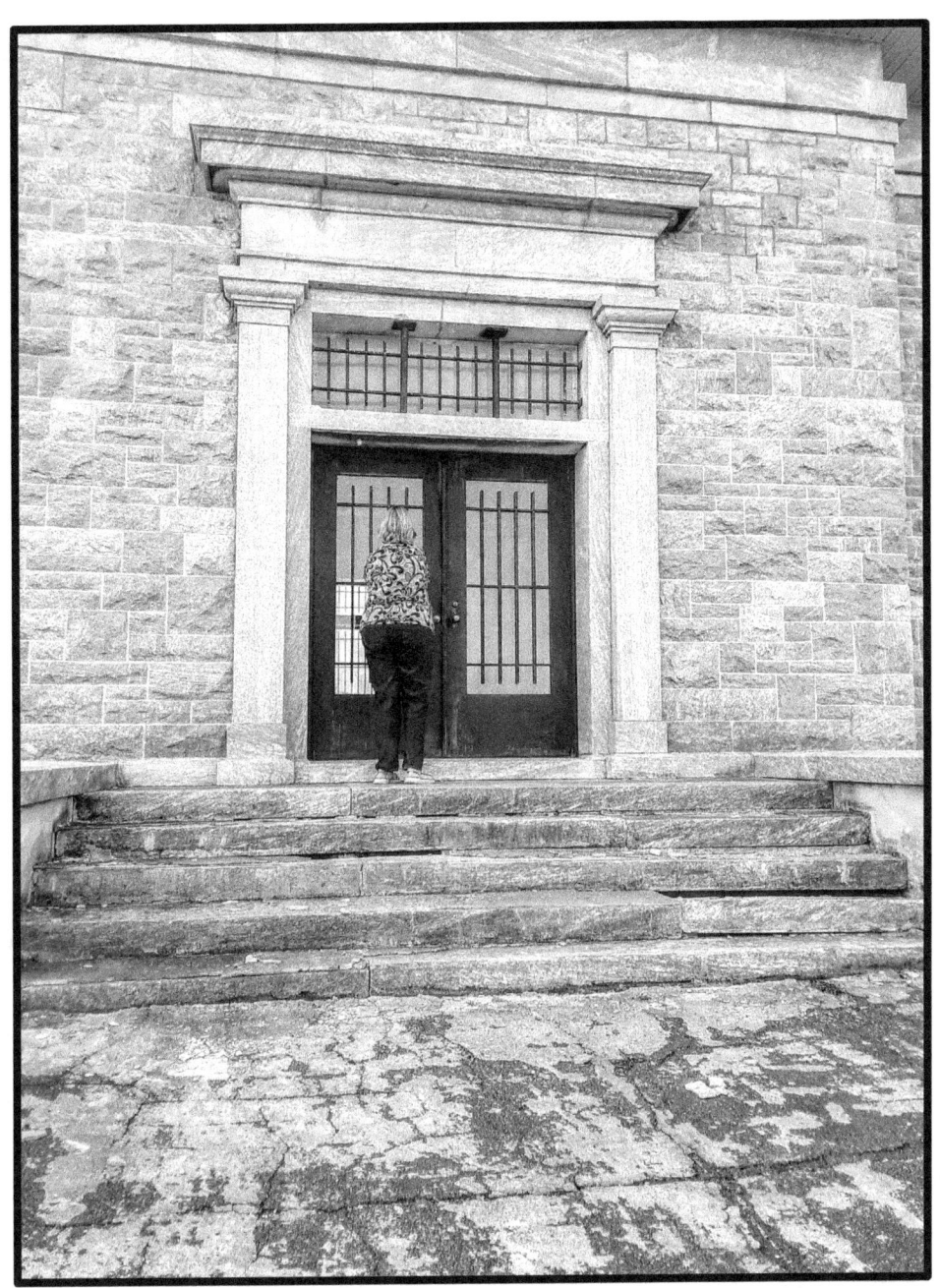

Ferndale Cemetery, Johnstown, NY

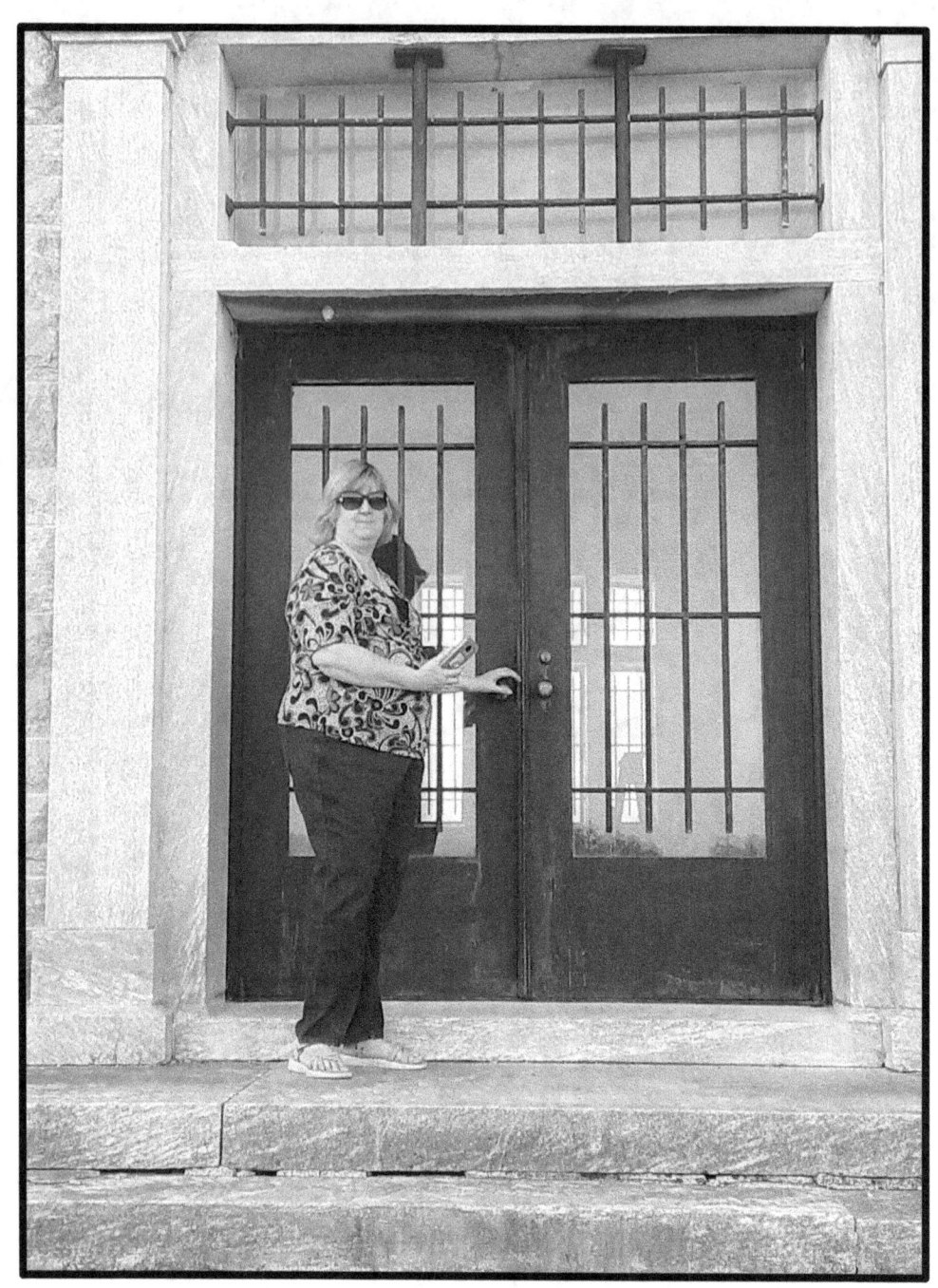

Ferndale Cemetery, Johnstown, NY

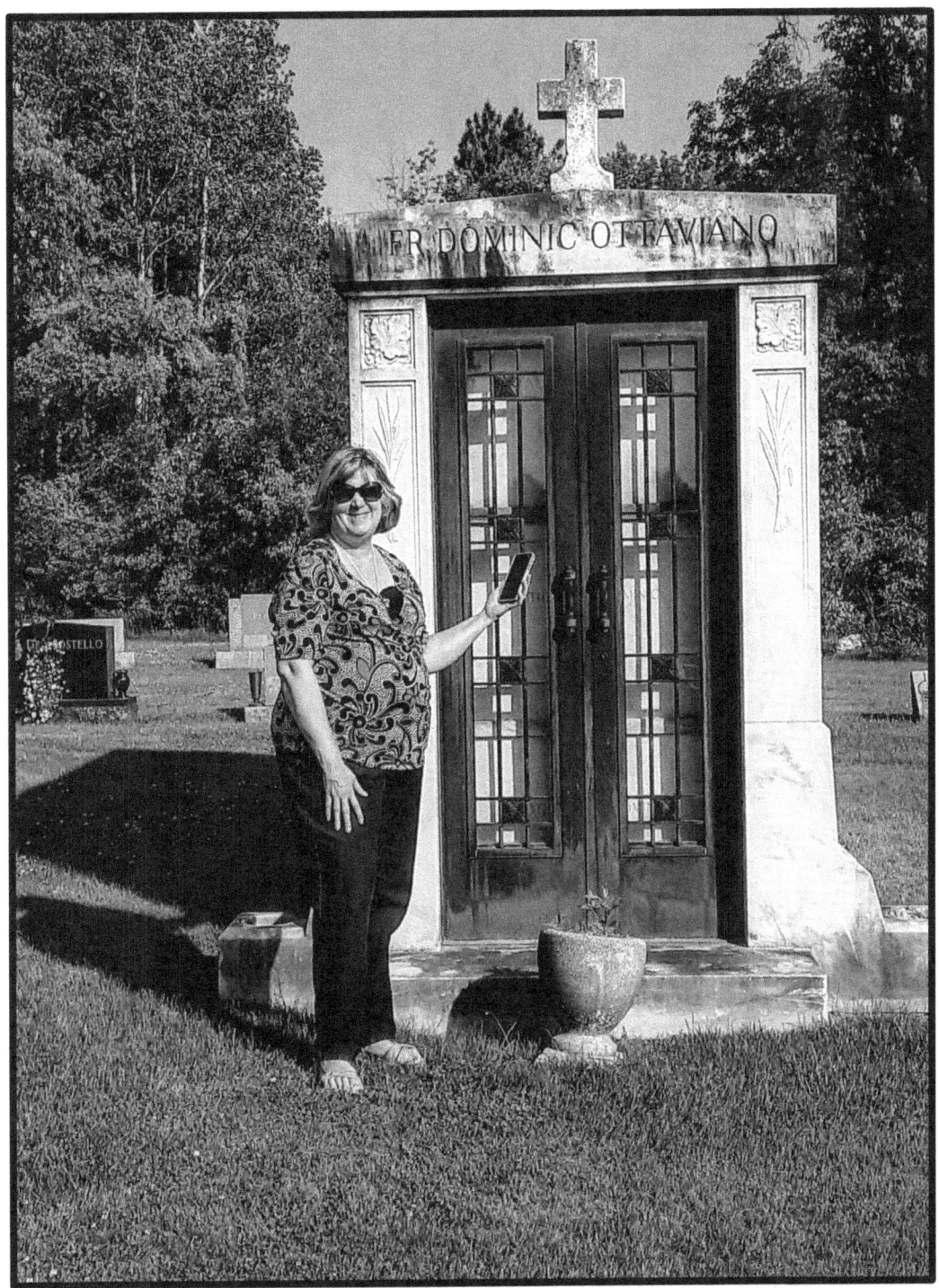

Ferndale Cemetery, Johnstown, NY

This particular style of mausoleum has intricate detail to it adding to its natural beauty.

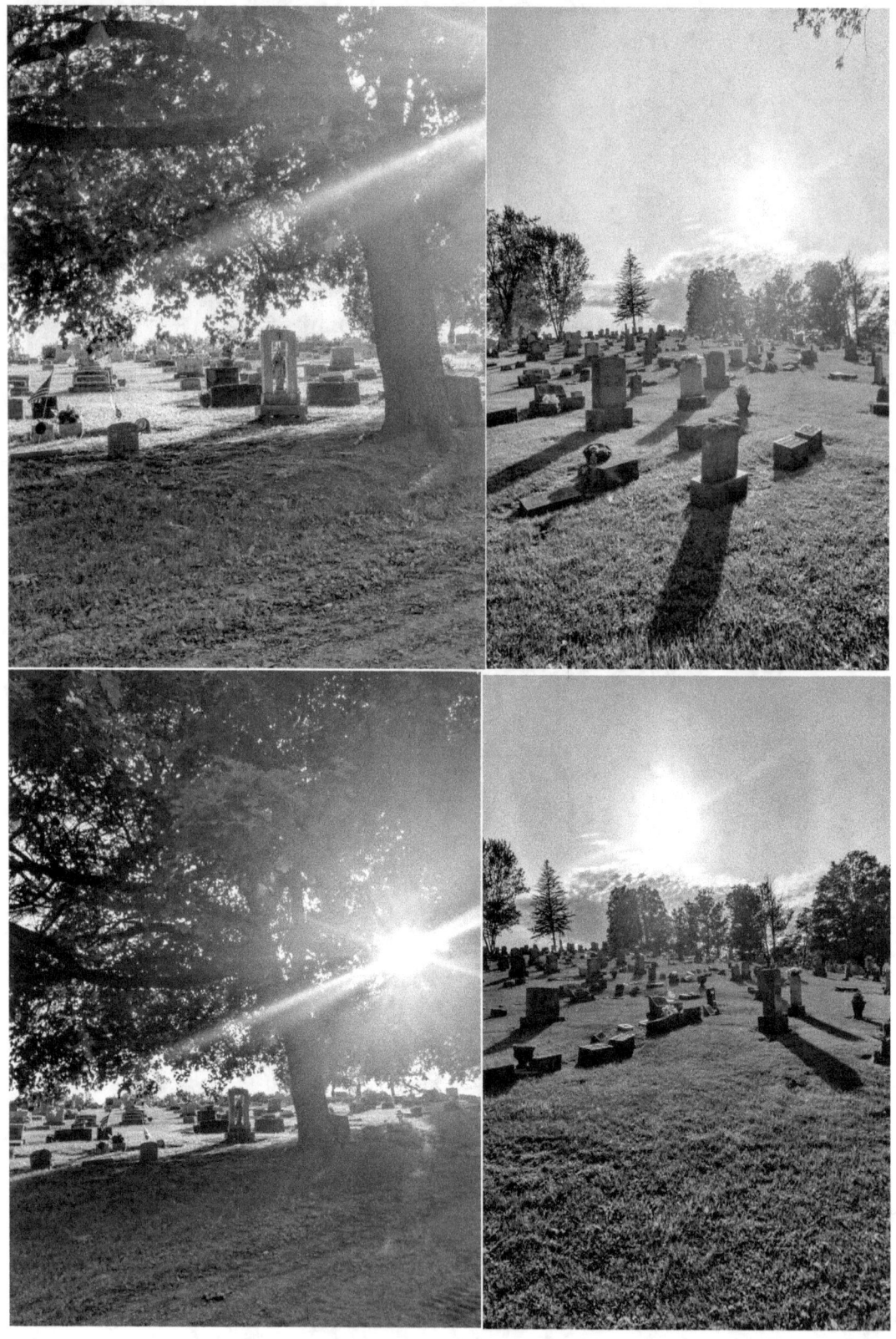

Ferndale Cemetery, Johnstown, NY

The sunsets were beautiful shining through the trees and in between the gravestones created a reminder of the natural sites to be grateful for.

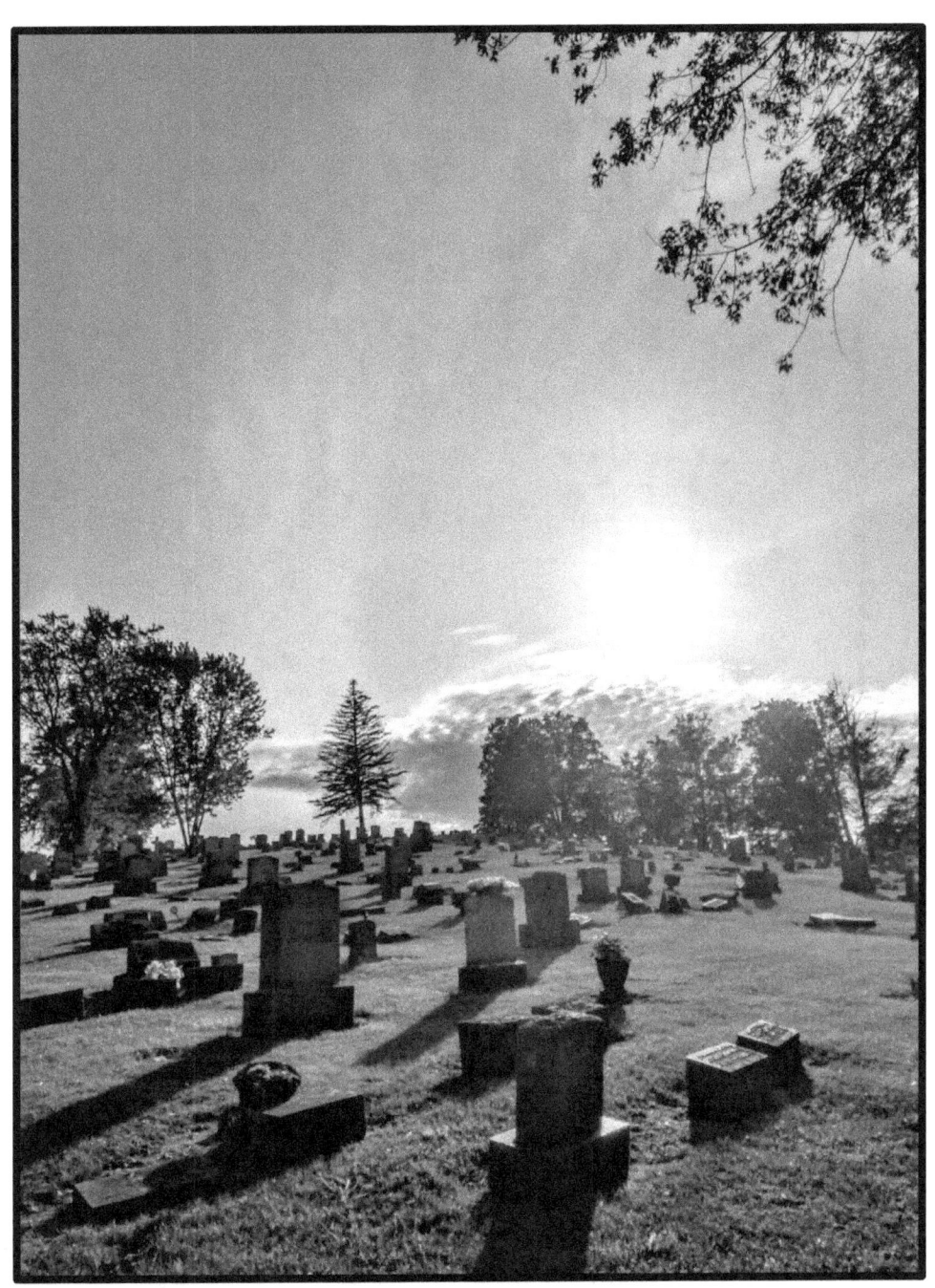

Ferndale Cemetery, Johnstown, NY

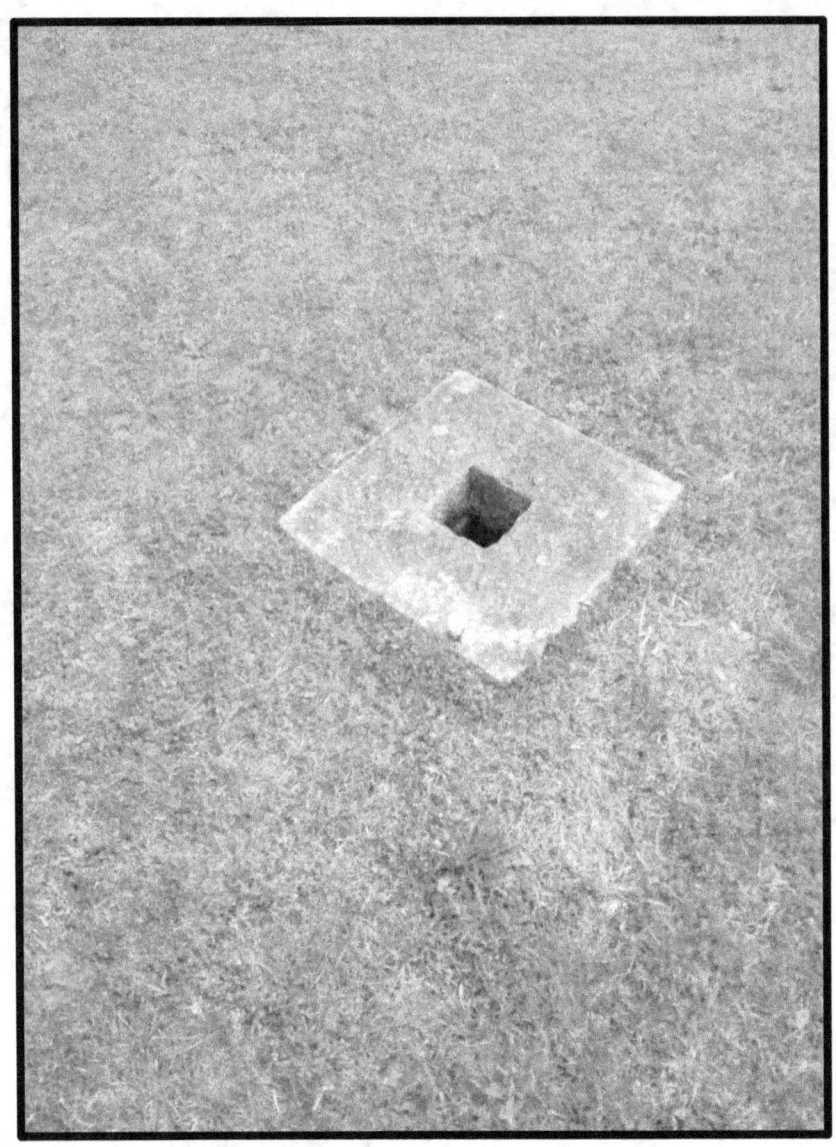

Ferndale Cemetery, Johnstown, NY

Do you know what this is? I didn't either till now. It's creepy but makes sense. Look what is underneath it on the following page.

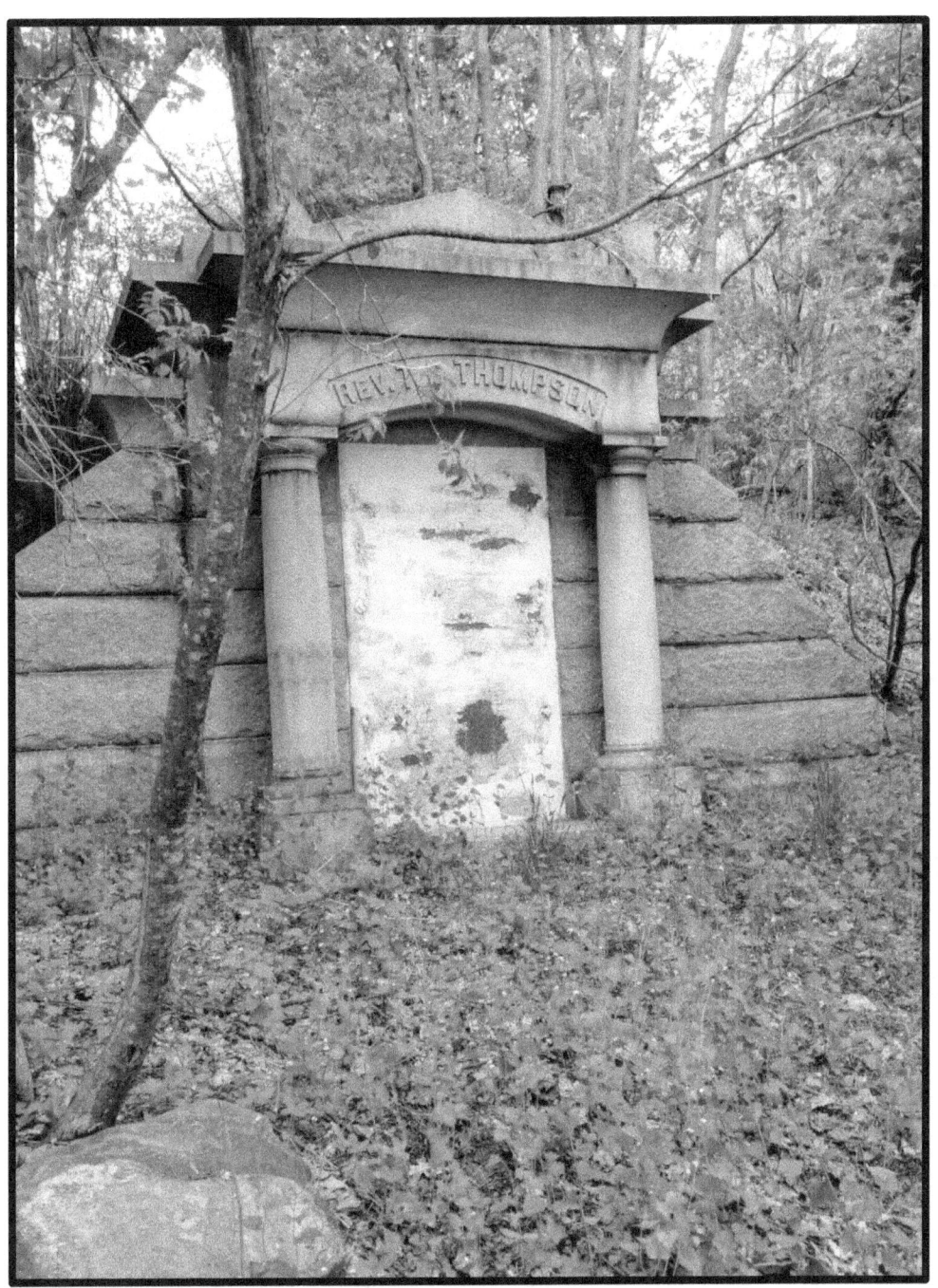

Ferndale Cemetery, Johnstown, NY

That cement piece with the hole in it is for ventilation from inside the above like burial place. It's still a mausoleum but there are many kinds apparently. This particular on is on the furthest point up on a steep hill overlooking Ferndale Cemetery. Research showed he was the person to oversee the cemetery, whether in death or alive, I am not sure.

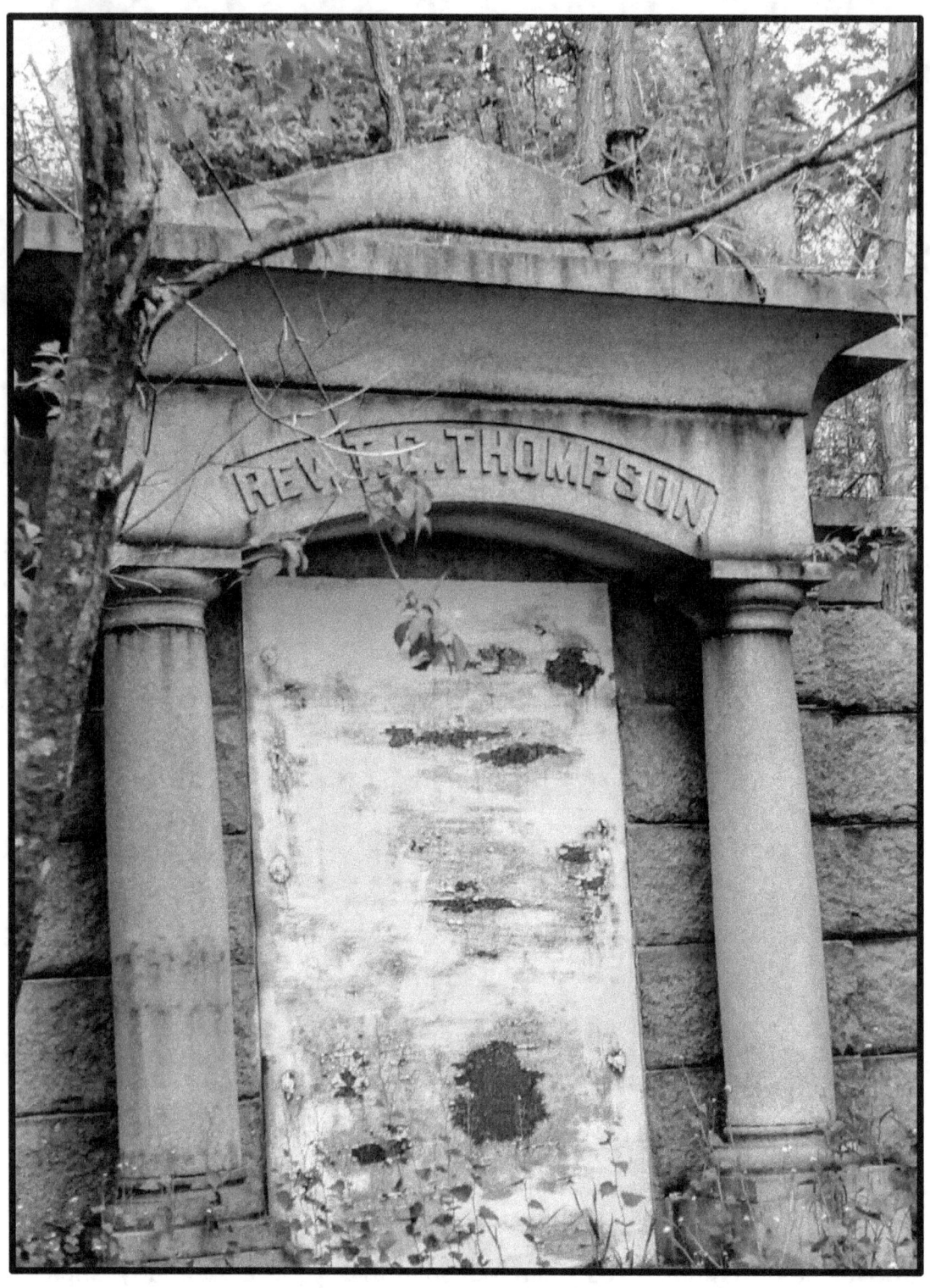

Ferndale Cemetery, Johnstown, NY

Our team member, Eric, actually got an EVP from this resting place.

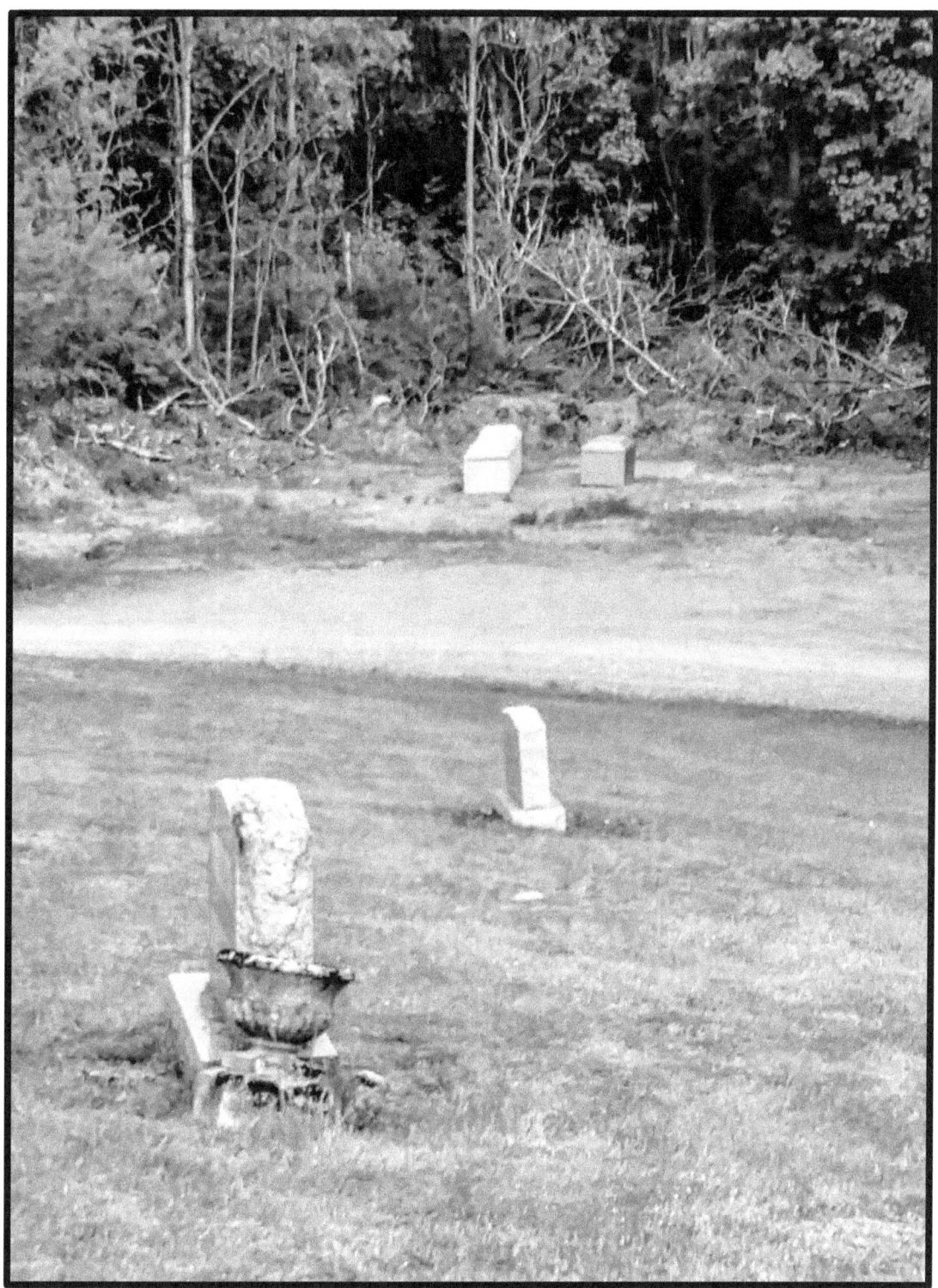

Ferndale Cemetery, Johnstown, NY

This scene was something we didn't expect to see sitting out in the open! In the far back of this picture you can see two coffin holders sitting out in plain sight! I know I am not using the proper terminology for these pieces but you know what I mean.

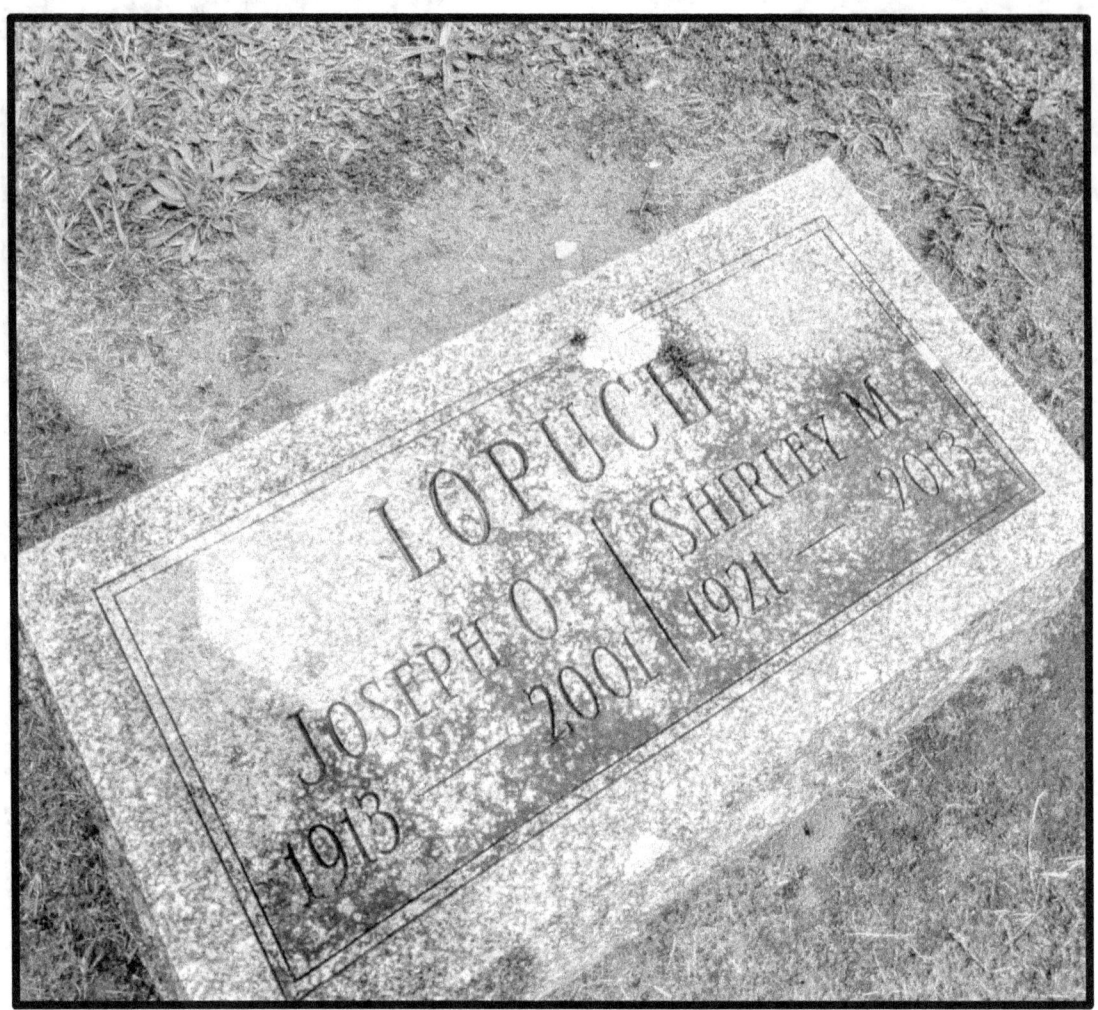

Ferndale Cemetery, Johnstown, NY

This is my great aunt and uncle's plot. They were great people.

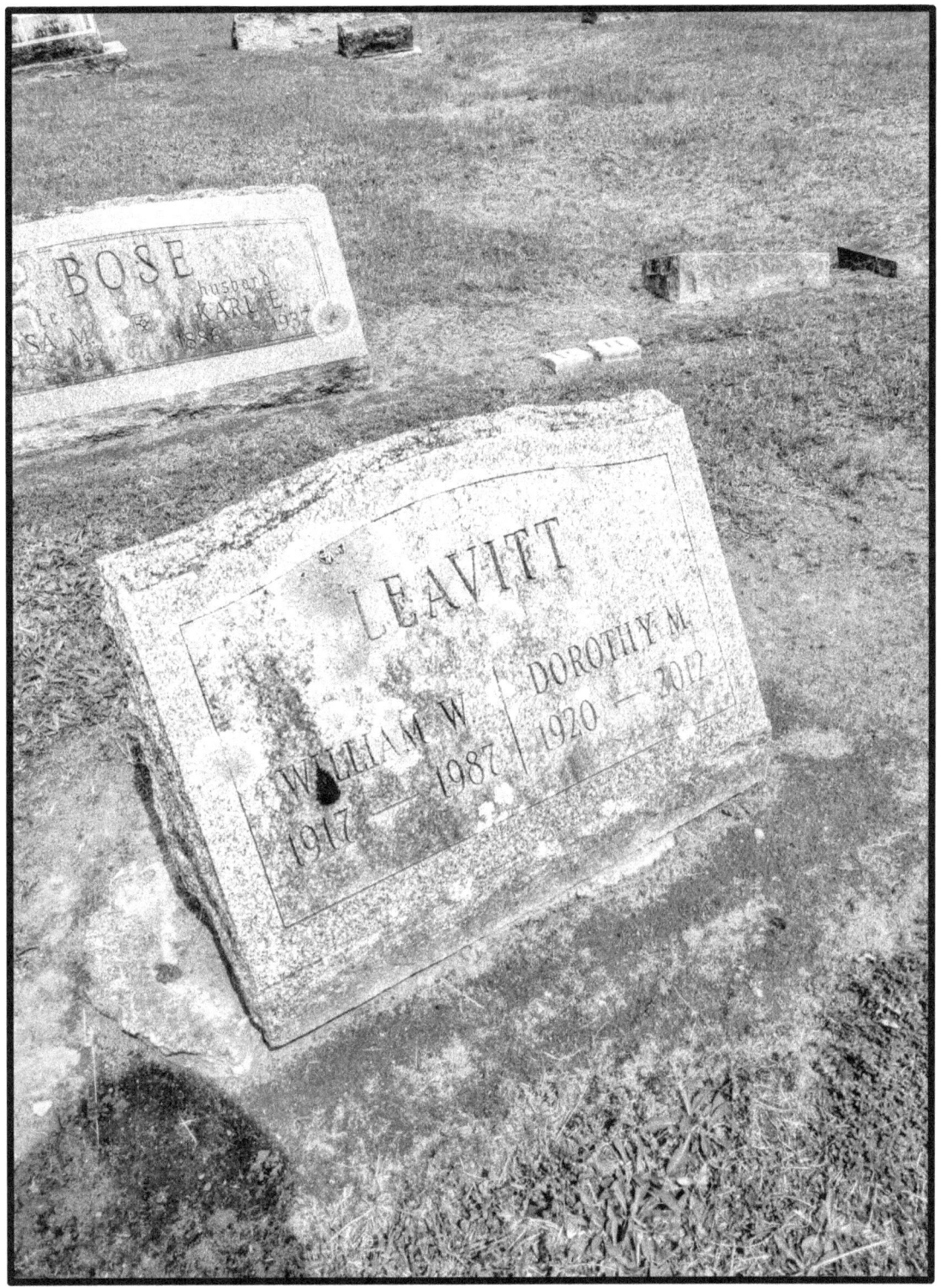

Ferndale Cemetery, Johnstown, NY

This was my great aunt from the previous photo, her sister and her brother in law. These two people I remember very well. Great Uncle Bill and Great Aunt Dorothy. When I was little at Christmas time, we would go to there house and visit. They would have a real tree and huge candy canes hanging off the branches. They wanted my sister and I to pick any one we wanted and of course, we did! Uncle Bill would be sitting in his rocking chair and Aunt Dot nearby. It was almost like they were Mr. And Mrs. Santa Claus! Aunt Dot would have candy in dish for us or ribbon candy! She would serve hot chocolate and my sister and I would play there while our parents visited with them. So many Christmases like that. A great memory I carry in my heart and mind always.

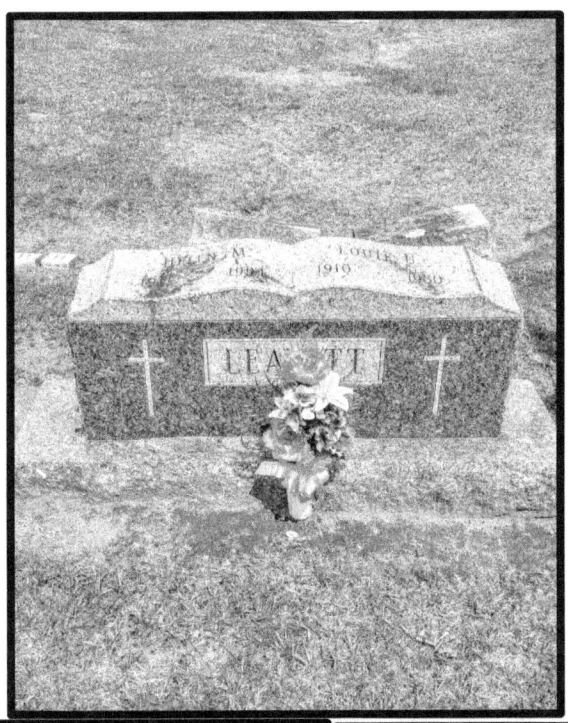
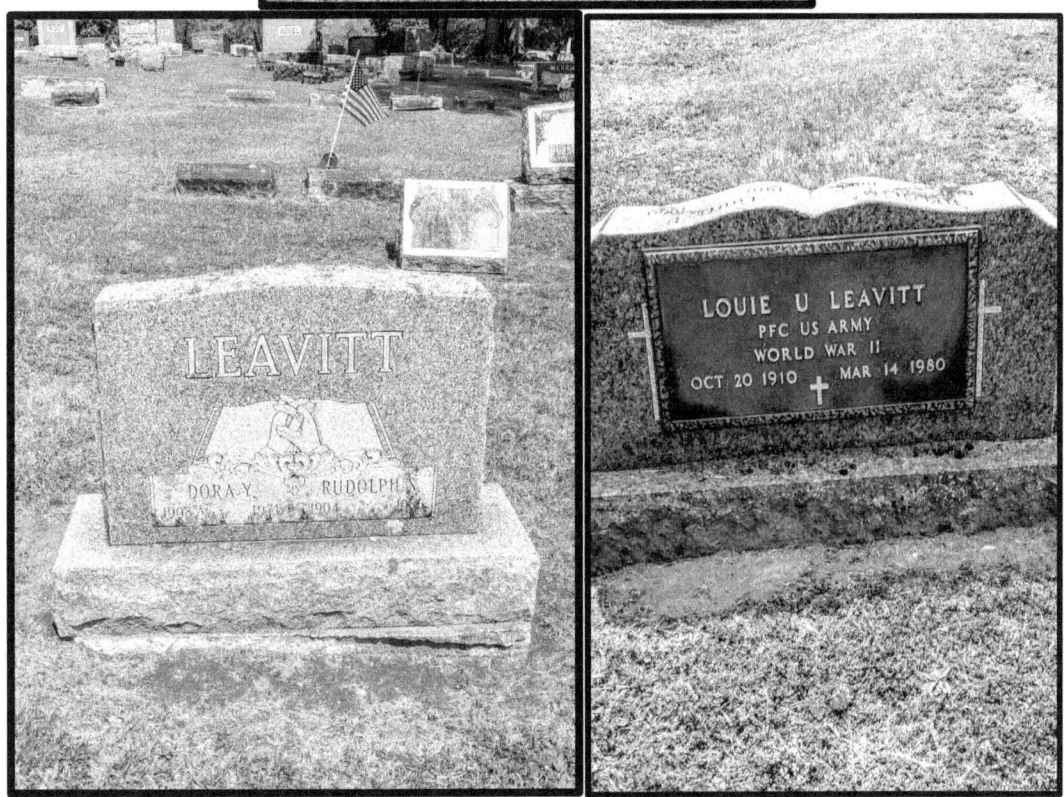

Ferndale Cemetery, Johnstown, NY

R. I.P. Aunt Shirley and Aunt Dot

Uncle Joe and Uncle Bill

The good old days!

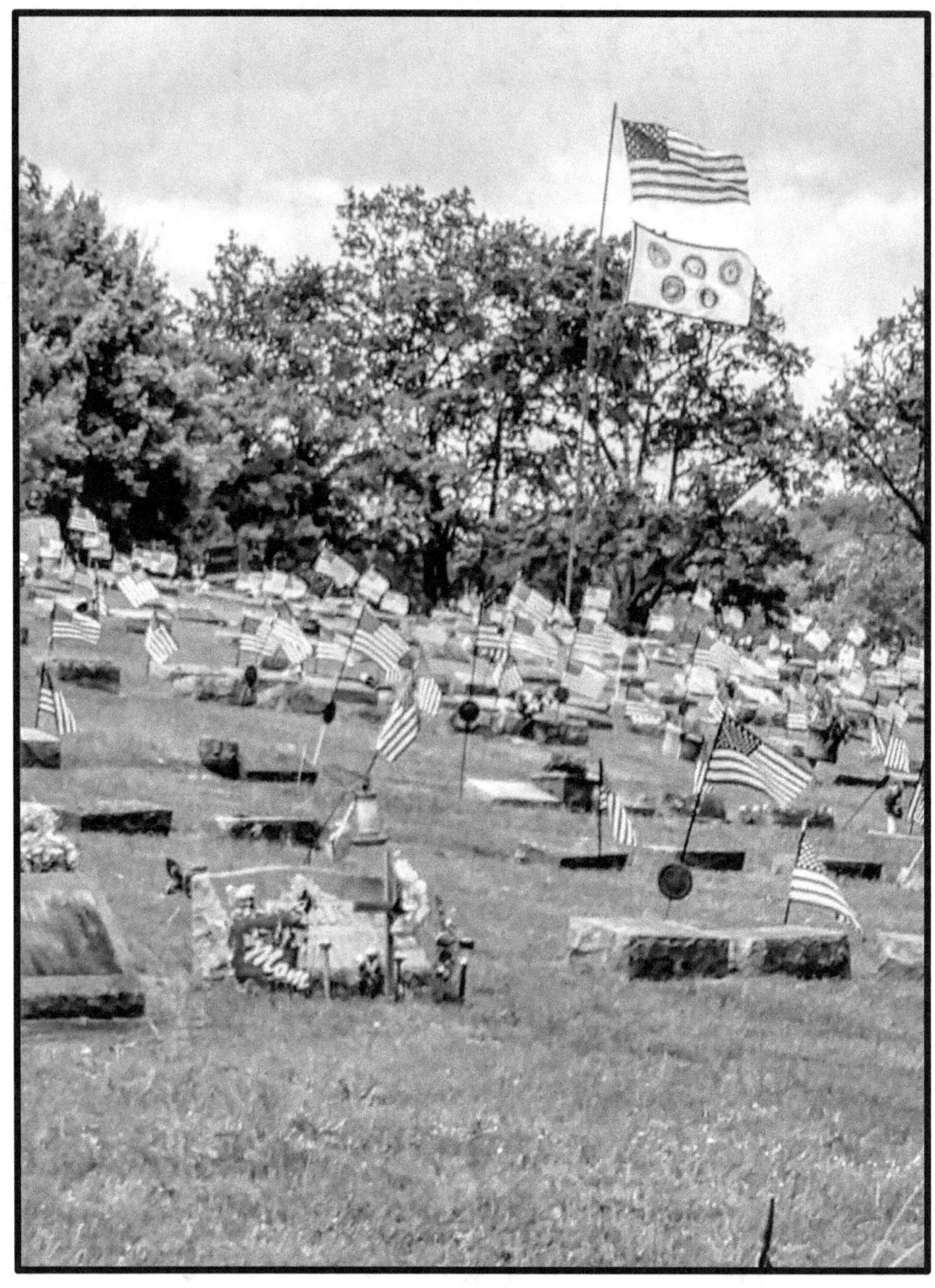

Ferndale Cemetery, Johnstown, NY

I thought this picture was especially poignant. So many veterans here.

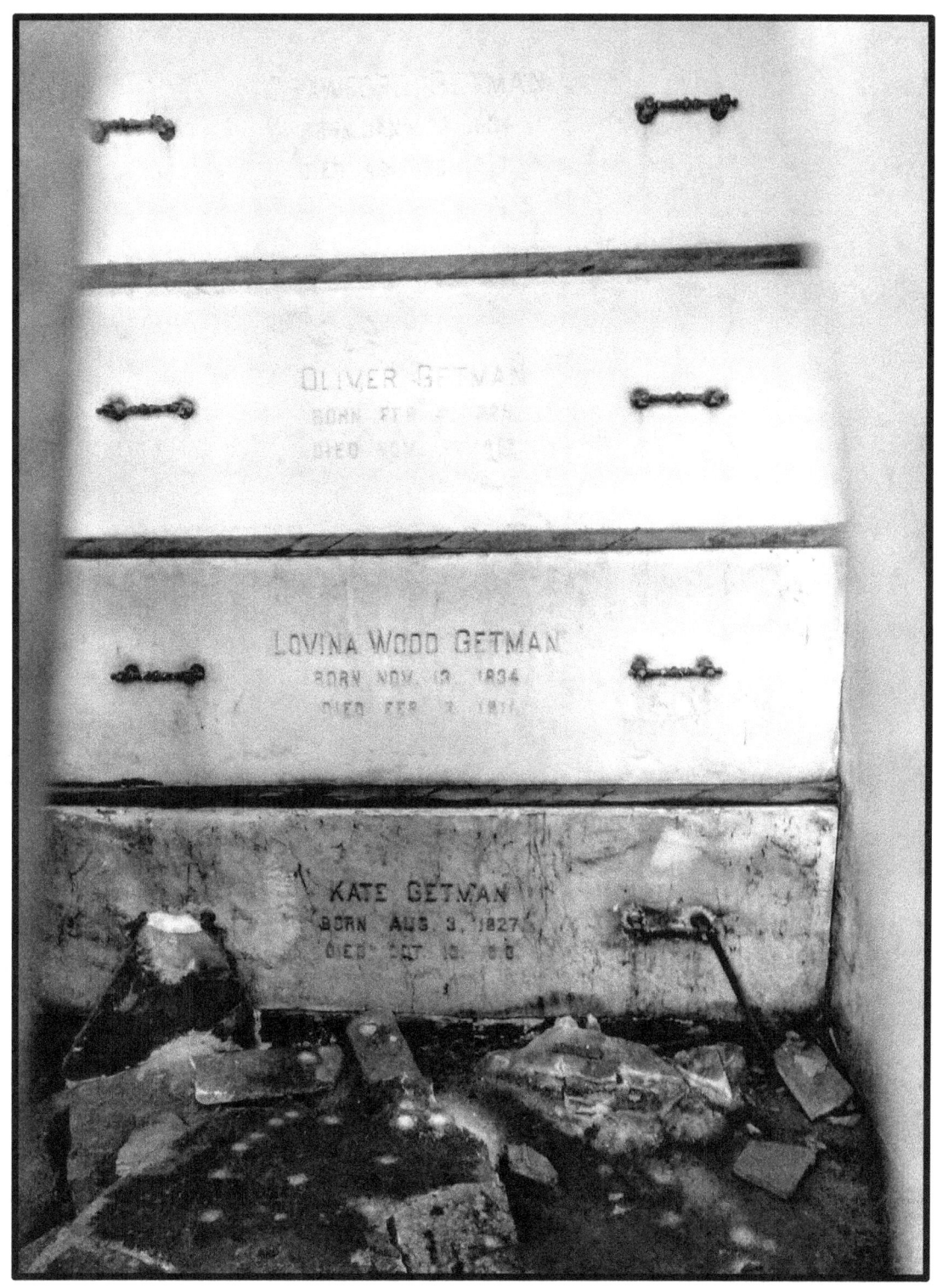

Ferndale Cemetery, Johnstown, NY

Another example of inside a mausoleum. Sad disrepair.

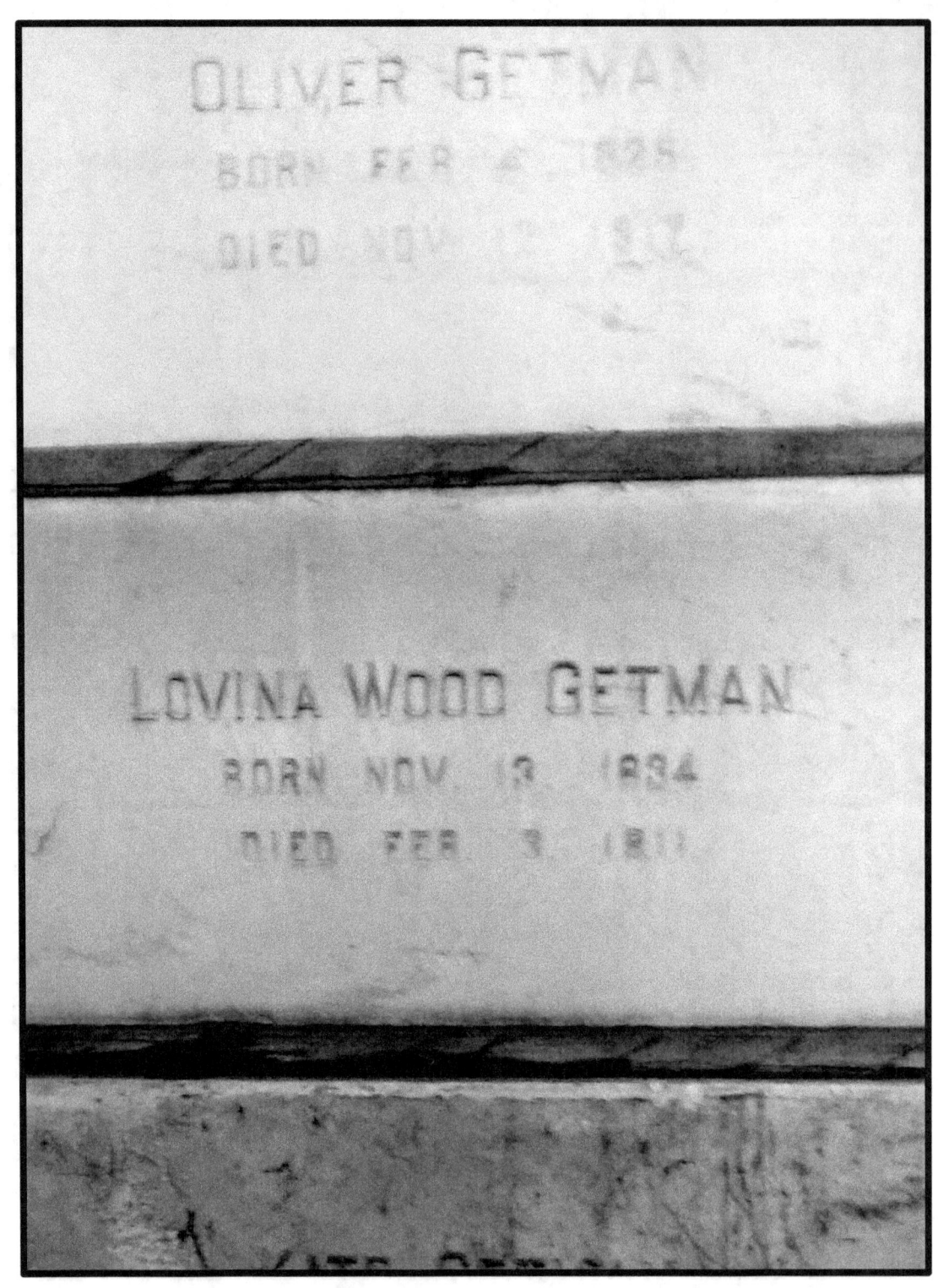

Ferndale Cemetery, Johnstown, NY

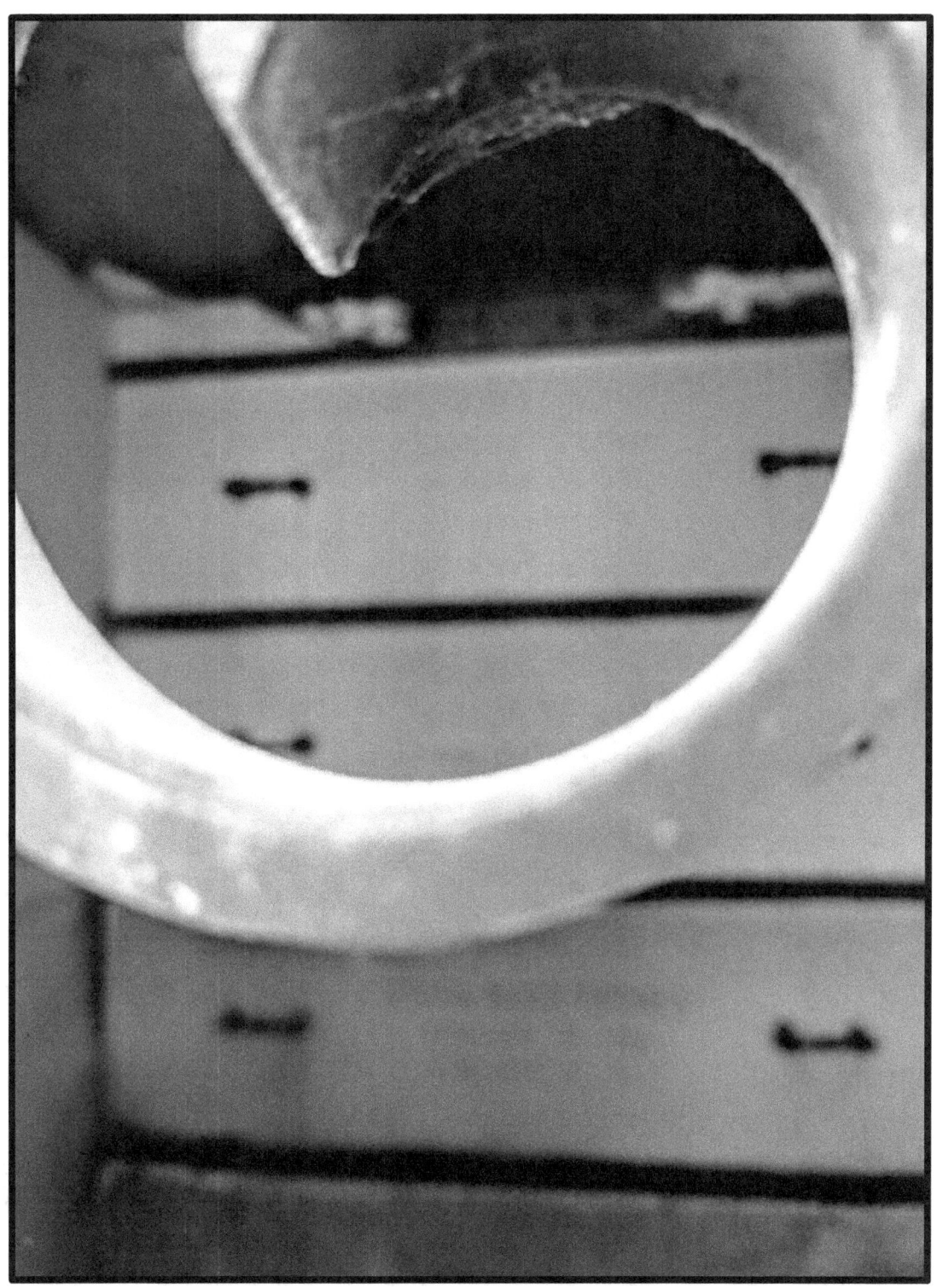

Ferndale Cemetery, Johnstown, NY

Looking through the door inside a mausoleum.

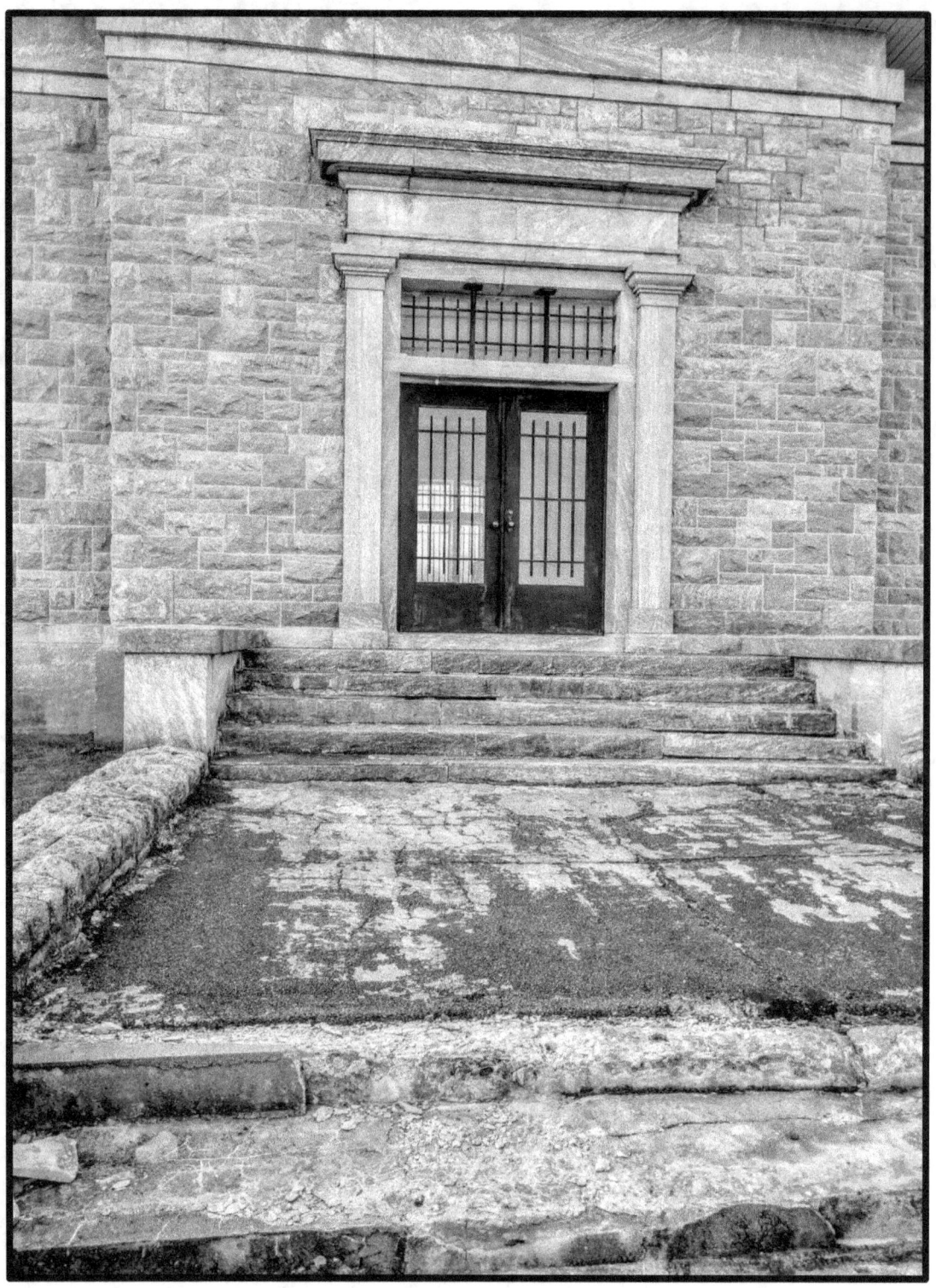

Ferndale Cemetery, Johnstown, NY

They said this was the place to hold bodies if they couldn't be buried quite yet in the ground. It's a huge building. We were able to get some great pictures of inside.

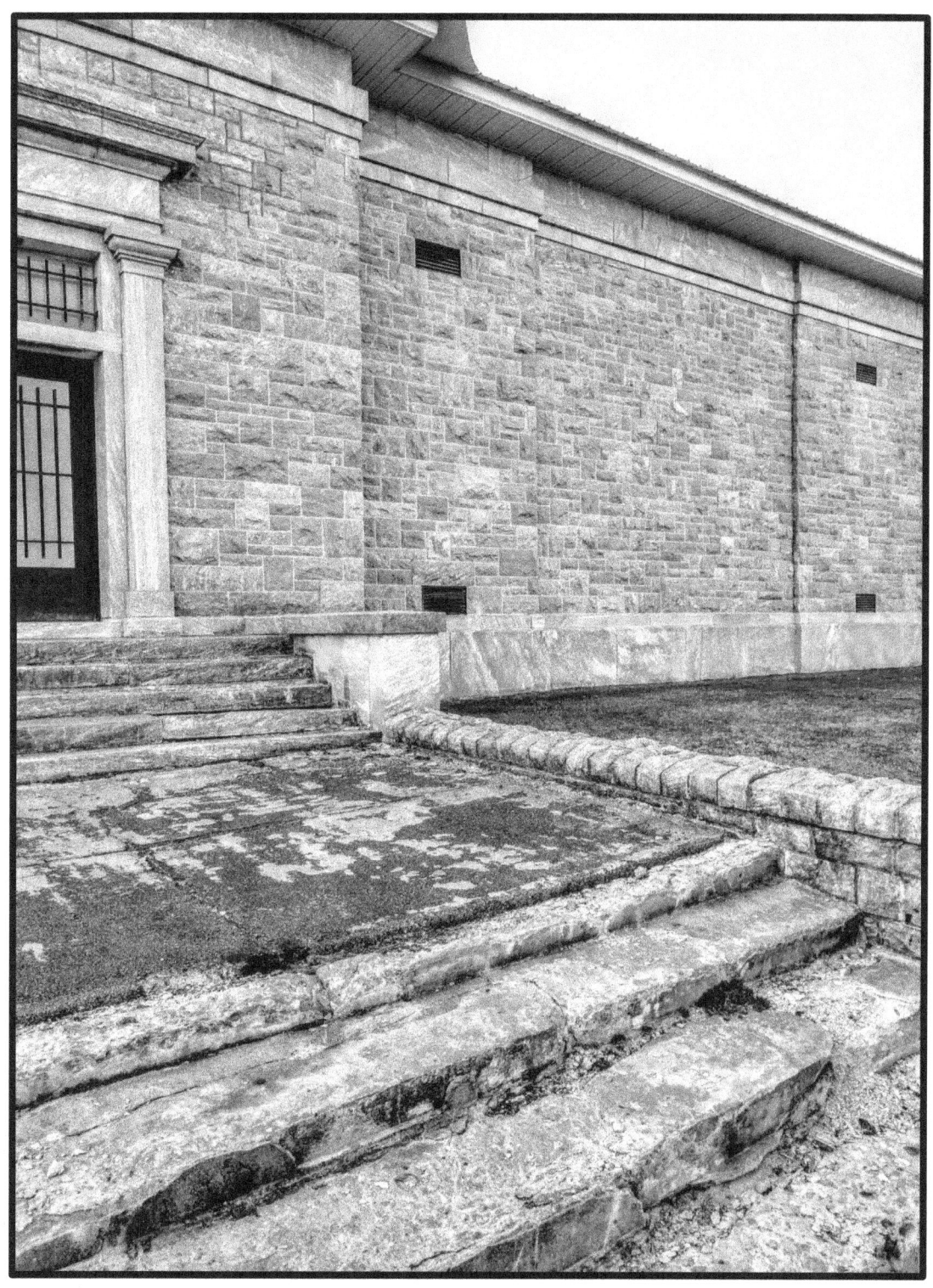

Ferndale Cemetery, Johnstown, NY

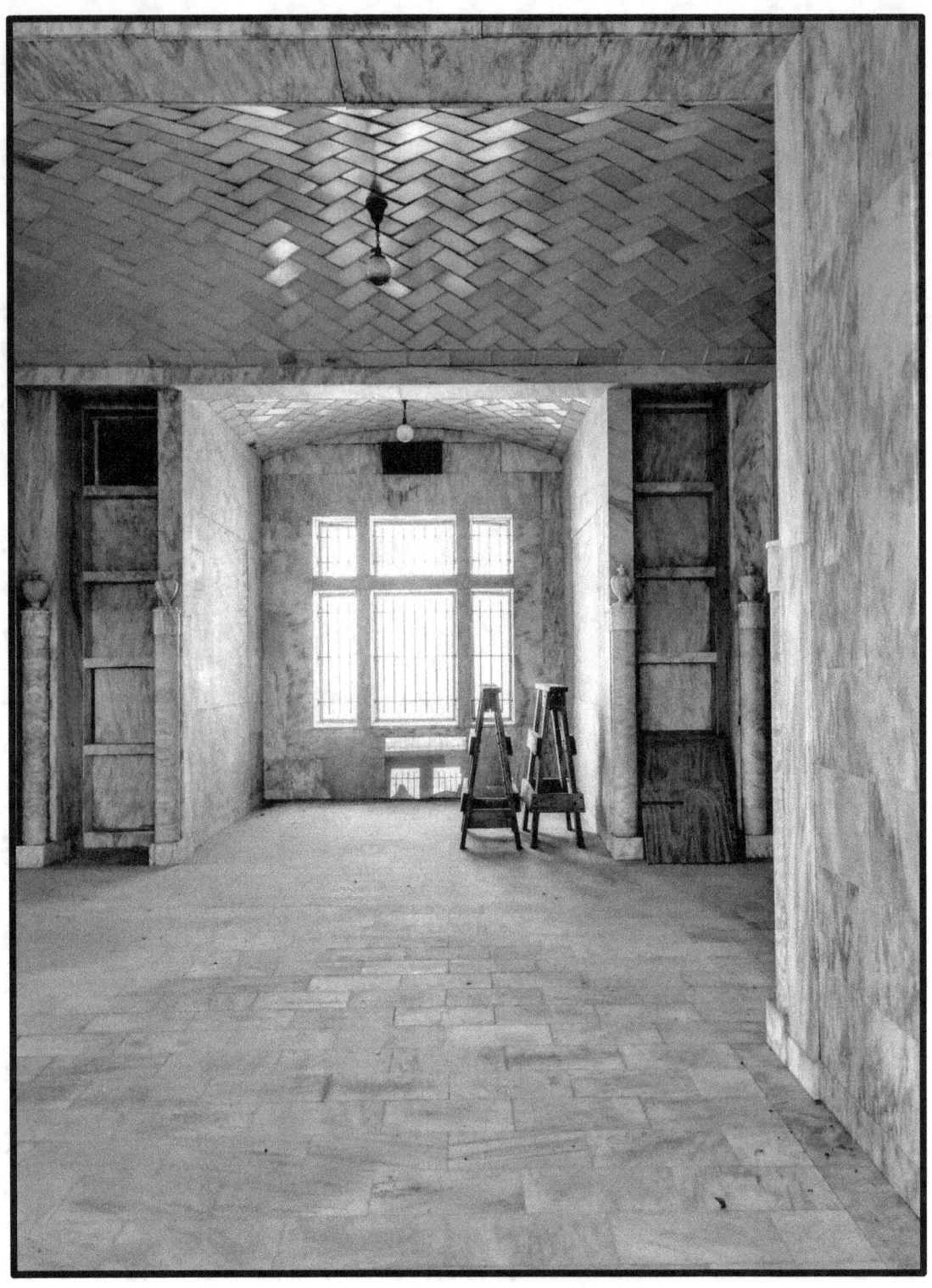

Ferndale Cemetery, Johnstown, NY

Inside this mausoleum, you can see its beauty. All marble floors and walls. A shiny ceiling made with a different color marble. Each wall is lined with a different name of a deceased person. I'm not sure if this is a findal resting place or a holding place. Either way, this is a beautiful building inside.

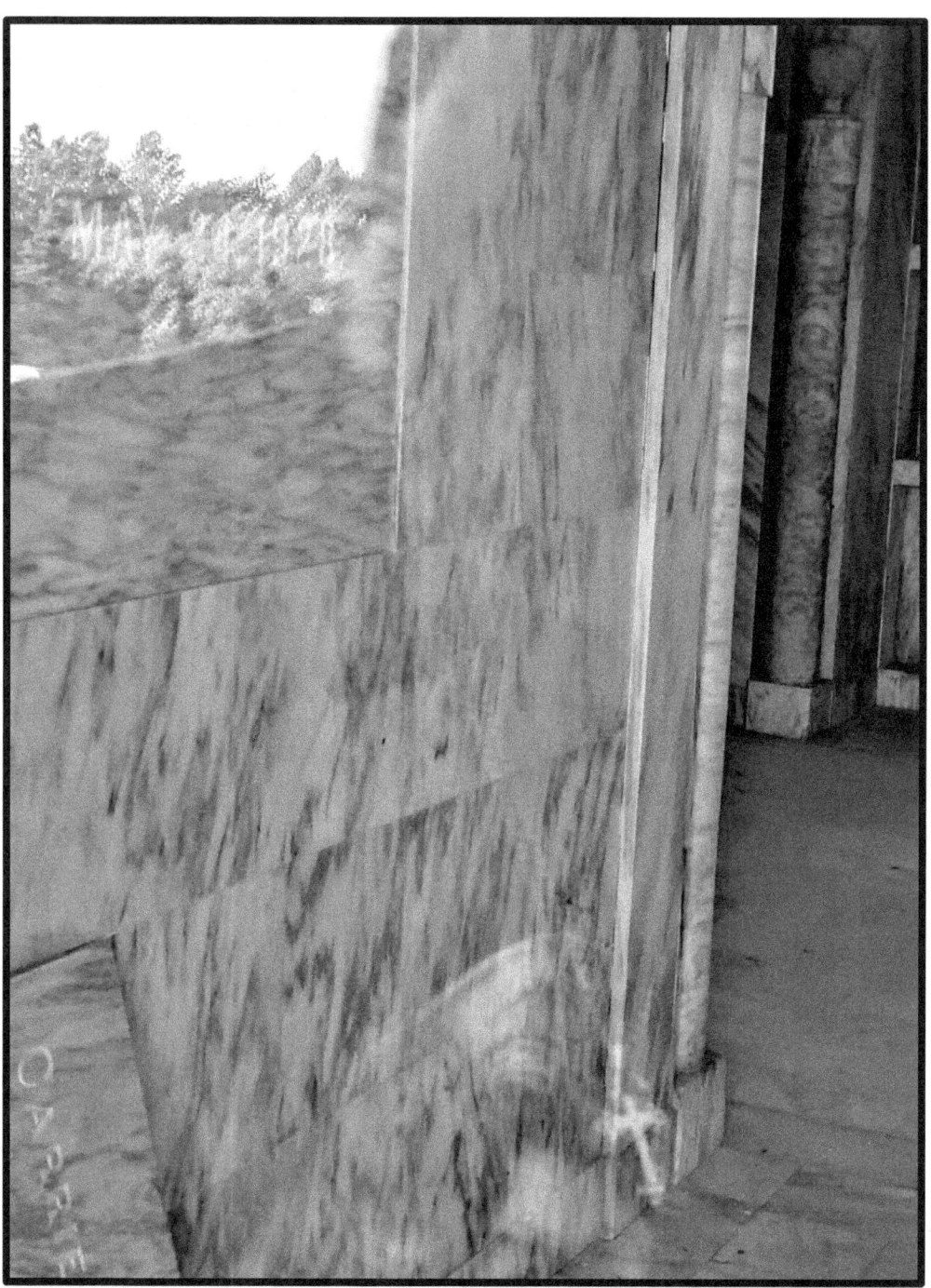

Ferndale Cemetery, Johnstown, NY

If you look carefully at this picture, you will see a date in the window. This had us baffled for some time. It reads May ?, 1928. We thought how could this be possible when we were taking a picture from the outside in, a date wouldn´t just appear...or could it?

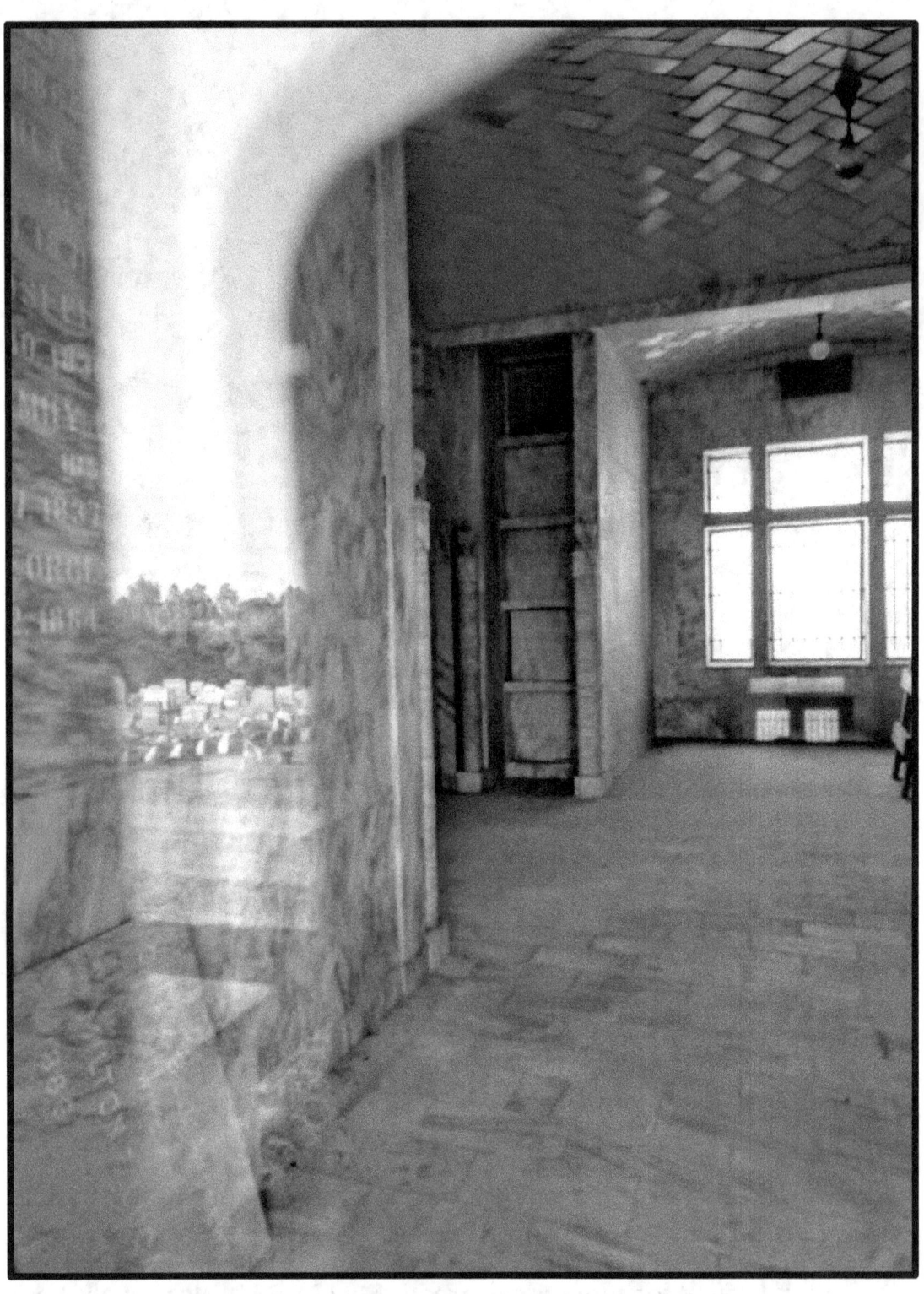

Ferndale Cemetery, Johnstown, NY

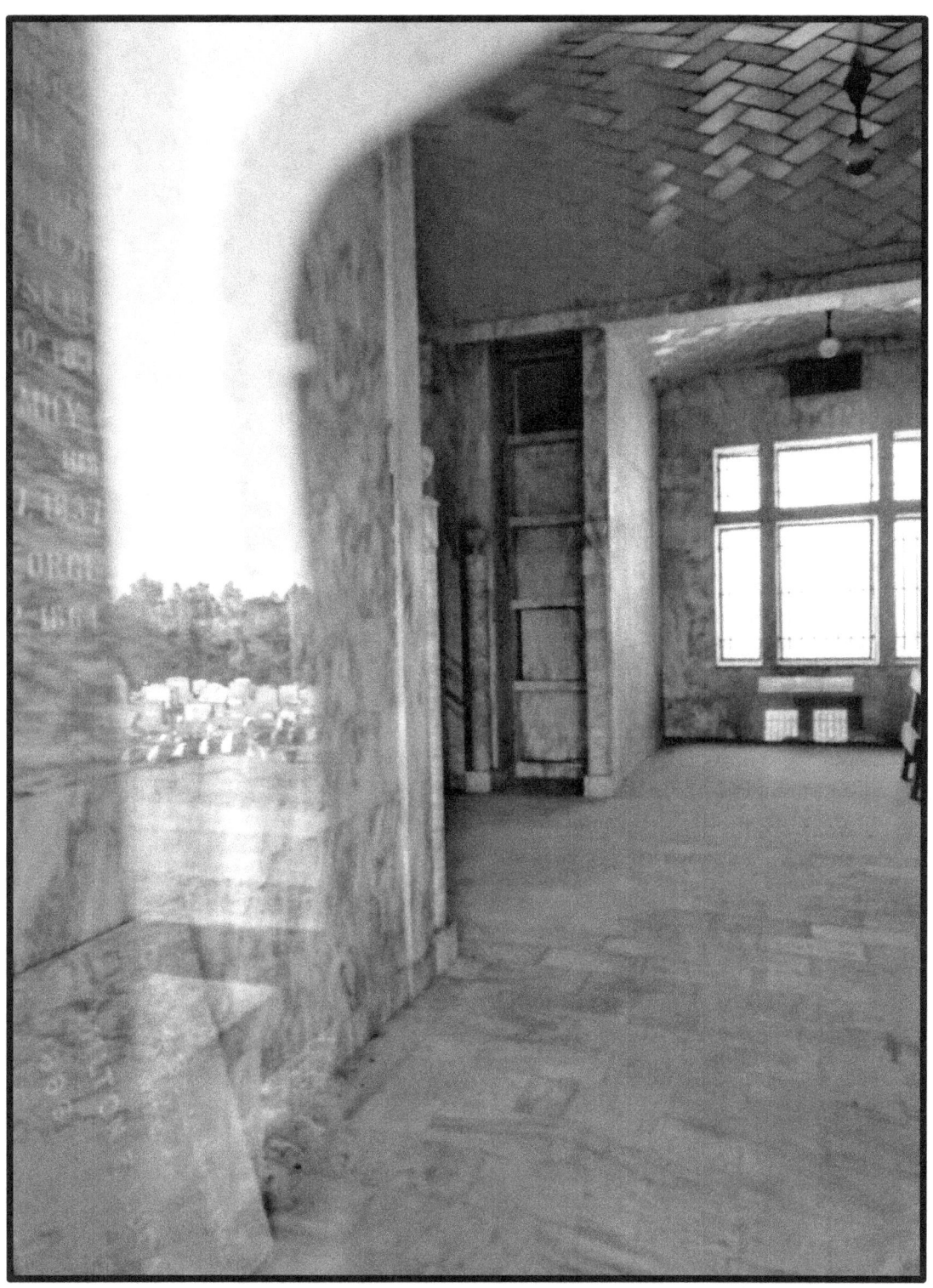

Ferndale Cemetery, Johnstown, NY

Upon looking at the pictures more clearly we figured out it was a reflection of the other side of the room to the right, which had engravings of other deceased persons with their resting spot in the side wall! Every wall was a person! This place was huge.

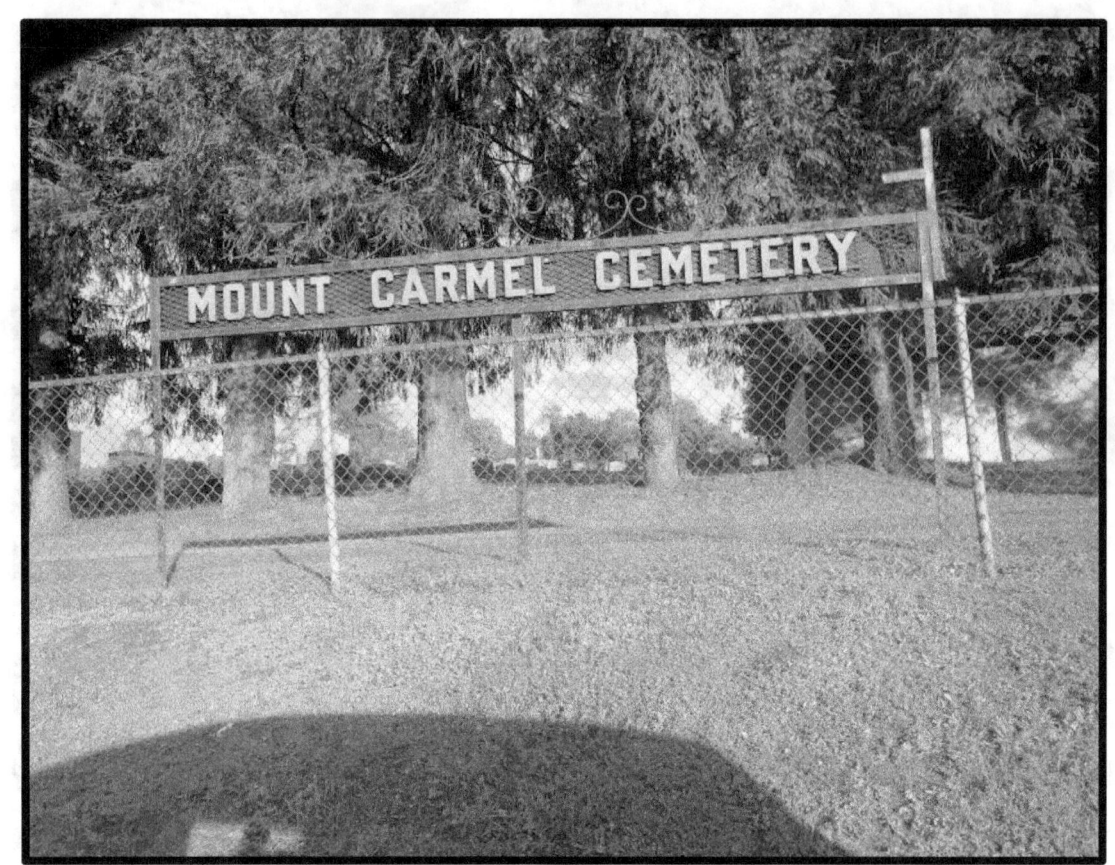

Mount Carmel Cemetery, Johnstown, NY

Mount Carmel Cemetery is a large, peaceful place.

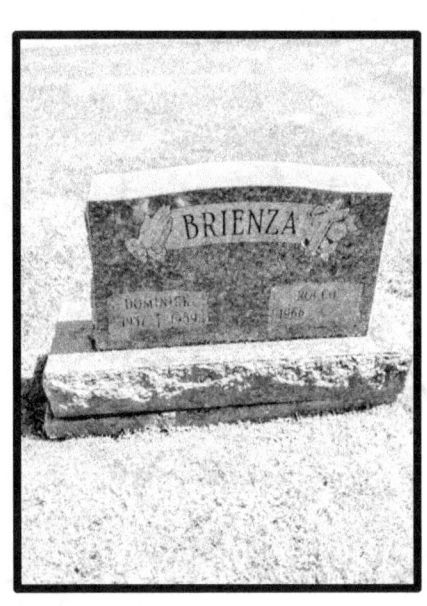
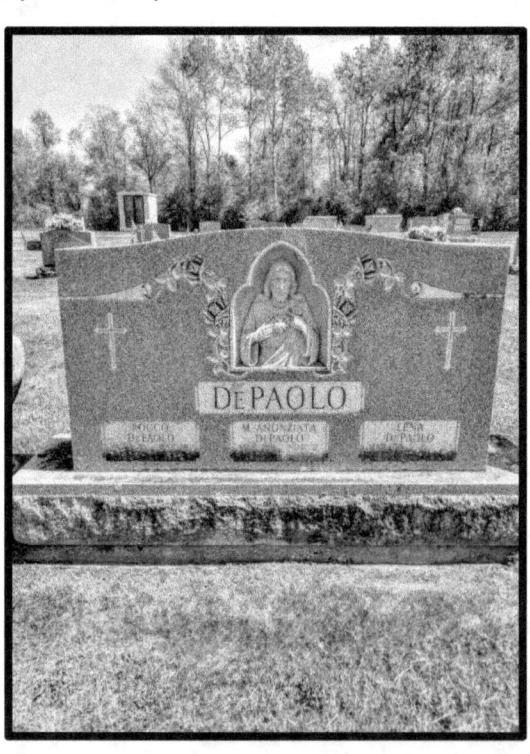

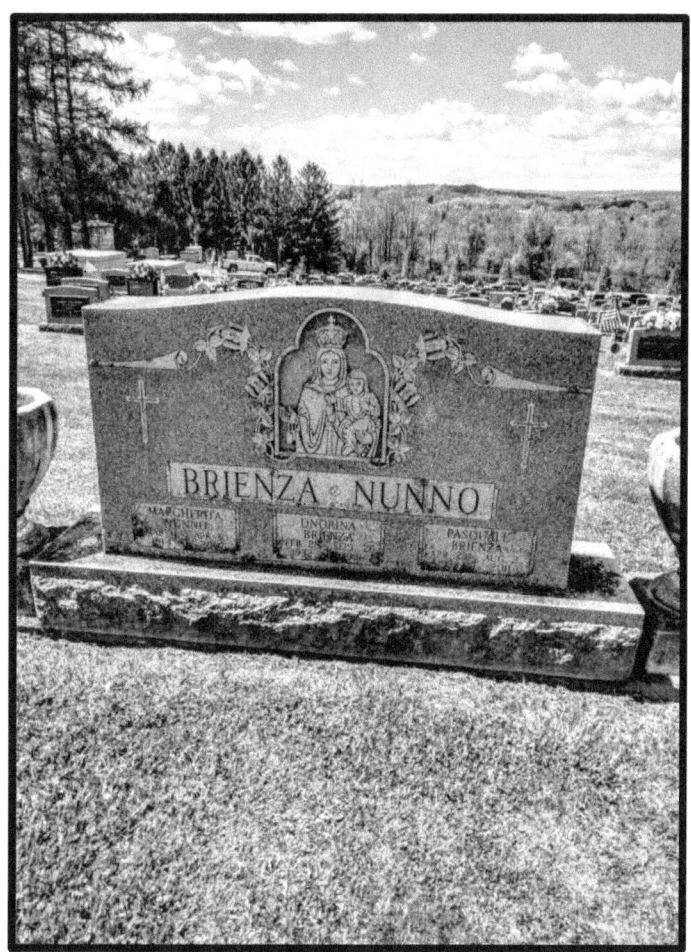

Mount Carmel Cemetery, Johnstown, NY

This stone is highly decorated as you can see. This is an Italian family known to this area. Yes, my former family member.

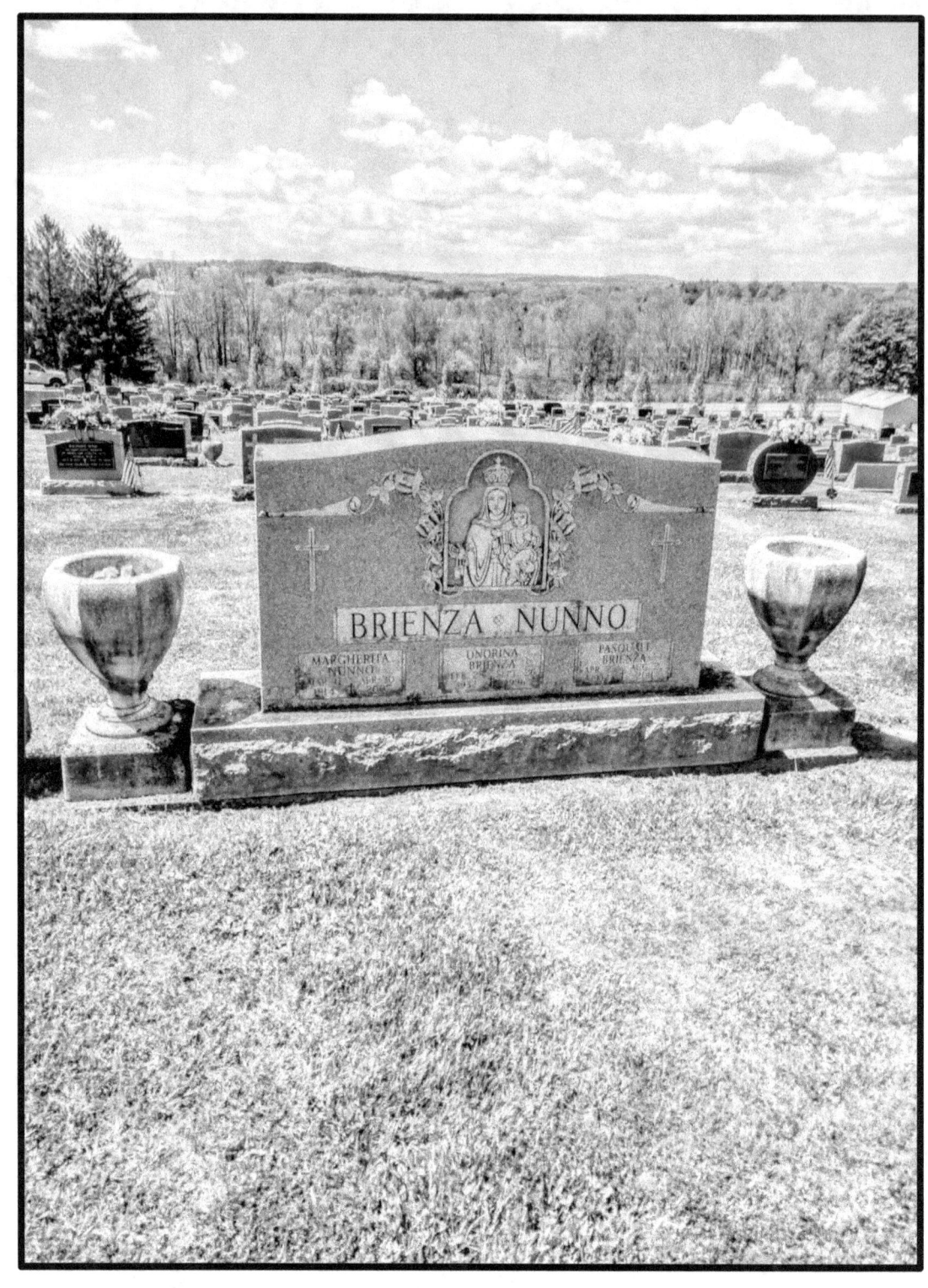

Mount Carmel Cemetery, Johnstown, NY

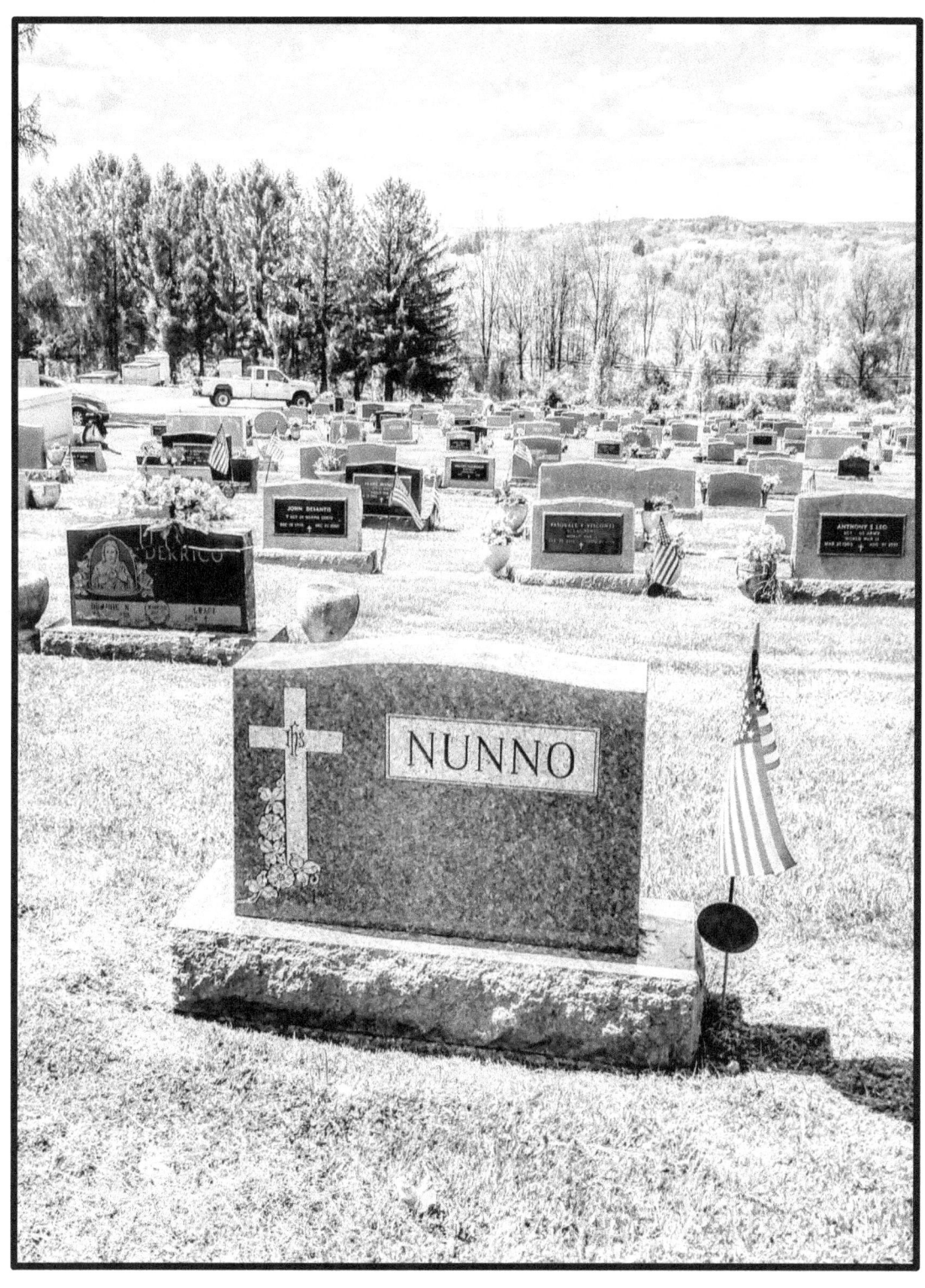

Mount Carmel Cemetery, Johnstown, NY

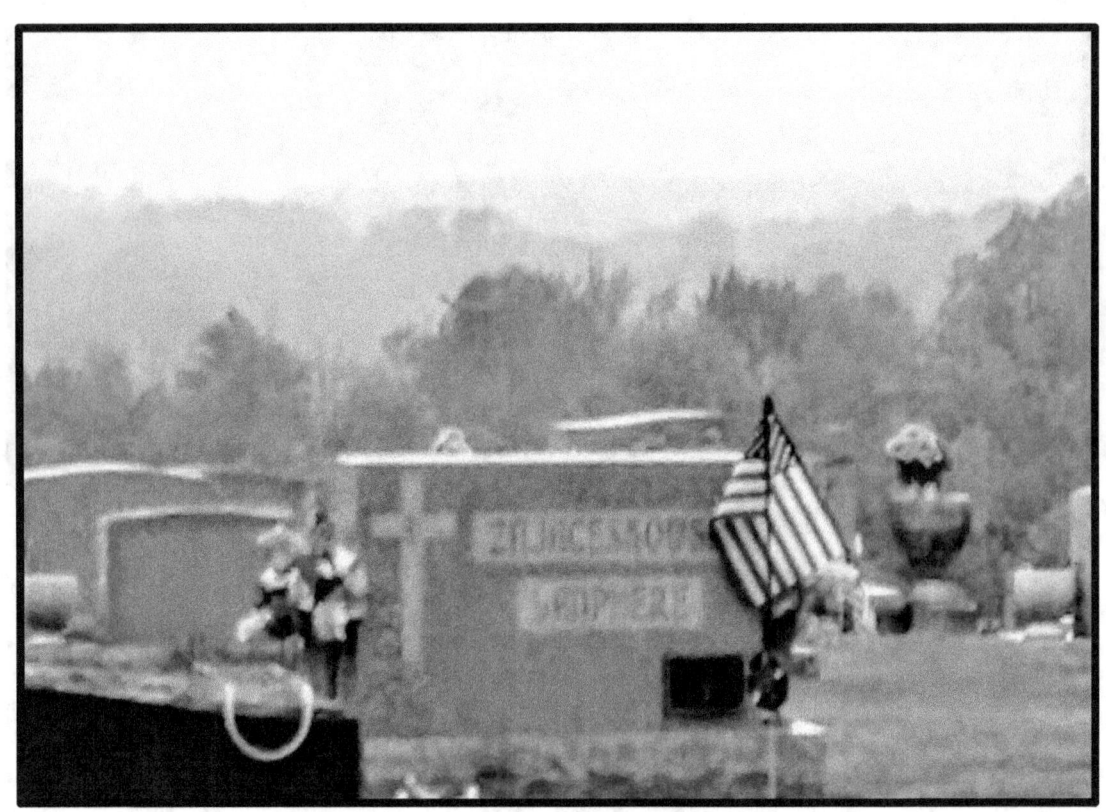

Mount Carmel Cemetery, Johnstown, NY

This was cool to see the fog rolling in. These are more family gravestones but notice the different types of designs each stone has. This one was part of my family also. Zajaceskowski

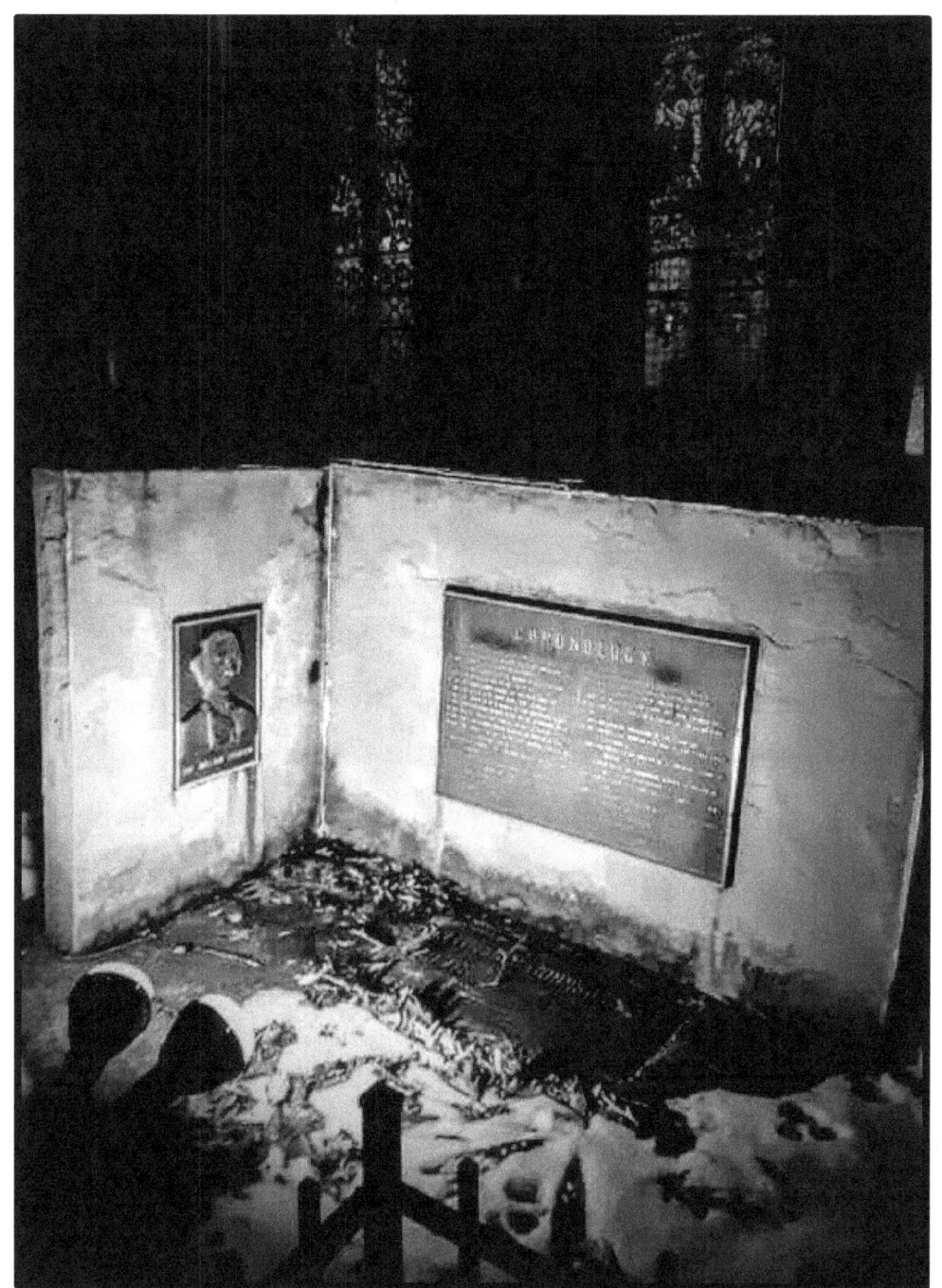

Sir William Johnson's burial place, Johnstown, NY

In 1738 at the age of twenty-three, William Johnson arrived in America from Ireland to oversee his Uncle Peter Warren's land holdings south of the present day city of Amsterdam. Despite his promise to his uncle not to start a settlement of his own, William purchased a tract of land north of the Mohawk River in 1739. He moved there, building a house in 1743 called Mount Johnson. At the same time, he began prosperous trade with the Mohawk Indians on his own behalf. He and Catherine Weissenberg had three children - Ann, John and Mary. Trade with the Indians flourished, for Johnson was an efficient, diplomatic businessman. More importantly, he adopted Indian customs and dress and learned the Indian language, and dealt fairly in the exchange of both furs and advice, fur trade being the basis of his fortune.

Johnson soon became involved in colonial politics. He provisioned British military posts, kept the Indians friendly to the British, served in the New York colonial legislature. Johnson won military fame as a major general of the provincial militia and a commander when the French forces under Baron Dieskau' were defeated at the Battle of Lake George in 1755. Largely as a result of this victory, Johnson was made a baronet by King George II. In 1759 and 1760, Sir William won greater renown for military achievements at Fort Niagara and Montreal. During the long years of conflict which culminated in the French and Indian Wars, Johnson rose from the rank of colonel (1745) to major general (1755). His increasing influence with the Indians secured their assistance as powerful military allies. In 1755 with the help of the Mohawks, among them Joseph Brant, Johnson turned back the French at the Battle of Lake George. For his many years of faithful service, the British Crown made Johnson a baronet in 1755. The following year Sir William was appointed "Superintendent of all the affairs of the Six Nations and other Northern Indians" (north of the Ohio River) a position he held until his death.

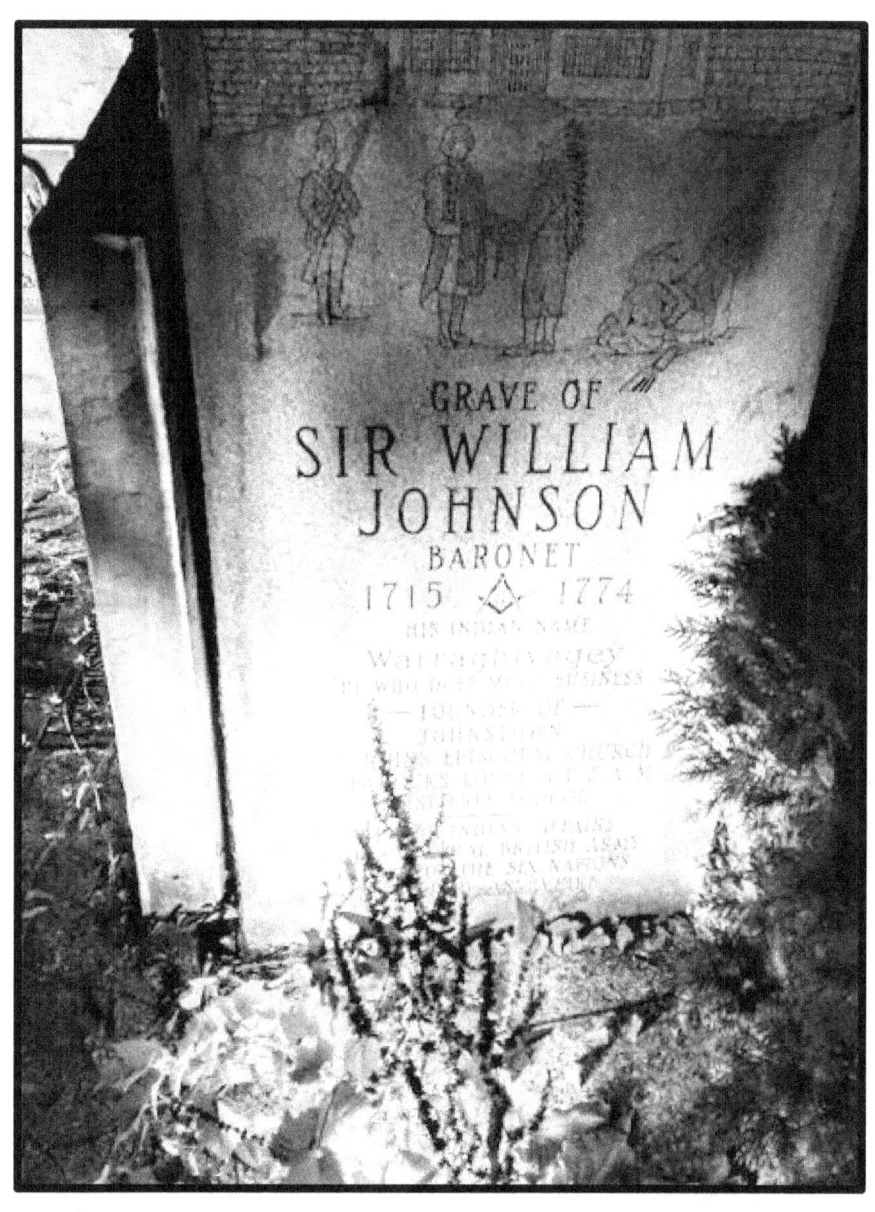

Sir William Johnson's burial place, Johnstown, NY

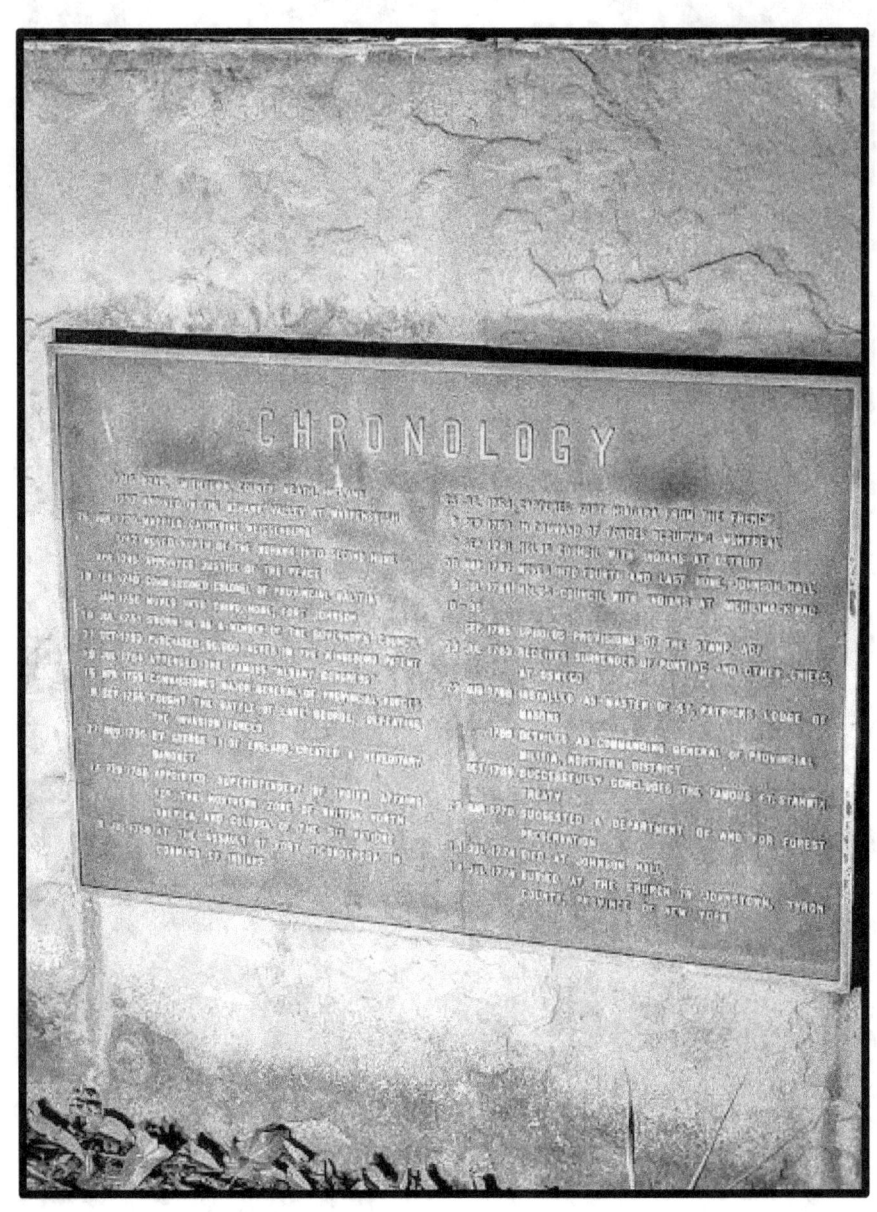

Sir William Johnson's burial place, Johnstown, NY

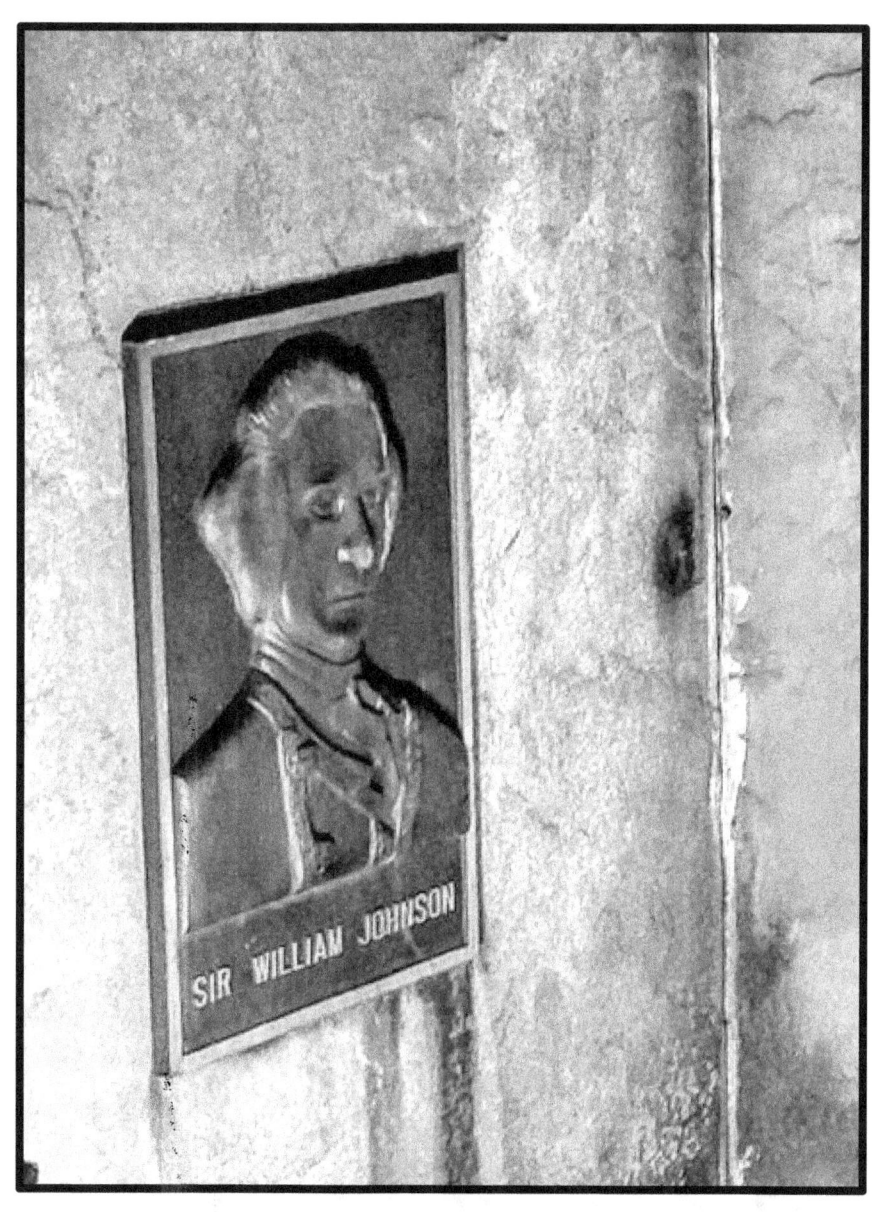

Sir William Johnson's burial place, Johnstown, NY

Sir William Johnson by John Wollaston, Albany Institute of History and Art.

Johnson sat for this portrait in New York City in 1750. John Wollaston, the artist, had been a pupil of a well known English painter whose expertise was silks and expensive drapery. Johnson supposedly criticized the portrait, saying that his OWN shoulders were broad and square. This work is in the Albany Institute of History of Art.

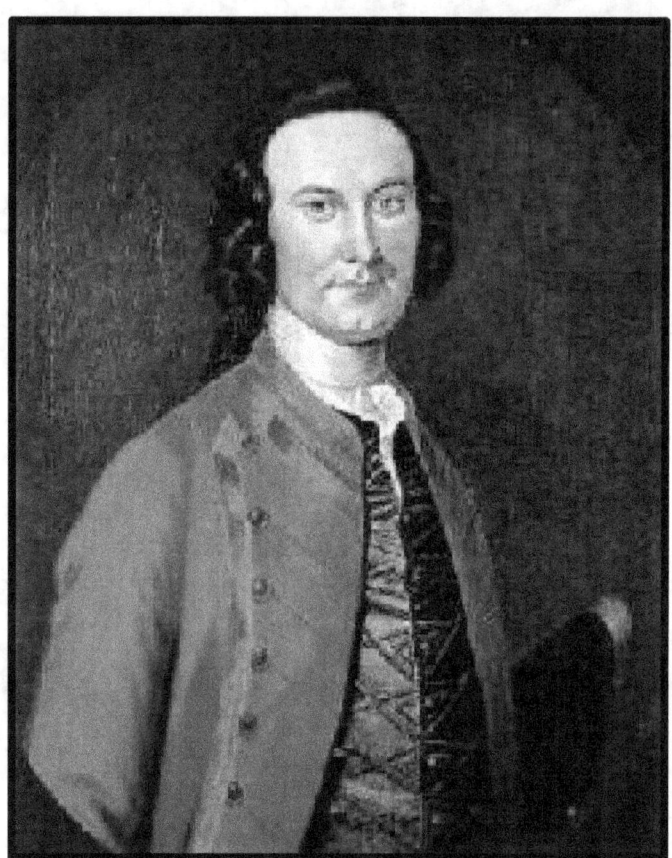

https://tryon.nygenweb.net/johnson.html

Johnstown Colonial Cemetery
Green Street, Johnstown, NY

Within this cemetery lie many of Johnstown's earliest citizens. Many notable colonial, Revolutionary War era and early 19th century citizens are interred here. A number of explanatory guides within the cemetery point out notable graves. The cemetery contains one contributing site and two contributing structures. The cemetery was established in 1766, and the district and cemetery was listed on the National Register of Historic Places in 1998.

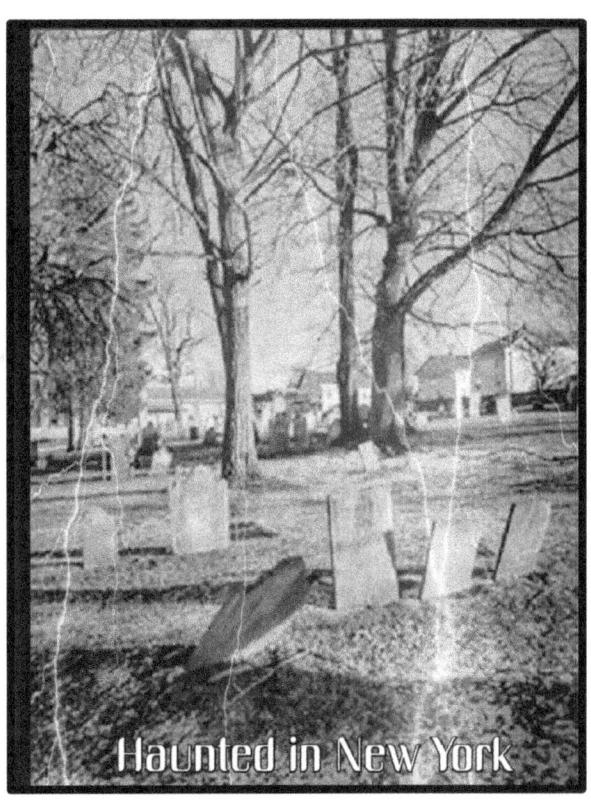

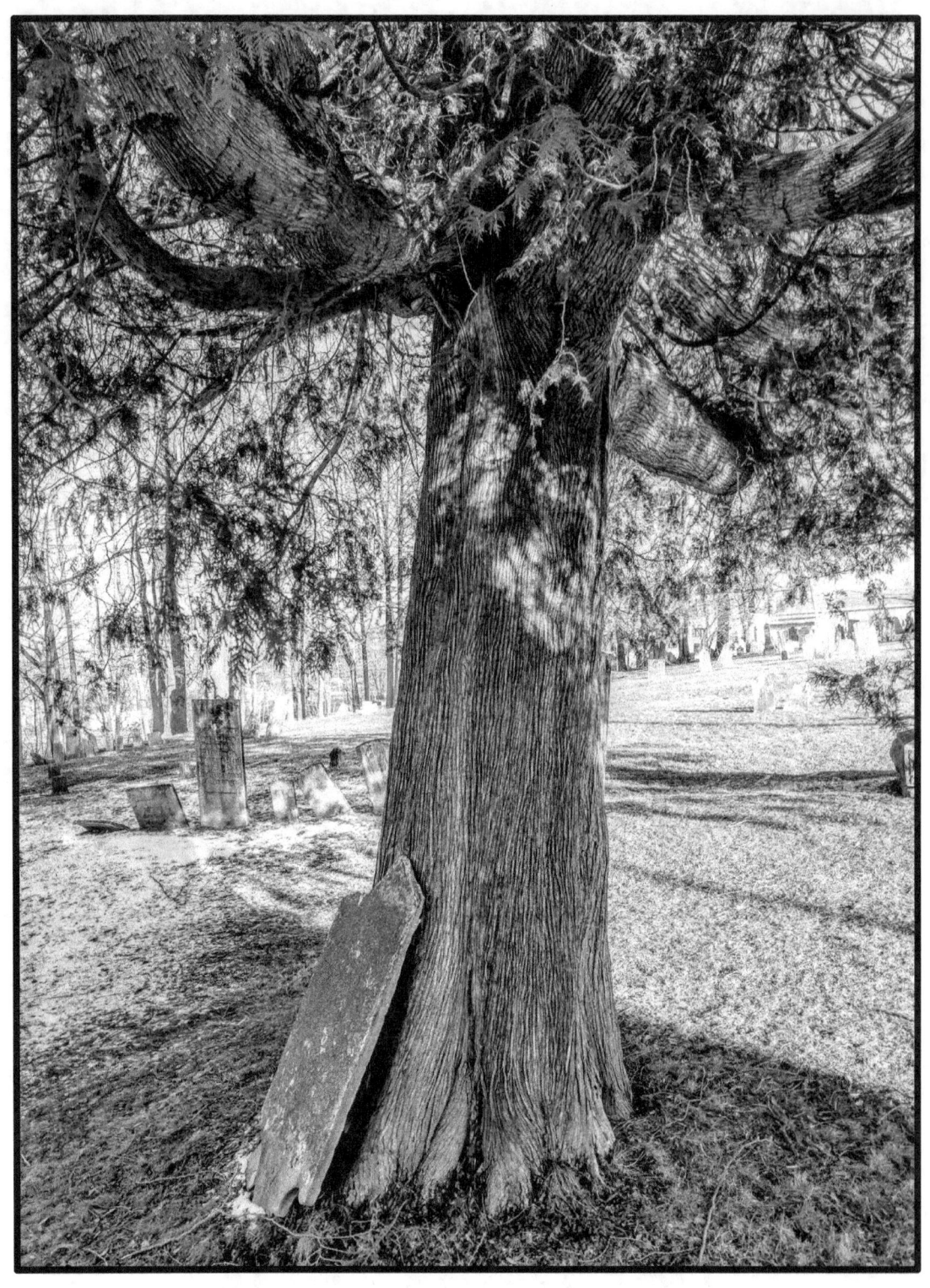

Johnstown Colonial Cemetery

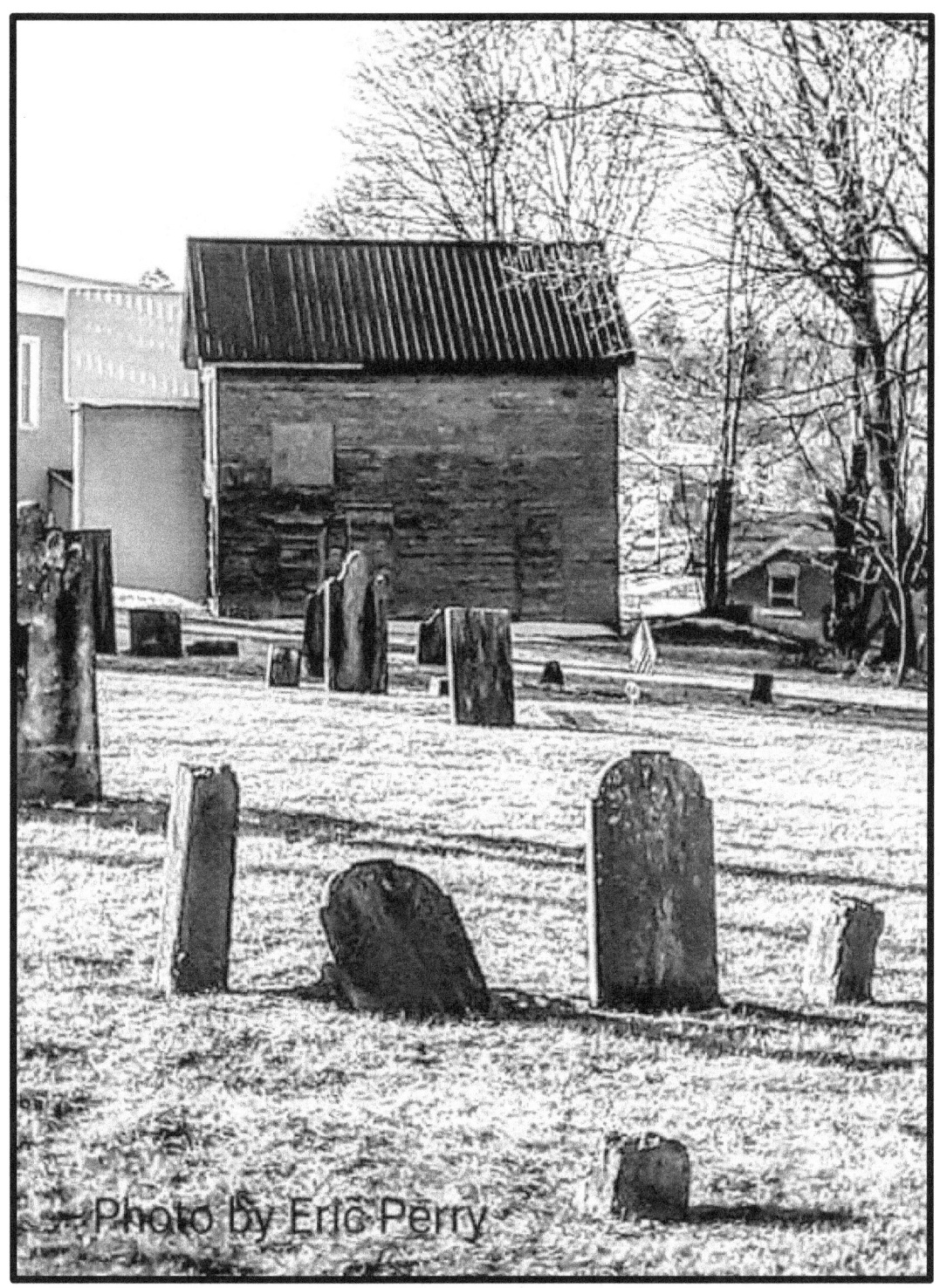

Johnstown Colonial Cemetery

This cemetery is very old and I felt that it was an honor that I could step foot in there just to see all those who fought for our freedom. On the paranormal front, it is spirited. I don t use the the term haunted because that makes people feel fear. So I use the term I like to use just suggests that there is energy there that we could "feel" or hear via out ghost hunting tools.

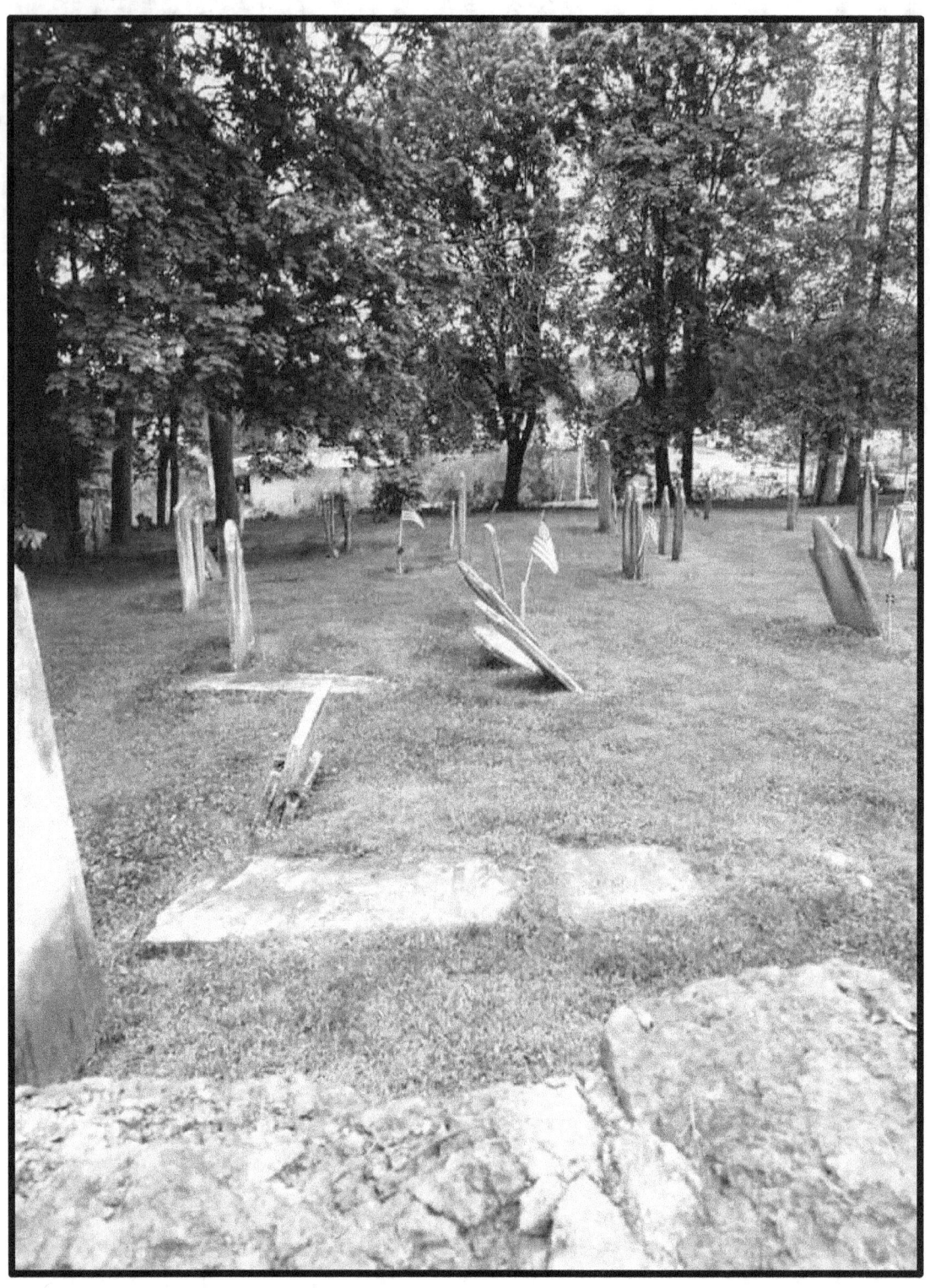

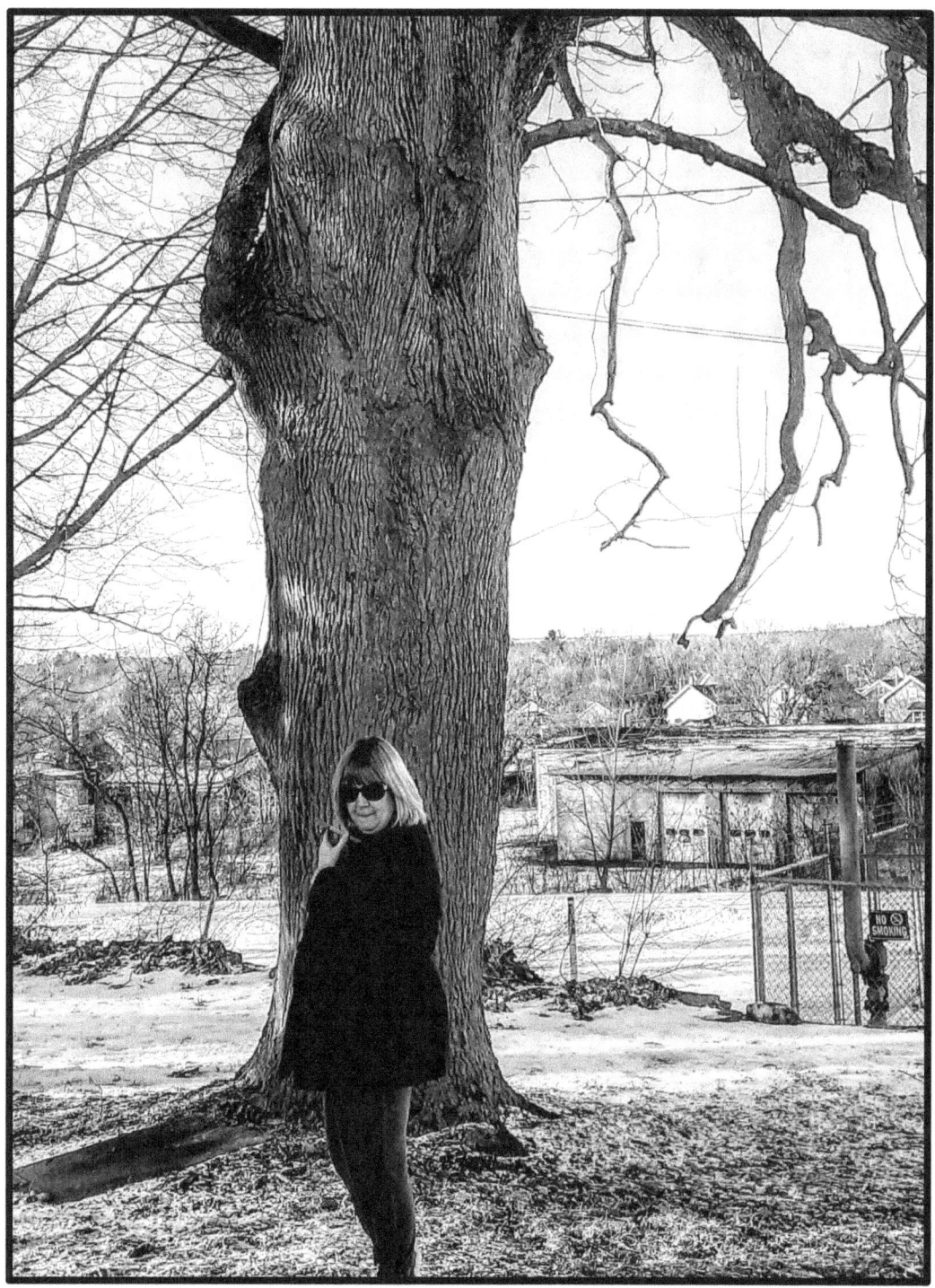

This is me listening to the spirit talking to me. I would ask questions and wait for a response and often would get one.

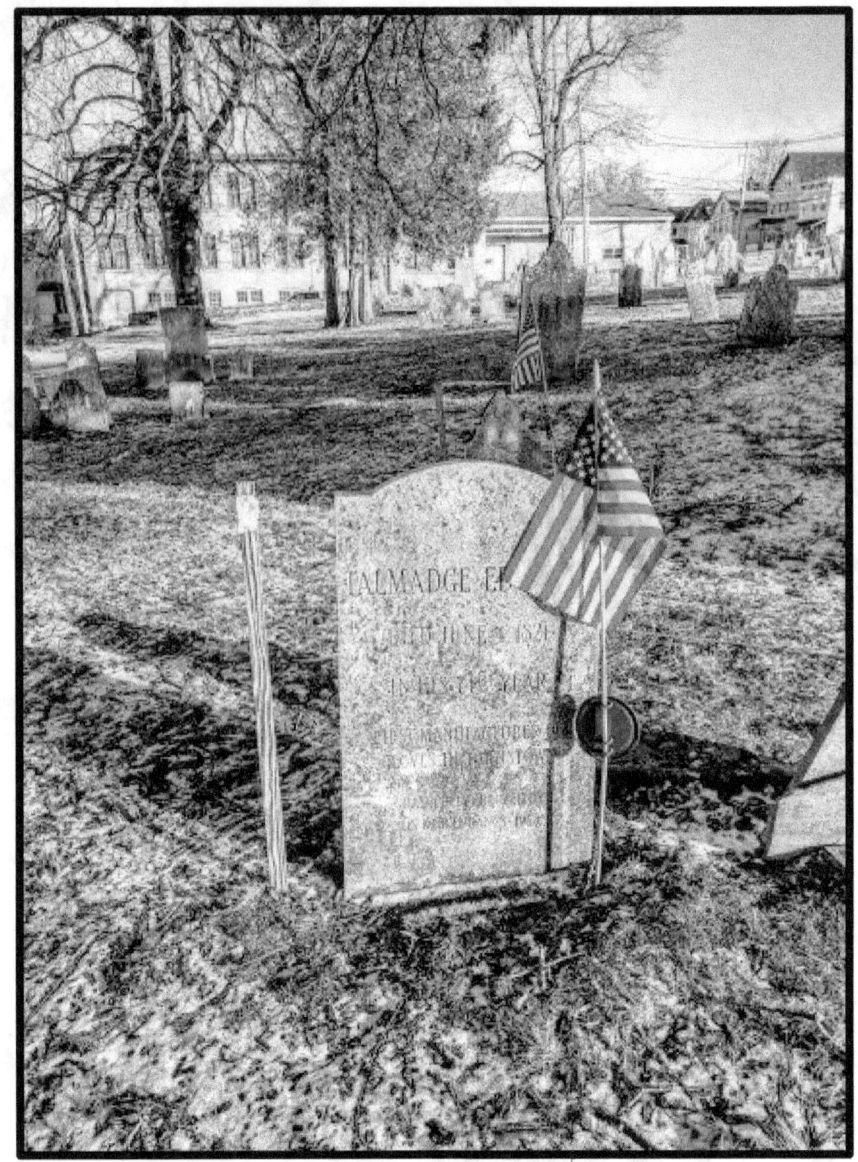

Johnstown Colonial Cemetery

This cemetery contains many prominent names to our communities. There is much history in here if you like to read very old stones. They also have a "trail" you can follow on an app on your phone that leads to learn more about different prominent persons. You can find out more about this IN the cemetery.

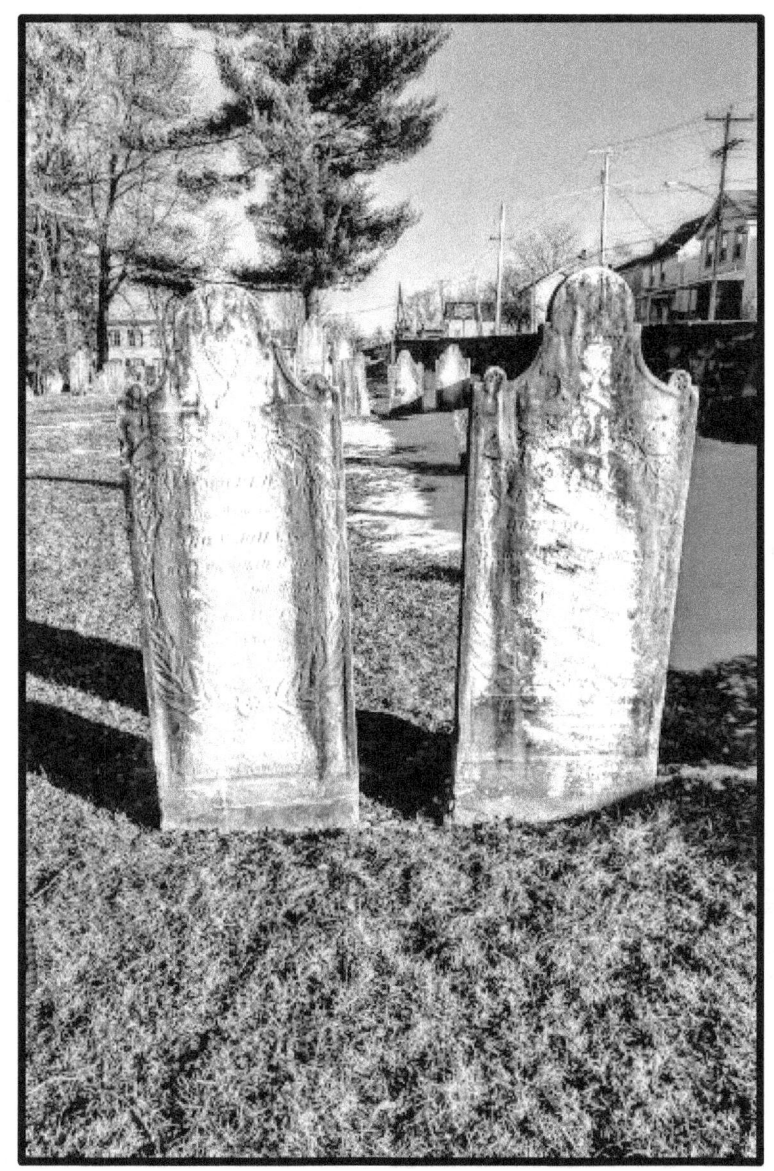

Johnstown Colonial Cemetery

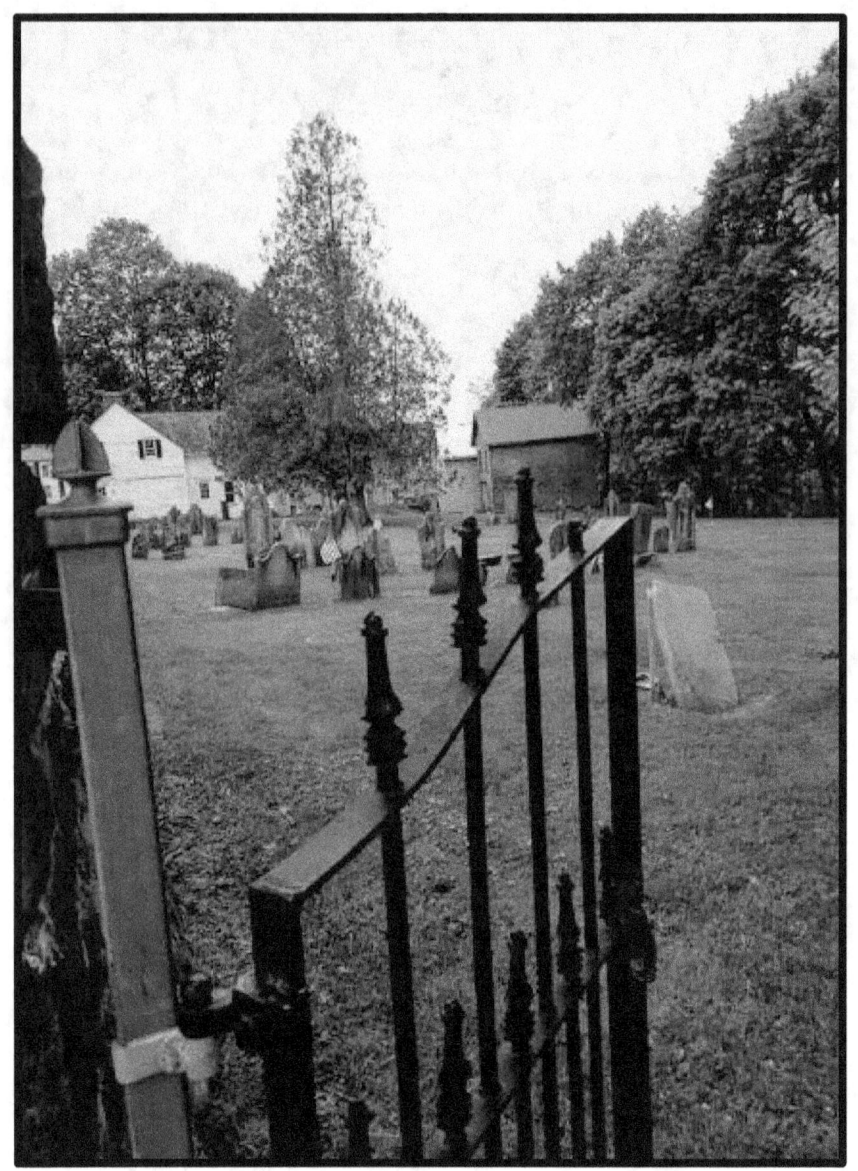

Johnstown Colonial Cemetery

I love taking pictures in black and white as it accenturates the stones in the cemetery that makes this place up. This gate was very photogentic.

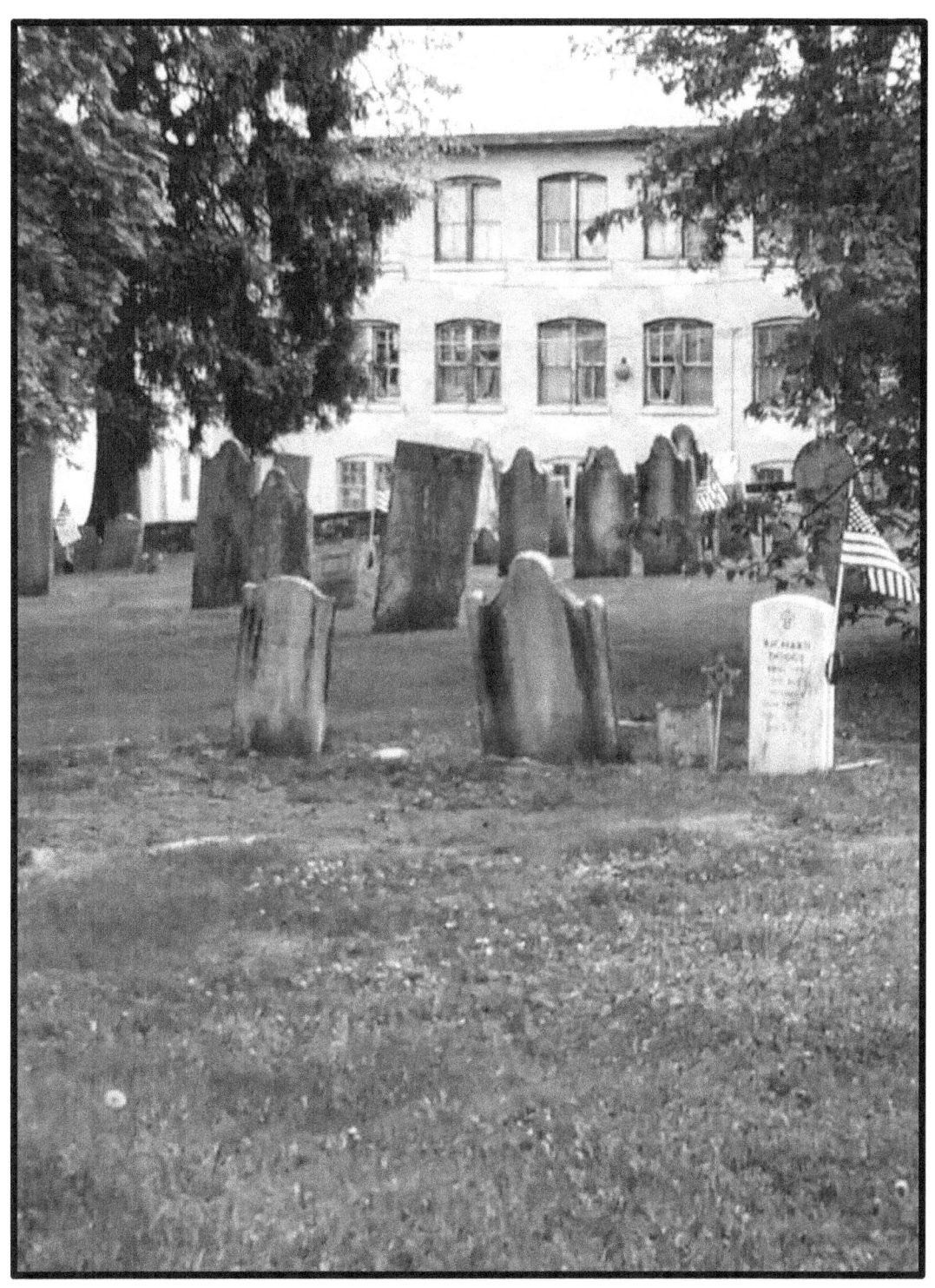

Johnstown Colonial Cemetery

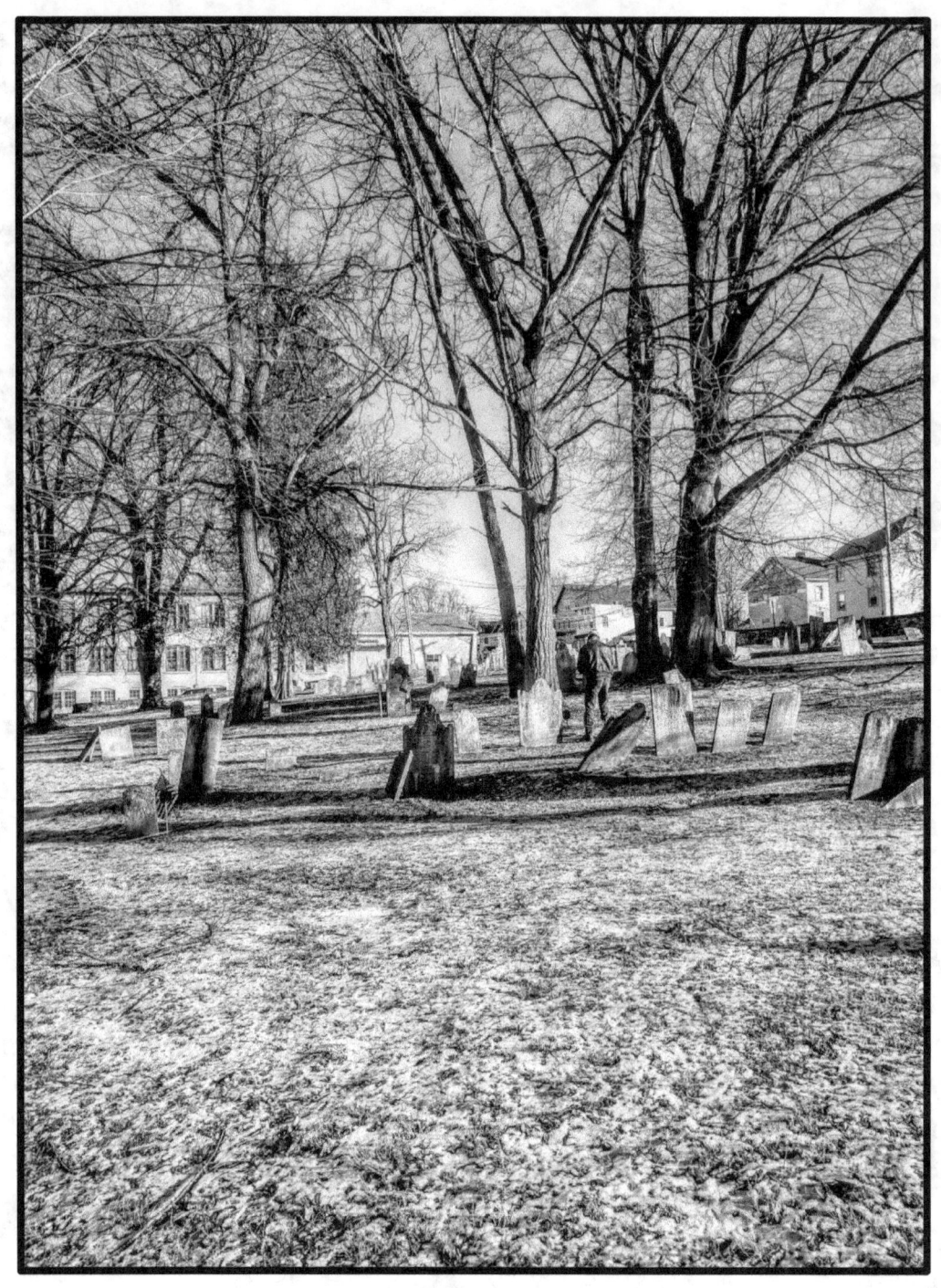

Johnstown Colonial Cemetery

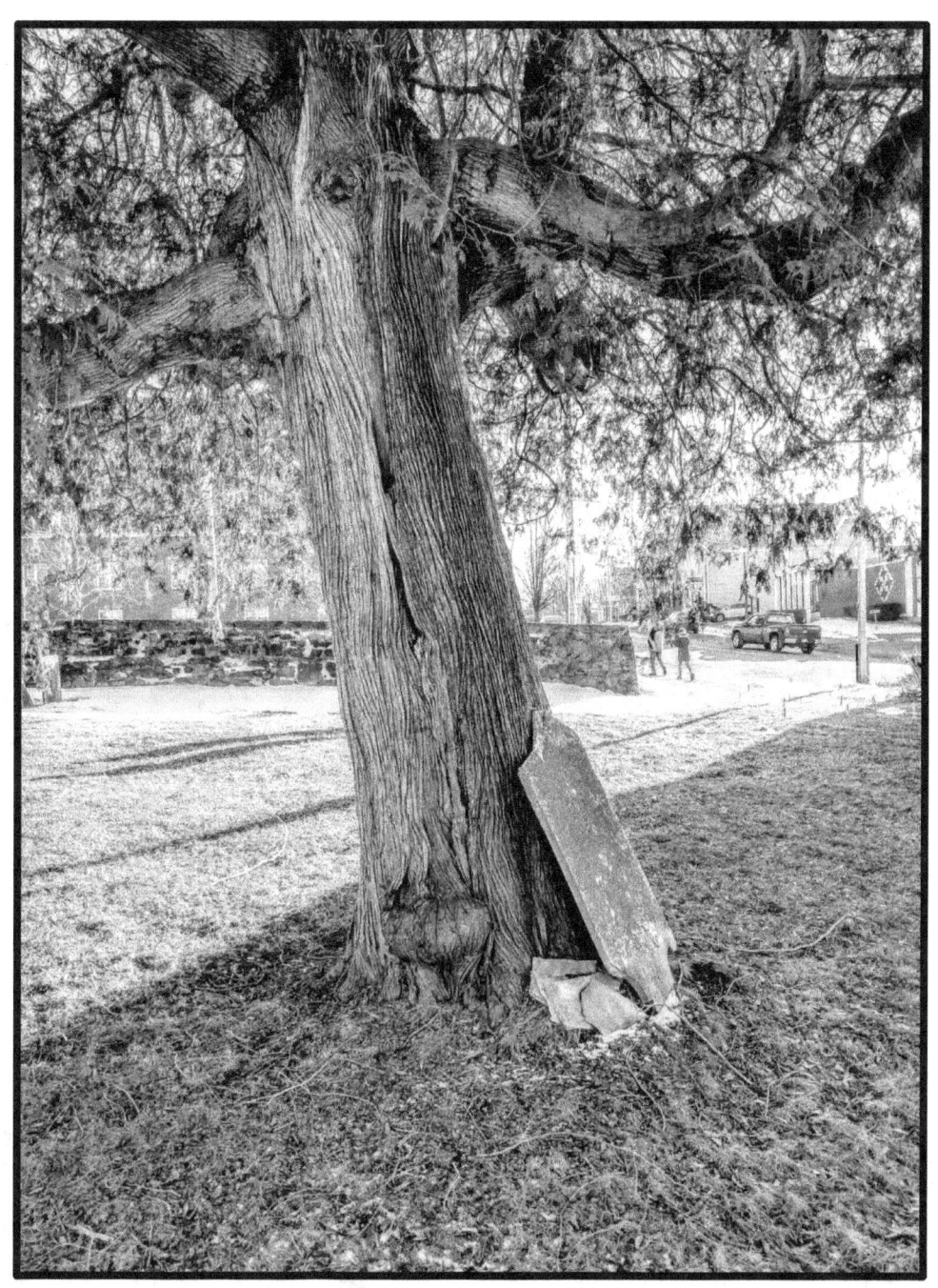

Johnstown Colonial Cemetery

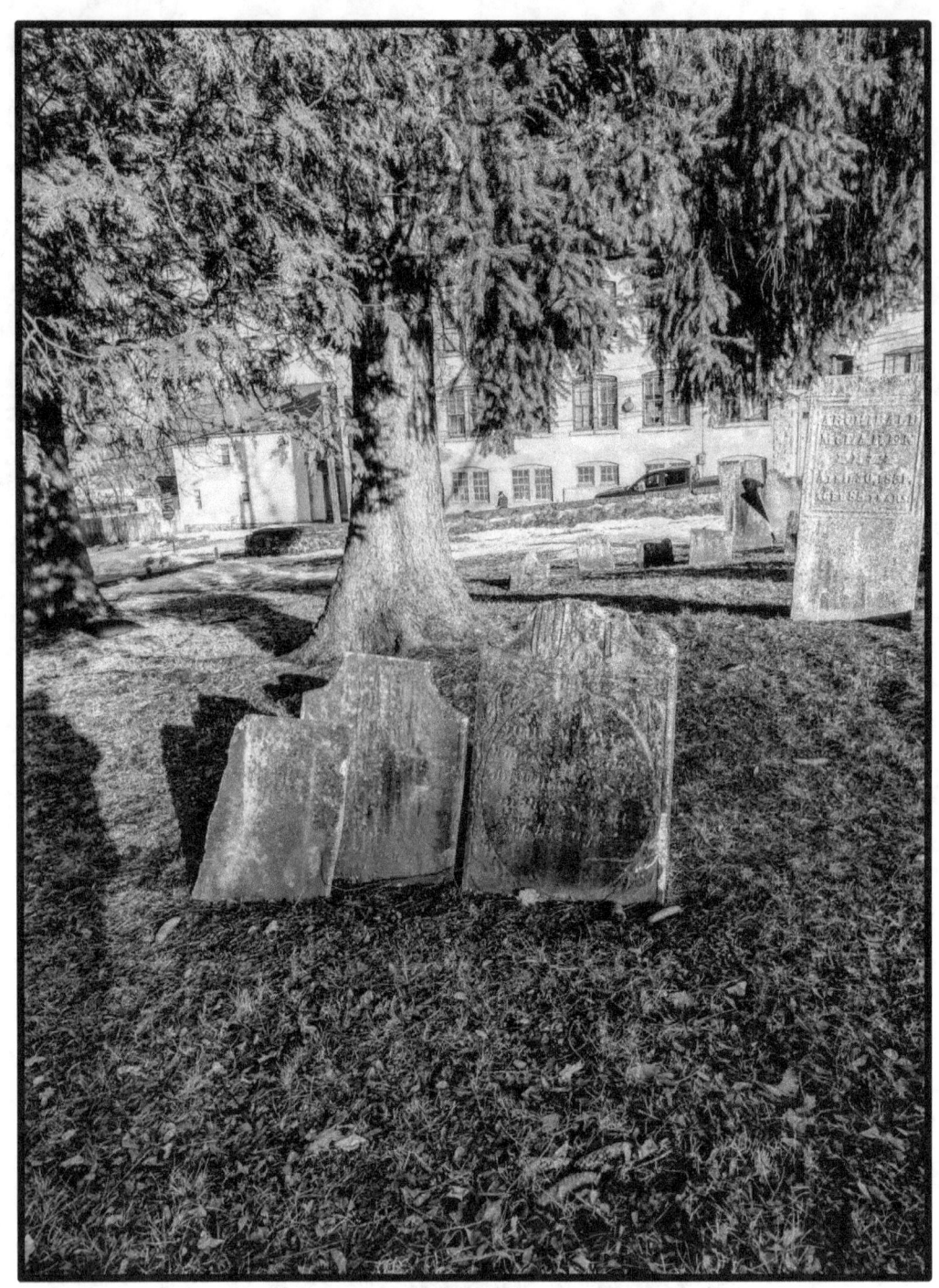

Johnstown Colonial Cemetery

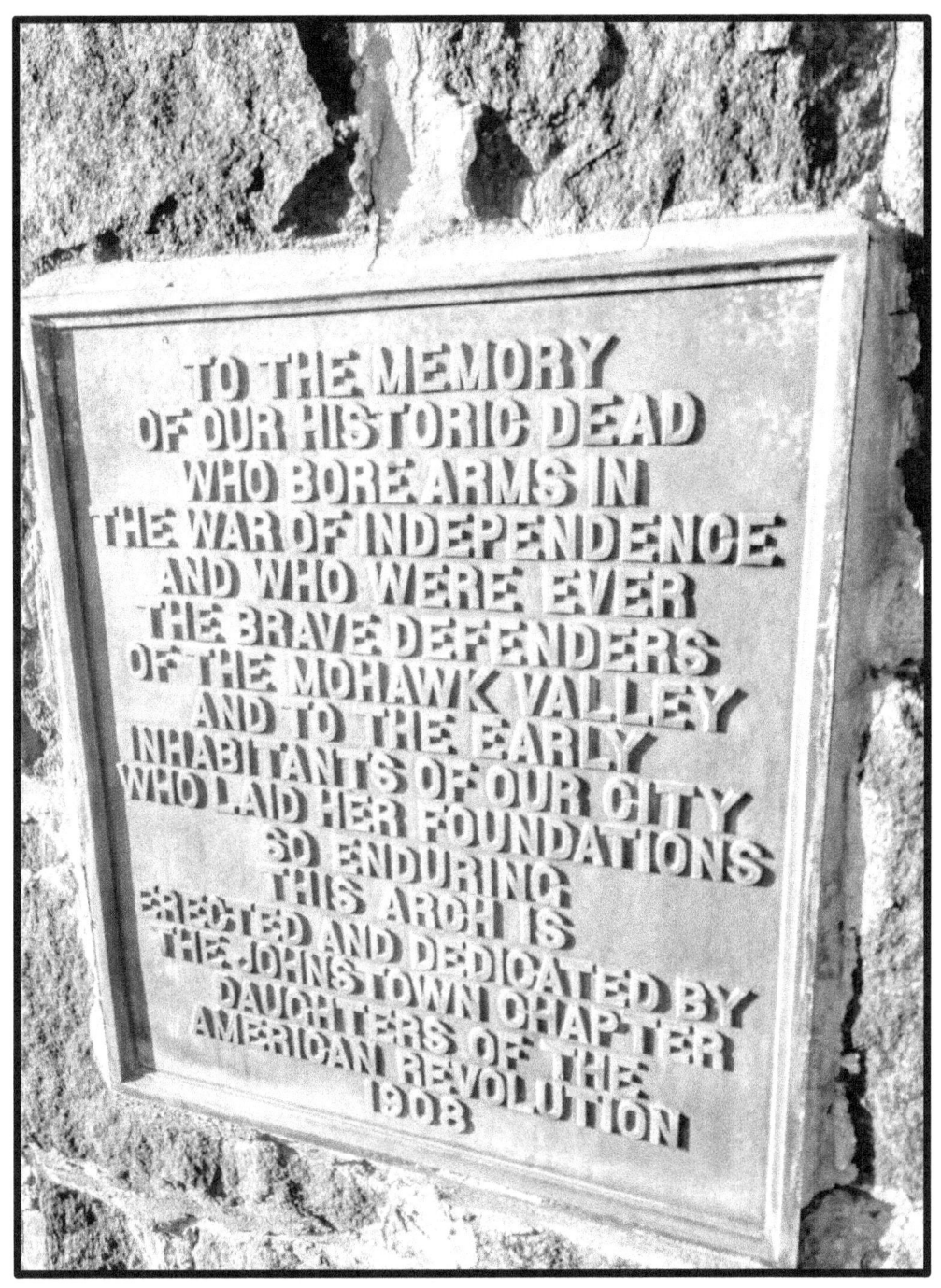

Johnstown Colonial Cemetery

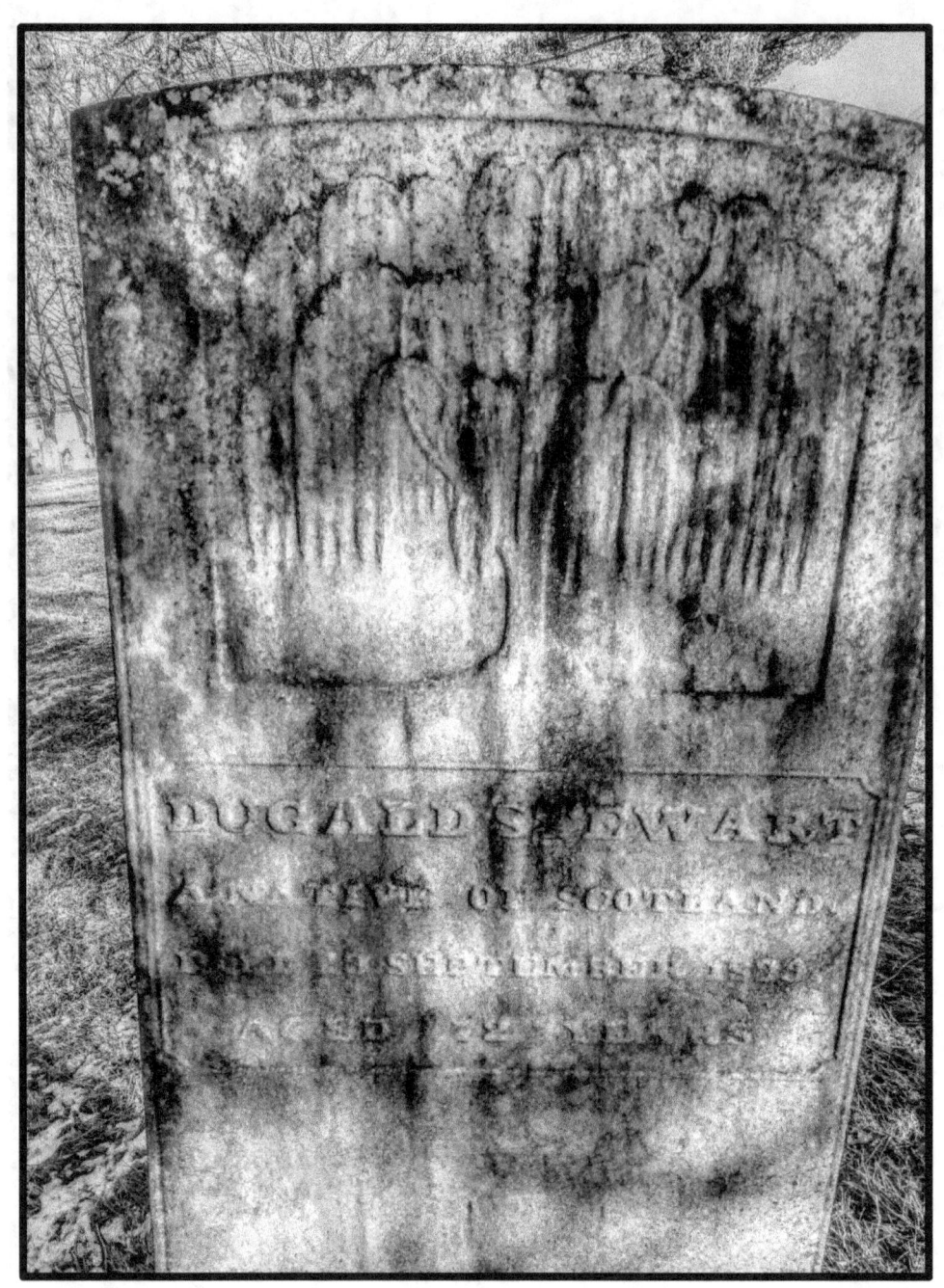

Johnstown Colonial Cemetery

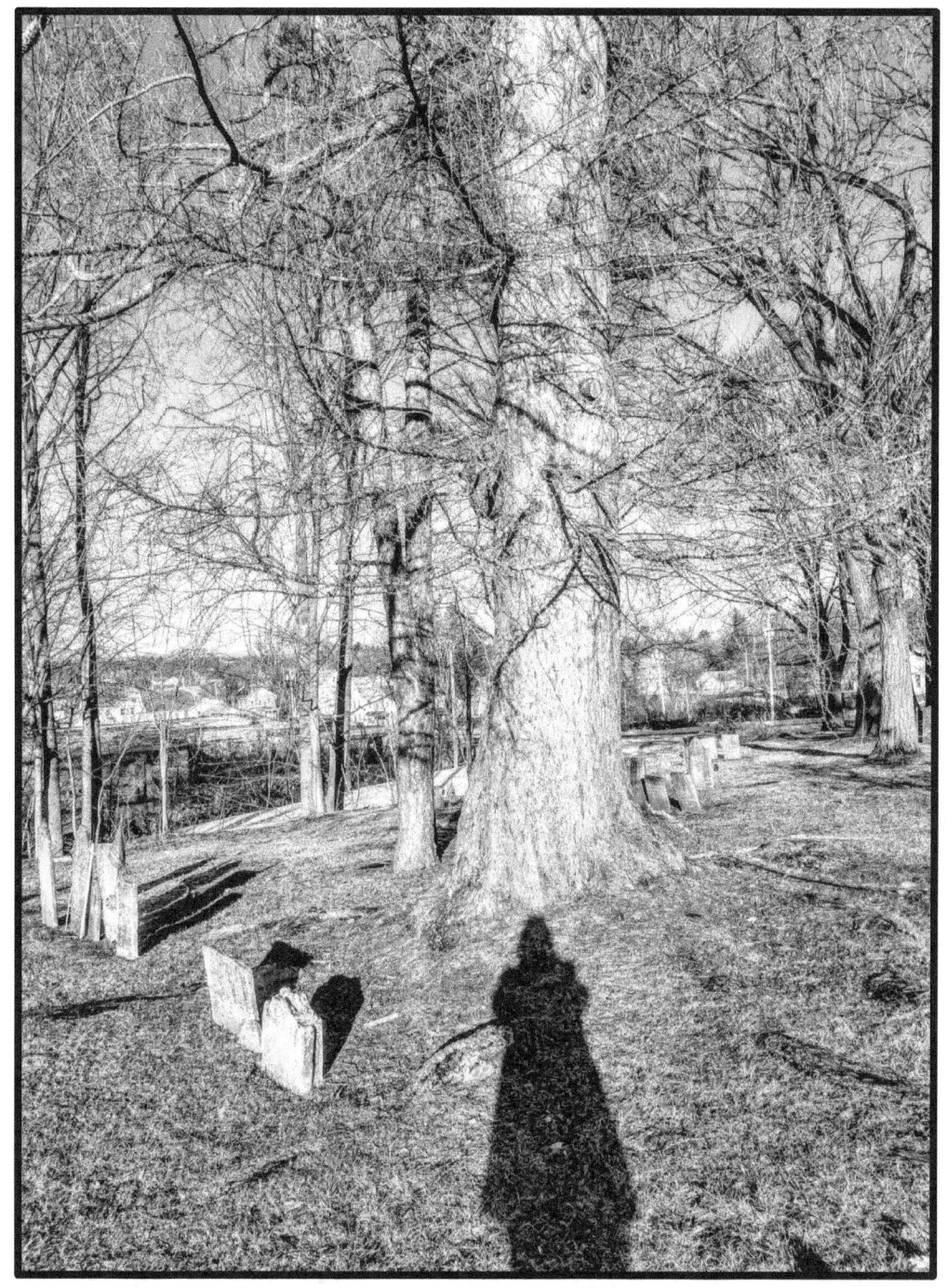

Johnstown Colonial Cemetery

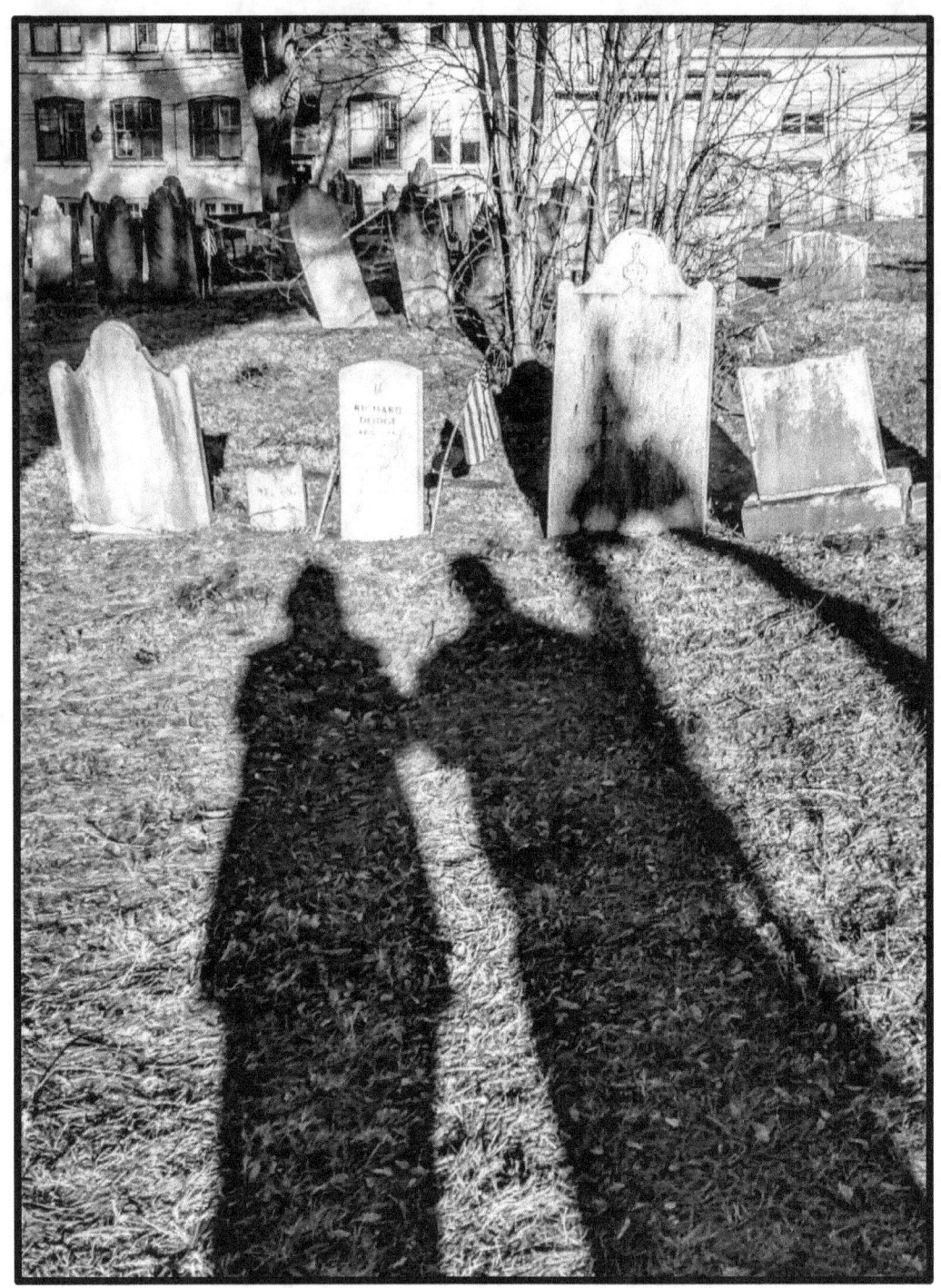

Johnstown Colonial Cemetery

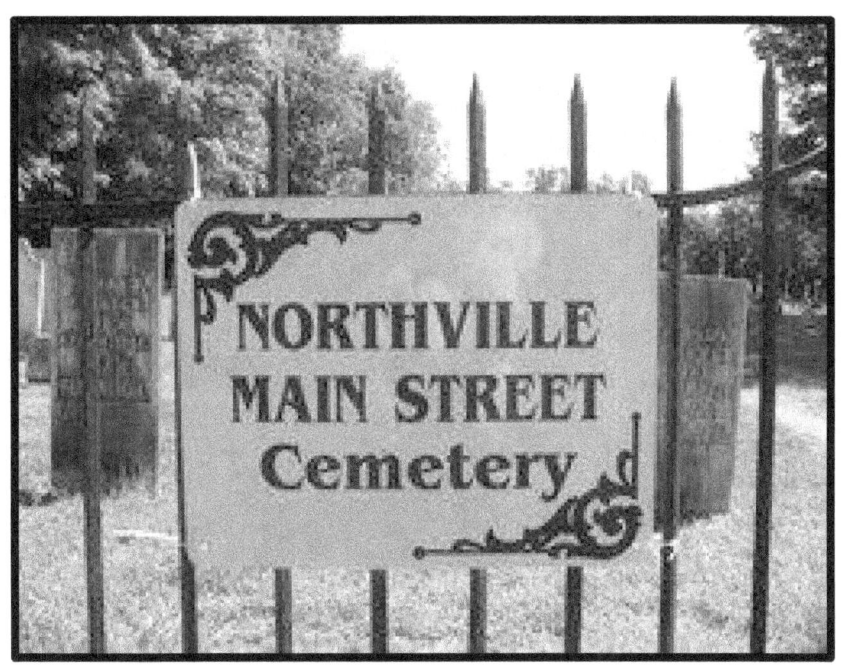

Northville Main Street Cemetery

This is a very historical location. You can see many very tall and very old gravestones. This goes back to Civil War era.

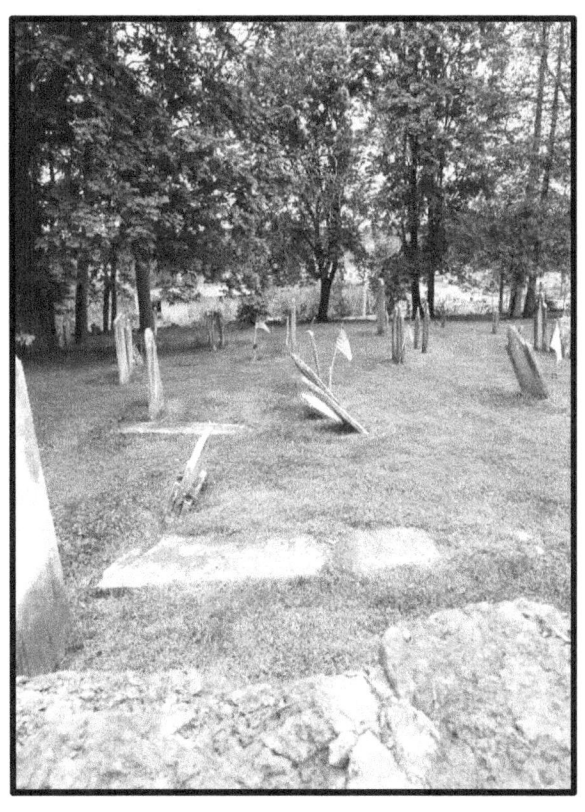

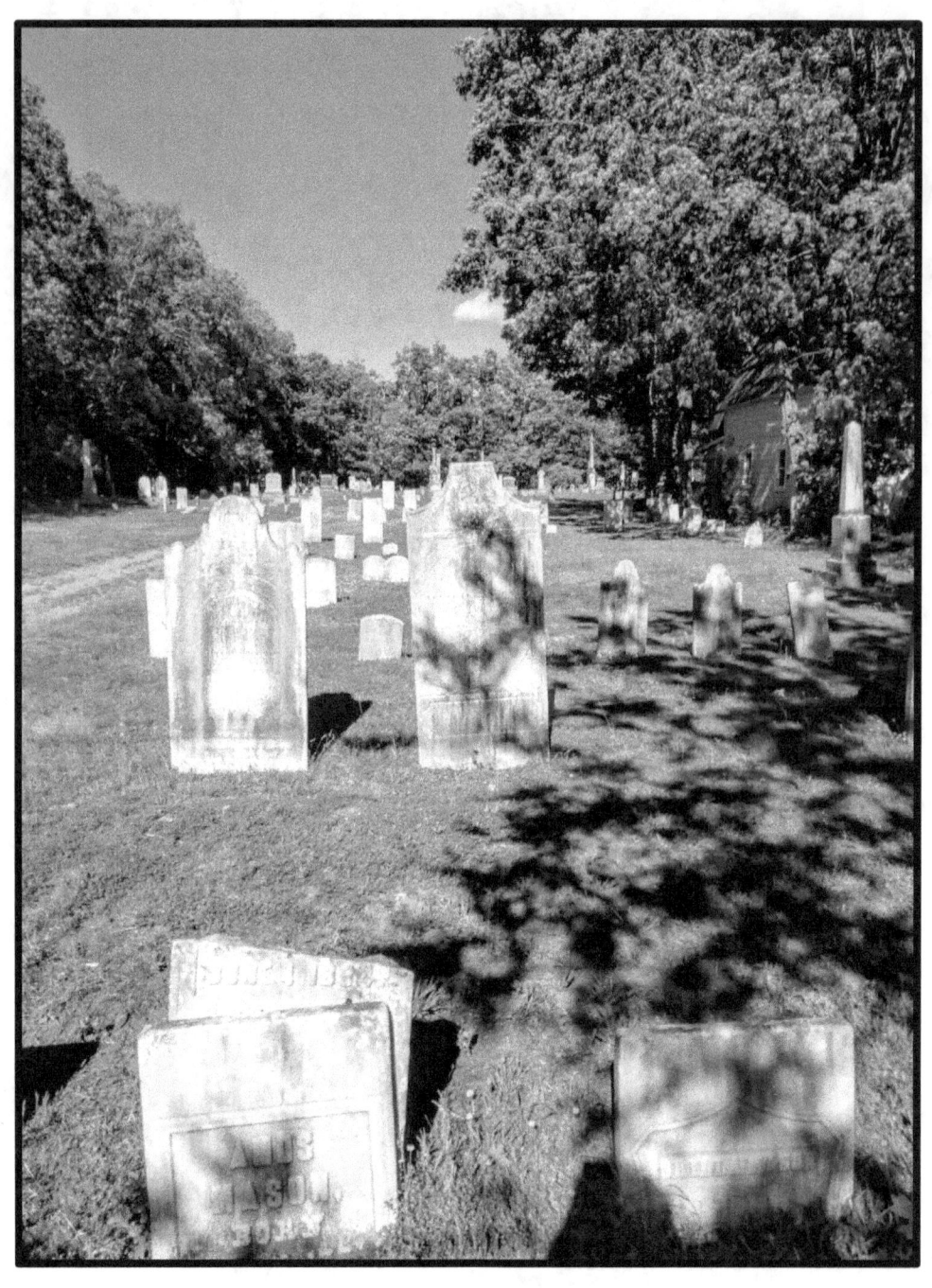

Northville Main Street Cemetery

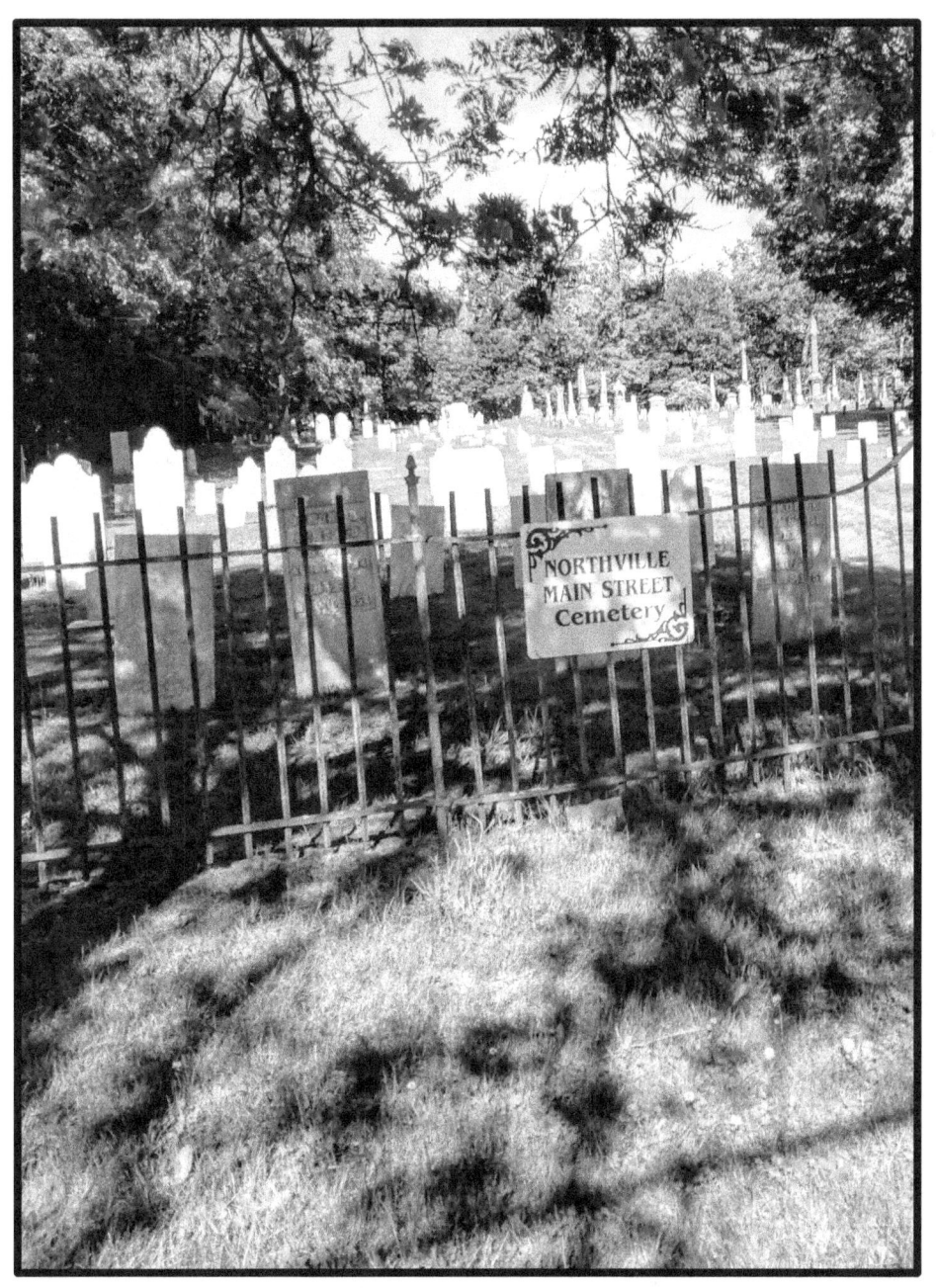

Northville Main Street Cemetery

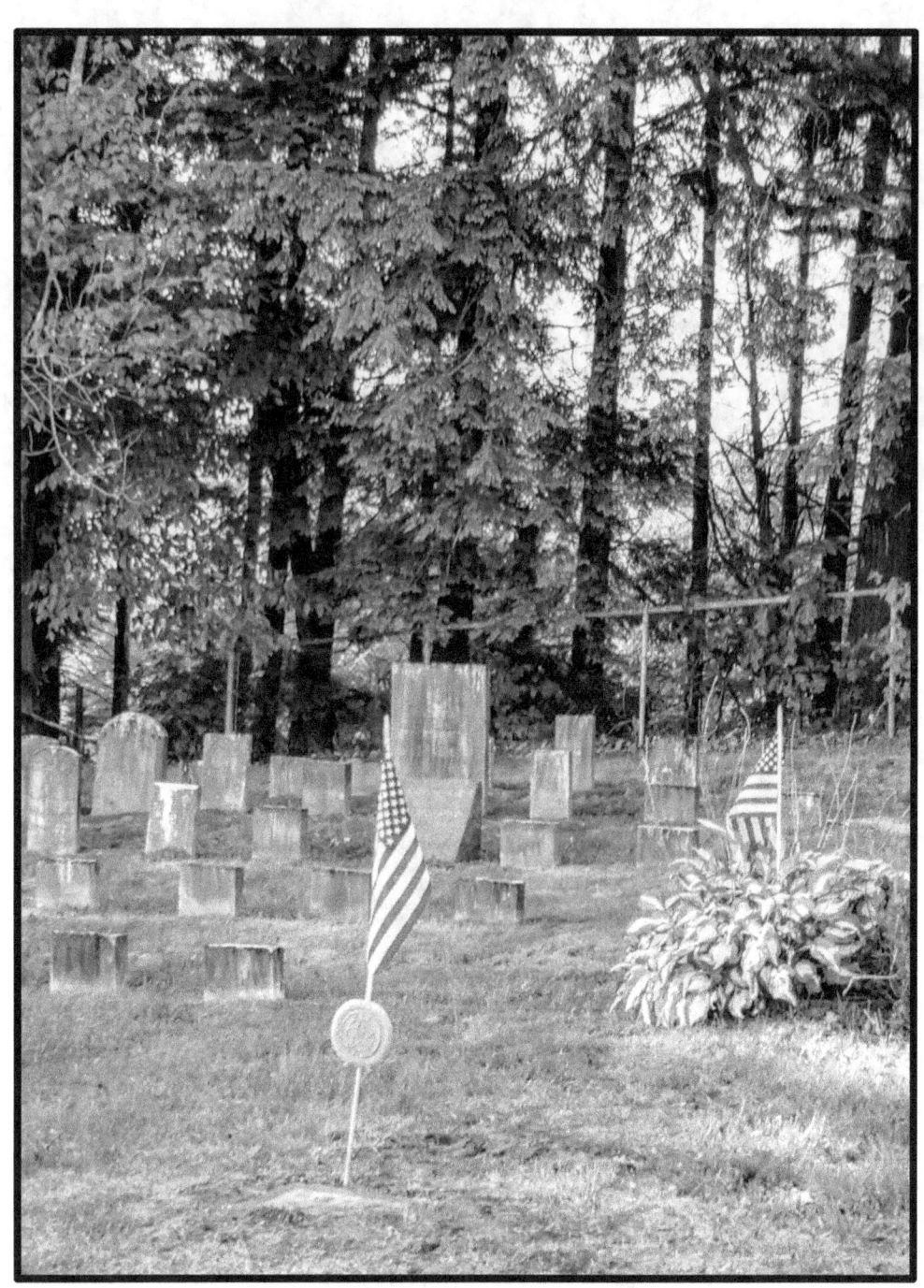

Edinburg Cemetery

Co. Road 4

Northville, NY

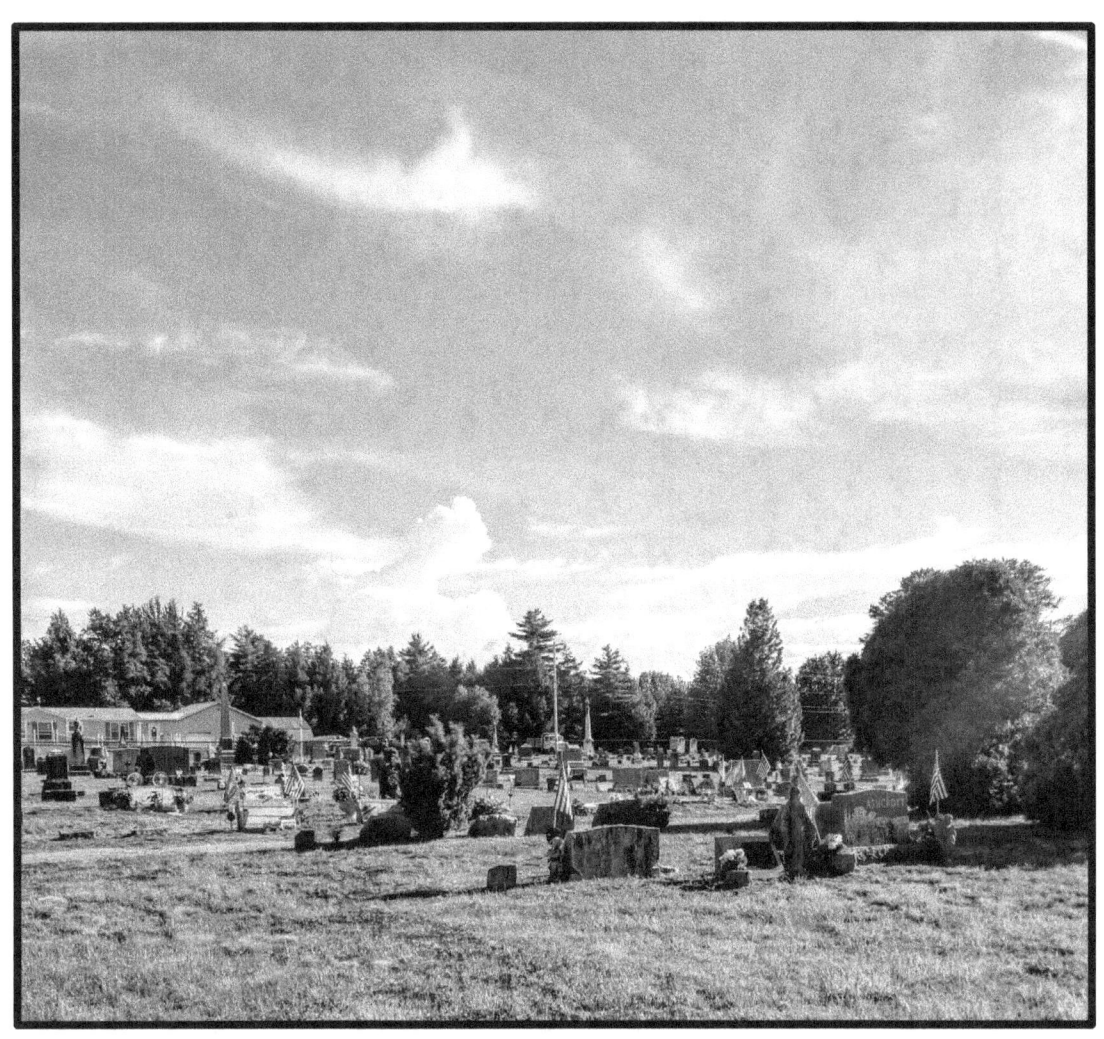

Edinburg Cemetery

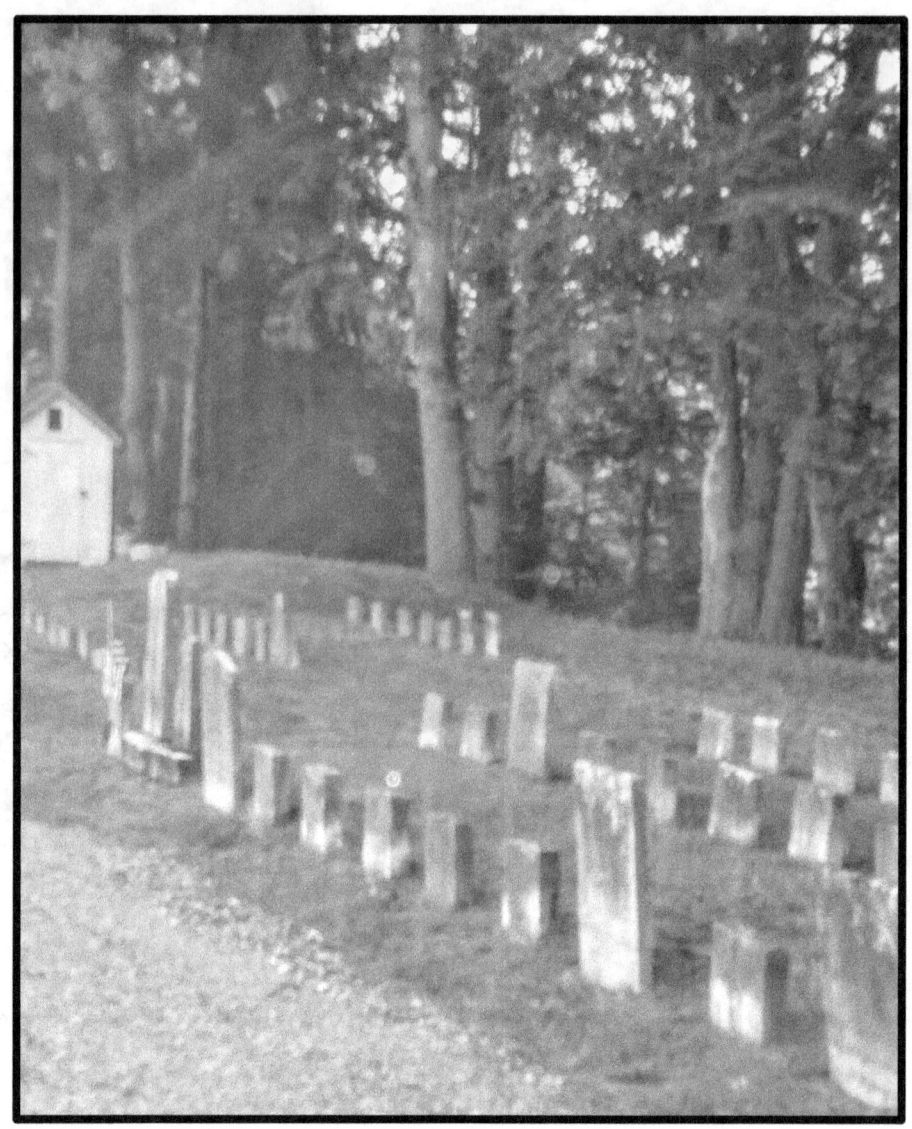

Edinburg Cemetery

This particular cemetery is haunted I feel. My team and I went here and used our investigative equipment. This particular area in the back by the maintenance shed has several ummarked headstones. Well, they are marked but with only numbers, not names. It is my understanding that you can look up these people by number perhaps at the historical society. I´m not really sure but I remember reading that somewhere. In this picture if you look closely you can see some little circles, one on the bottom of the picture and two by the edge of the woods. To us, an Orb is a Spirit of a person letting itself be shown.

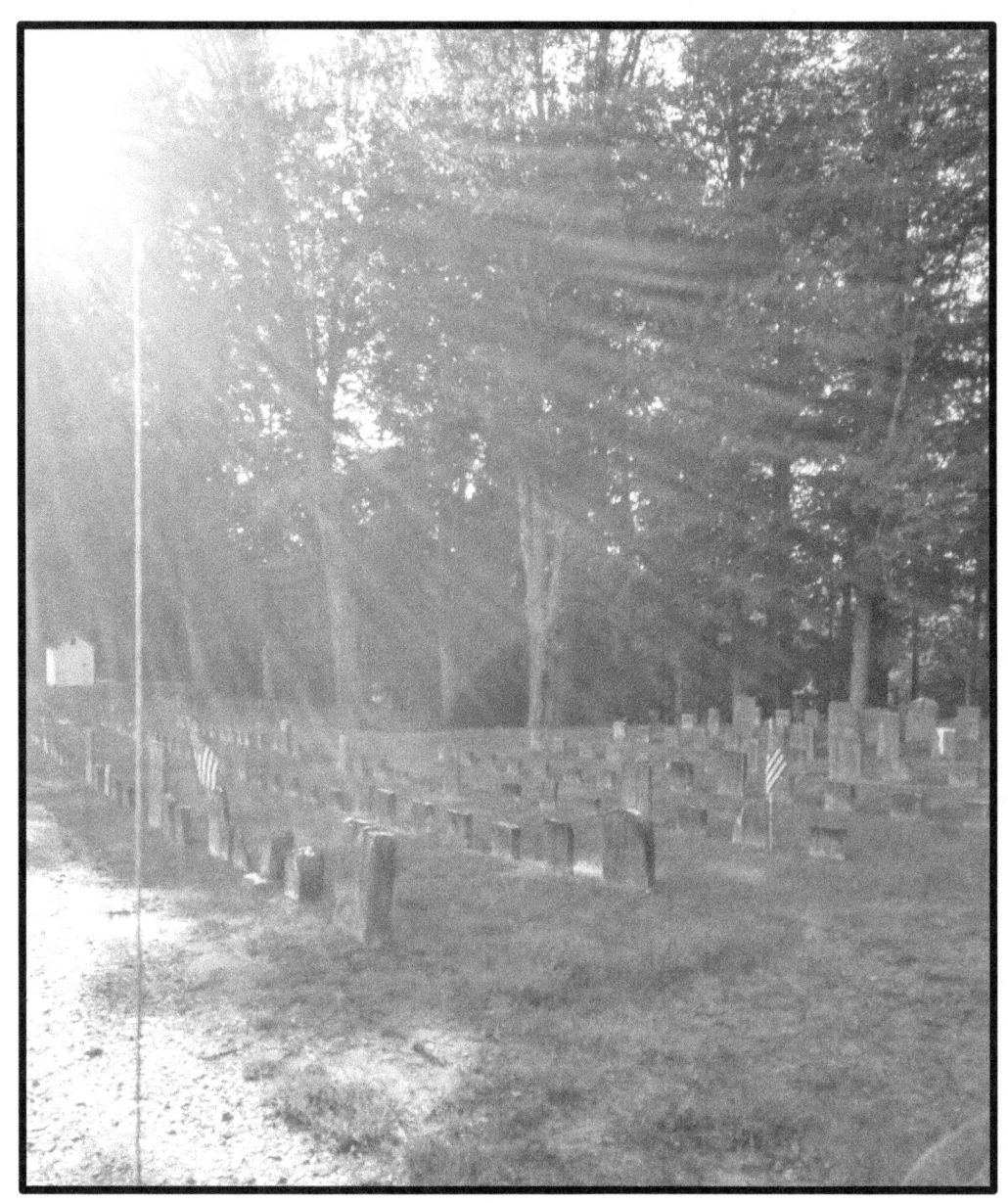

Edinburg Cemetery

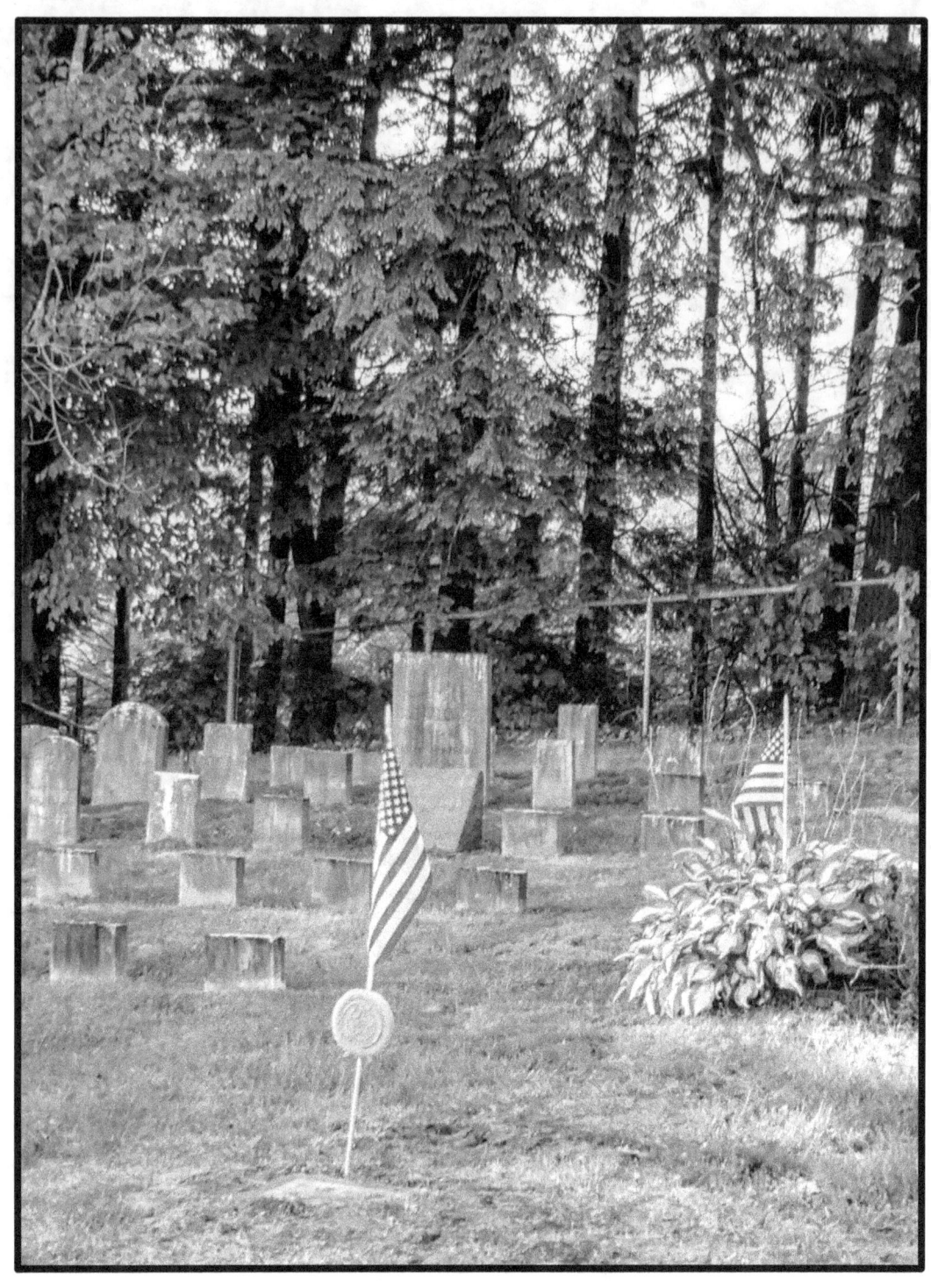

Edinburg Cemetery

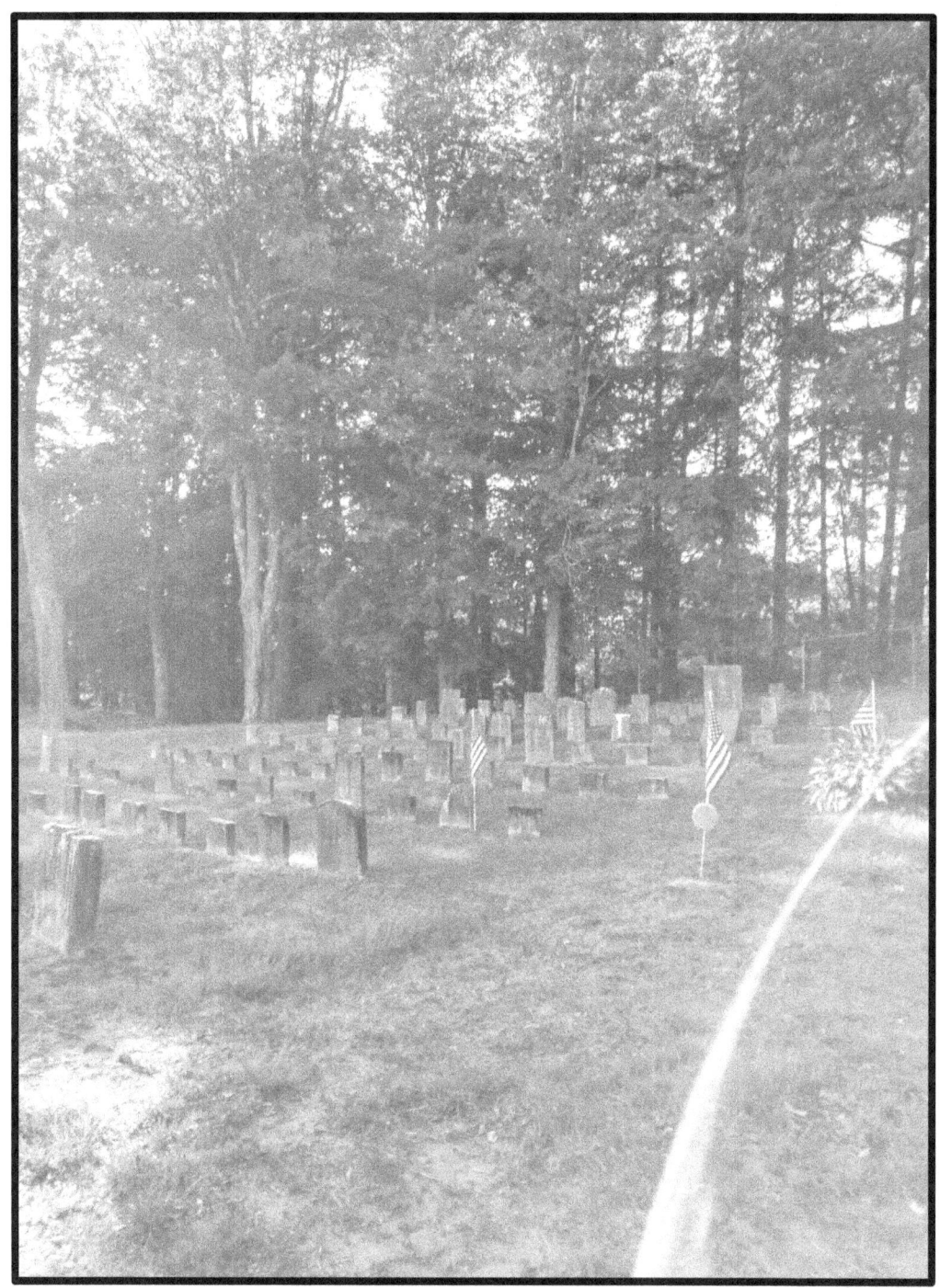

Edinburg Cemetery

When taking pictures with your cell phone as I did here, beware of camera flares like this greenish streak. A lot of people want to believe it's a spiritual entity but unfortunately it's just your camera reflecting from the sun.

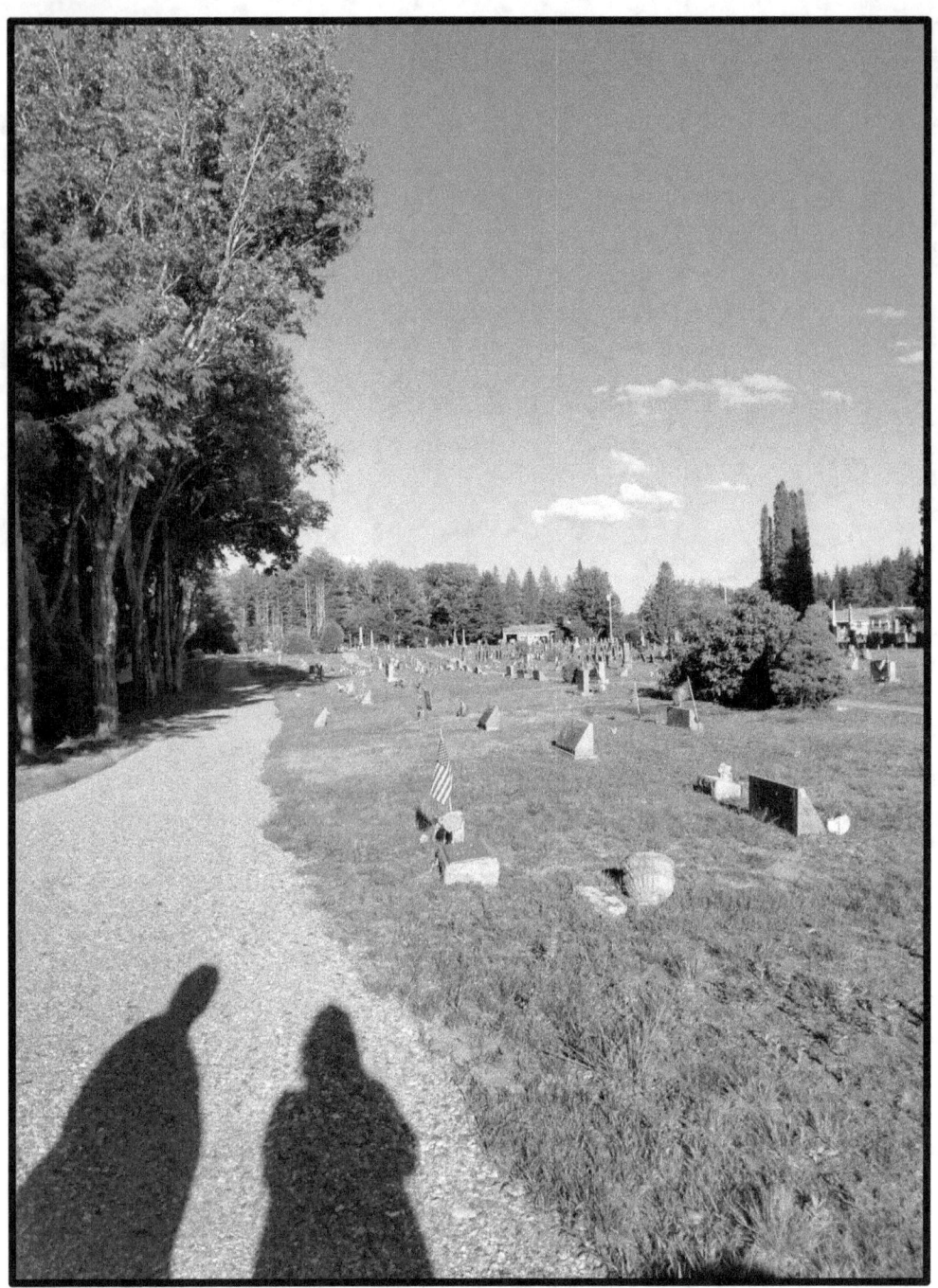

Edinburg Cemetery

In closing this book, I hope you have enjoyed looking at my pictures as much as I did in taking them. This turned out a lot bigger than I anticipated but at least a few things are documented. I´m going to do a

Montgomery County Edition next and then perhaps some individual editions as they had a lot of paranormal activity in them.

Mohawk Valley Cemeteries Series One

Look for other editions coming soon!